S. Teackle Wallis

Spain

Her institutions, politics and public men. A sketch.

S. Teackle Wallis

Spain
Her institutions, politics and public men. A sketch.

ISBN/EAN: 9783337245795

Printed in Europe, USA, Canada, Australia, Japan

Cover: Foto ©Suzi / pixelio.de

More available books at **www.hansebooks.com**

SPAIN

HER

INSTITUTIONS, POLITICS

AND

PUBLIC MEN

A SKETCH

By S. T. WALLIS
AUTHOR OF "GLIMPSES OF SPAIN"

BALTIMORE
JOHN MURPHY & CO
1896

TO

THE HONORABLE JOHN GLENN,
U. S. JUDGE FOR THE DISTRICT OF MARYLAND,

IN

G<small>RATEFUL</small> A<small>CKNOWLEDGMENT OF</small> M<small>ANY</small> K<small>INDNESSES.</small>

PREFACE.

WHEN writing the "Glimpses of Spain," the author supposed it scarcely possible that he should ever return to that country. The work, however, was still in the press, when he was honored by an invitation from the Secretary of the Interior of the United States, to visit Madrid upon an important professional errand. The offer was too flattering to be declined, and the present volume is one of the results of its acceptance.

Though the author did not occupy any recognized relation to the Spanish government, the nature of his duties, and the intercourse and connections resulting from his position, afforded him many and excellent opportunities of knowledge and observation. He does not profess to have availed himself of his advantages as fully as he might, had his duties been less engrossing; but he trusts it will be found that they have enabled him to give the work which follows a less ephemeral character than that of an ordinary book of travels. In the attempt to do this, he has sought to communicate, as far as practicable, such information in regard to Spain, as is not, to his knowledge, accessible elsewhere.

Much of this volume was prepared, as the whole should have been, soon after the writer's return to the United States. Having had no control over the circumstances which delayed its completion, he has endeavored to countervail them by keeping pace with the intermediate progress of Spanish affairs, and is persuaded that he has thus been able to present, on the whole, a fair contemporary view of his subject. The reader will, of course, make allowance for the generalities of both statement and reflection which it was impossible to avoid in a sketch. The favorable reception of his former work gives the author some confidence that the present volume will not meet with the less consideration because he has again attempted to portray the national characteristics of the Spaniards, without underrating their intelligence, depreciating their morals, or caricaturing their manners and religion.

It would be unpardonable to send forth the record of a most agreeable sojourn in the Spanish capital, without acknowledging the indebtedness of the author to the officers of the United States Legation there, and especially to the Hon. Mr. Barringer, for all the pleasure and advantage which courtesy and kindness could give to personal and official intercourse.

BALTIMORE, *January*, 1853.

CONTENTS.

I.
Journey to Madrid 1

II.
Lodging-Houses, Lodging, and Life in Madrid.—Servants, &c. 4

III.
Foundation, Locality, Climate, Dress, Health, &c. of Madrid 12

IV.
Puerta del Sol.—Public Habits of the Madrileños.—The Prado.—Equipages.—Horsemen.—Atocha Walk.—Women of Madrid 20

V.
Constitutional History and Epochs.—Constitutions.—Ferdinand the Seventh.—Duc d'Angoulême.—Cristina.—Don Carlos.—Estatuto Real.—History of Parties.—Espartero.—Narvaez 28

VI.
Constitution of 1845.—Its Provisions and Character.—The Cortes.—Elections.—Pay of Members.—Executive Influence.—Its Benefits.—Republican Propagandism 40

VII.

The Executive and Judiciary.—Juries and the Trial by Jury............ 53

VIII.

Jurisprudence.—Codes.—Colonial System.—Administration of Justice.
—Escribanos.—Judges.—The Legal Profession........................ 62

IX.

The Press. — Newspapers. — Sartorius. — The Puritans. — Pacheco.—
Party Organs......... 76

X.

Cuba and the United States.—The Crónica Newspaper.—Parties in
Cuba.—Public Sentiment there.—Abuses and their Remedy.—
Annexation... 90

XI.

The Chamber of Deputies.—Teatro de Oriente.—Ministers and Opposition.—Council of Ministers.—Seats of Ministers in the Legislature.. 105

XII.

General Narvaez.—Ministerial Profits.—Marquis of Pidal.—Asturian
Nobility.—Sr. Mon.—Prohibitive Duties and the Catalans........... 113

XIII.

Sr. Arrazola.—Bravo Murillo.—The Budget.—Ministerial Movement.
—The Senate.—Moderado Principles.—Bravo Murillo's Speech..... 127

XIV.

General Figueras.—Roca de Togores.—Alexandre Dumas.—Southern
Oratory.—Olozaga.—Escosura.—Benavides.—Donoso Cortés.—
Their Speeches.. 137

XV.

The Senate.—Alcalá Galiano.—The Cortes of 1823.—The Athenæum.
—Galiano's Lectures there 155

XVI.

The Ex-Regent Espartero and his Rival, Narvaez.—The Carlist War
and its Conclusion.—Downfall of Espartero, and its Causes.—Love
of Titles and Honors.—Orders of Knighthood 164

XVII.

Loyalty.—The Queen.—Guizot and Infante.—Regicides.—Necessity of
an able Prince.—The Queen's Embarazo.—Public Rejoicings and
Ceremonial.—Diplomatic Congratulations and Reception.—The
King 173

XVIII.

Social Customs in Madrid.—Entertainments.—Society and its Spirit.—
Imitation of the French.—The Academy and the Press.—Socialism.
—Etiquette.—Social Frankness and Cordiality 184

XIX.

Theatres and Dramatic Literature.—Actors and their Style.—Romea
and Matilde Diaz.—Breton de los Herreros and his Plays.—Rubí.
—Isabel la Católica.—Historical Dramas.—Theatrical Police.—
Literary Rewards.—Copyright.—Count of San Luis 196

XX.

Literature.—Books, Booksellers, and Book-Stalls.—Book-Hunting in
Madrid.—Publishers.—Standard Works.—Historical and Geographical Dictionary of Madoz.—Cheap Publications.—Mr. Ticknor's History of Spanish Literature.—Its Character and Translation.—Gayangos.—Vedia 206

XXI.

Quintana.—The Junta Central.—Quintana's Political and Literary Life and Works.—Nicasio Gallego.—His Political Career and Poems.—Debates on the Inquisition.—Clerical Liberality.—Dos de Mayo.—Martinez de la Rosa.—His Political and Literary Life and Works.—Estatuto Real... 219

XXII.

Standing Armies.—The Spanish Army, its Condition and Political Influence.—Immense Number of Generals.—The Scientific Corps.—Their Organization and Merits.—The Navy, its Improvement and Personnel.—Its Organization.—The Cuban Expeditions.—Discriminating Duties under our Act of 1834.—Development of Agriculture and Internal Improvements in Spain, in Consequence.—Santander.—Railroads.—The Canal of Castile.—Competition...... 235

XXIII.

Ecclesiastical System and Reforms.—Abolition of the Inquisition.—Its Character.—Llorente.—Campomanes.—Floridablanca and Jovellanos.—The Monastic Orders.—Their Suppression.—Confiscation of Church Property.—Reforms of the Church System.—Pay of the Clergy.—Character of the Secular Clergy.—Clerical Influence.—Toleration in Spain.—Protestant Travellers and Prejudices.—Exaggerations, &c... 249

XXIV.

Education.—Statistics.—System of Instruction.—Schools.—Universities.—Census of 1803.—University of Madrid.—of Alcalá.—Complutensian Polyglot.—Manuscripts.—Prescott's Ferdinand and Isabella.—Sabau's Translation of it.. 274

XXV.

Taxes and Modes of Collecting them,—Reforms in Taxation.—The Provincial Deputations and Ayuntamientos.—Grievances and

Abuses.—The Customs.—Low Salaries.—Gate Money.—Tax on Consumption.—National Debt.. 284

XXVI.

Internal Improvements.—Agricultural and Mineral Wealth.—Natural Obstacles.—Present Facilities for Travel and Transportation.—Safety of the Roads.—Police.—New Roads and Canals.—Administration of Roads and Canals.—Railroads projected and completed.—Railroad Committee of the Cortes.—Royal Decree and Participation of the Government in the Management of Railroads.—Influx of Capital, and its Results... 295

XXVII.

Improvement in Agriculture and its Causes.—Improved Value of Land.—Territorial Wealth and Production.—Practical Farmers.—Espartero.—Agricultural Education.—Economical Societies.—Agricultural Bureau and its Action.—Irrigation.—Geological Chart.—Colonization of Waste Land.—Irish Colonists.—Dairy of Madrid.—Advancement of Manufactures and Commerce.—Prohibitory Duties.—Exports and imports.—Steam Coasters and Coasting Trade.—Manufactures.—Catalan Monopolies.—Manufacturing Resources of Spain.—Modifications of the Tariff.—Silk and Woollen Fabrics.—Flax, Hemp, and Iron.—National Arsenals and Foundries.. 309

XXVIII.

Fine Arts.—Galleries.—The National Museum and its Treasures.—Academy of San Fernando.—Marshal Soult.—Murillo.—Architecture.—Public Edifices.—Domestic Architecture.—The Escorial.—Fountains of Madrid.—Bronze Equestrian Statues.—Spanish Academy.—Academy of History.—National Library.—The Armory.—Bull-Fights of 1850.—Montes, his Exploits, Death and Story... 325

XXIX.

Valladolid.—Simancas and its Archives.—Blasco de Garay and the Application of Steam to Navigation.—His Invention a Fable.—Burgos.—Vergara.—Visit to Azpeitia.—Valley of Loyola.—Jesuit College and Church.—The Basques.—Their Character, Agriculture, and Institutions.—Tolosa.—Ride to Bayonne.—The Gascon 343

XXX.

Conclusion.—Political Prospects of Spain.—Effects of Peace.—Espartero.—The Moderados.—The Queen Mother.—The Nobility.—Monarchy.—Republicanism.—Independence of National Character and Manners.—Loyalty.—Tendency to Federalism.—Reasons therefor, and Probability of a Confederation.—Its Benefits.—The Basque Fueros.—Effect of Internal Improvements and Development of Industrial Resources.—Empleomania.—Reasons for American Sympathy with Spain.—Justice due Her........................... 356

Postscript 373

SPAIN.

I.

Journey to Madrid.

IT was in the beginning of December, 1849, that I approached the Pyrenees, from Bayonne, for the first time. Had it been a matter of discretion with me, I should, of course, have selected a season for crossing them, in which the proprieties of the barometer and thermometer would have been more likely to be observed. The weather, however, was not the only thing that promised disagreeable contingencies. The whole gossip of the hotel population in Bayonne was terrible with tales of robbery upon the highway of the Spanish capital. My previous visit to the Peninsula had made me rather sceptical, it is true, in such matters, but now the details were so vivid and circumstantial, that they could hardly be doubted without flying in the face of all road-side probabilities. A fat gentleman, at the *table d'hôte* of the Hôtel de Commerce, assured me,—with that air of certainty not to be questioned which belongs to age in its combination with the apoplectic diathesis,—that to his knowledge the diligence had been robbed near Lerma a few days before. The passengers, he said, had been made to lie shivering in the middle of the road, with their faces downwards, and with the scantiest possible allowance of under-clothes, until the thieves had made off with their outer garments and valuables, and the best mules of the team. "And so," added the old gentleman, helping himself to two cutlets, "they were many hours without any thing to eat!" It was not, therefore, without some chill forebodings, in spite of myself, that I surrendered my fortunes to the lumbering vehicle which was to bear them. As I looked at my watch, to see the time of our departure, it was tenderly and sadly, I own, as at the face of an old friend, from whom I soon might part in sorrow and for ever. On the 12th of December, nevertheless, at four in the morning, I awoke to find my journey and misgivings of seventy hours triumphantly at an end. I was at Madrid, in the huge hostelry of the Postas Peninsulares on the Calle de Alcalá, sorely exercised in mind and battered in body, but none the worse in estate, beyond the usual and lawful pillage of custom-house officers, landlords, and postilions. Whether the presence of two well-appointed *guardias civiles*, who had joined us some stages from the capital, had any thing to do with our safety, I am not clairvoyant enough to know; but I made up my mind, as I advise all travellers in Spain to do, that thenceforward and for ever no story of highwaymen—though as long and romantic as the Chronicle of the Cid, and as authentic as the American news in Galignani—should prevent me from pursuing my business or pleasure in the Peninsula, with a light heart and as heavy a purse as needful.

The greater part of what attracted my attention on the journey, I saw again, in a brighter and more genial light, on my return. Only the stern mountain passes of Pancorvo and Somosierra seemed to derive a lonelier and sublimer wildness from the snow and leafless trees, and the congenial, tempest-laden clouds above them. As to the "entertainment for man" with which we were favored, under the auspices of the Postas Peninsulares in whose diligence I travelled, it is a matter of duty to those who may follow me to say, that it was as detestable as can be imagined. The humblest *ventorrillo* on the Andalusian hills, where I partook of game and salad in former days, while the fleas took reprisals from me, was a palace for a Sybarite, in comparison with some of the *paradores* into which we were now compelled to burrow. A cordon of such establishments would do more, I think, than martello towers and floating batteries, to check the march of an invading army, from any land where creature comforts are prized as they deserve.

But we were at Madrid, and, strange to note, in that proverbially clear, transparent atmosphere, there hung over the stately city what a stout curate, who dismounted with us, called *una niebla del Demonio,*—a fog of the Devil! If I had been the author of the *Pillars of Hercules*, I should have felt it my duty, as a Scot, to maintain, against all diabolical pretensions whatever, that the mist was a countryman of mine, and that I had seen its relations in Auld Reekie. As it was, I followed the legal maxim of believing every man in his business, and, on the faith of his clerical friend, gave credit to the *Demonio* accordingly.

II.

LODGING-HOUSES, LODGING, AND LIFE IN MADRID.—SERVANTS, &c.

THE Arcipreste de Hita—upon the principle of taking the lesser evil where we have a choice—commends us to the smallest women for our loves and wives:—

> "Del mal, tomar lo menos, díselo el Sabidor,
> Porende de las mugeres la menor es la mejor."

He will be a wise man who reads the principle backwards, and remembers that the Fonda de las Postas Peninsulares, being the largest tavern in Madrid, is of necessity the worst. It is quite an imposing establishment—when seen from the street, I was about to say; but the interior will impose upon you quite as much, in its way, if you will give it an opportunity. The edifice belongs or belonged to the Marques de la Torrecilla, and is adorned, as to its front, with sundry blazonries in churrigueresque, which aptly symbolize the highly feudal character of what you meet within. That it is considered quite a grand affair, and worthy of this attempt to forewarn the unwary in regard to it, will be seen by the commendation which Madoz bestows on it, in his *Diccionario Geográfico, Estadístico, Histórico*, a work of really great merit, which I shall have occasion to speak of hereafter. "All its apartments," says the patriotic Don Pascual, "which are many and good, enjoy excellent light and ventilation, and have just undergone notable improvement, as well in the papering and painting of the walls and ceilings, as in the complete array of furniture which adorns them. Its guests will find the service exact, the table choicely provided, and the beds and linen exquisitely neat." I should be happy if I had room for the whole passage in the original, if it were only to show, as a philological curiosity, how much a beautiful language can make out of a bad, dark, mouldy caravansera. The *fonda*, rhetoric apart, is served by Italians, whose national instincts are a guaranty against cleanliness, as all the world knows. The ground-floor is dedicated to the four-footed servants of the company, which of course secures to the rest of the mansion a liberally distributed odor of the stable and a lively circulation of fleas and horse-boys. The diligences, of which it is the great centre and emporium, arrive and depart at all hours of the night, especially at those when people with good consciences and unpacked trunks enjoy their sweetest dreams;—and let not any man with nerves delude himself by thinking that the cup of tribulation has visited his lips, till there has risen on his slumbers that forty-mule-power chorus of shouting, cursing, and whip-cracking, for which every departure or arrival is an awful signal. At the *table d'hôte*, which has considerable pretension, and which you reach through long, dark passages, dreary to tread, I found scarce any visitors but *commis voyageurs*, who, to judge from their manners and conversation, were, I am sure, the worst of the beasts not enumerated in the Apocalypse.

It will be readily imagined, that such quarters were not long to be endured; but, although I speedily fell among kind friends, who appreciated the sadness of my lot, and were willing to liberate me if they could, Madrid is not a place where a man may find pleasant lodging-houses as readily as the illustrious Manchegan fell upon adventures. "*No es este ramo en el que mas sobresale Madrid,*" candidly confesses Mellado, in his "Traveller's Guide,"—the tavern department is not that in which Madrid chiefly excels! The Spaniards themselves, who are exceedingly simple in their habits, and can get comfortably through the coldest winter by a dexterous combination of the *brasero,* the cloak, and the sunshine, will cheerfully stow themselves away, wherever there is a mat on the tiled floor, and a large window to let in the rays. A few chairs and a writing-table, with an alcove, and a plain but tidy bed, are "*lo que hay que desear,*"—all that a man could wish for lodging. For diet,—be it good taste or bad,—they are well content with the national *puchero,* more or less refined,—thinking, with Governor Panza, that, "in the diversity of things whereof the said *ollas* are composed, a man cannot help stumbling upon something that will please him and do him good." Nor is that dish altogether unworthy the great Sancho's praise, which may be expanded, if you will, into a compendium of natural history and botany, or be decent and respectable with only bacon and *garbanzos.* Entertainment of this sort is cheap and easy to find. You have but to look at the newspapers, or cast a glance at the intelligence-office which is wafered up, in manuscript, on the back wall of the post-office building, and you will find paradises of the kind tempting you by the score. "*No hay niños,*"—there are no children about the house,—say some of them; and with such a recommendation, and balconies on the sunny side, what more in reason could you crave?

Alas! reason, like most elementary substances, is rarely to be found in a pure state. Custom, somehow or other, manages to keep up a sort of chemical combination with it. People will wear boots and shoes, if they can get them, notwithstanding the "annoyance and vexation, astonishment and surprise," with which Mr. Urquhart regards so abnormal a condition of the extremities. Travellers who have become viciously accustomed to fires and carpets in cold weather, and are not prepared to appreciate a mixture of the entire animal and vegetable kingdoms, in one pot, for dinner, will seek to accommodate their prejudices, though ever so unreasonable. I do not mean to say that they are right, and Spaniards wrong; for Adam's unsophisticated palate might perhaps have found in turtle-soup and *patés de foie gras* much less of the eternal fitness, than in the wildest *gazpacho* that Iberian peasant ever supped. I only suggest it as a fact, that tastes differ.

Until late years, the number of foreigners visiting Madrid would hardly have justified any extensive or costly preparation for their special entertainment. Even now they are so few, in comparison with the throngs which fill the other capitals of Europe, that it would be altogether unreasonable for them to expect such a reception as elsewhere is afforded them. Indeed, in Spain itself I found no city, among those I visited upon the coast or near it, which was not greatly in advance of Madrid, in the particular referred to. Barcelona, Cadiz, Seville, and especially Malaga, were beyond comparison better provided. Nevertheless, with a little patience and the aid of a friend's experience, one may still be comfortable in Madrid,—nay, and have luxury too, if he be willing to pay for it. At the *table d'hôte* of the Vizcaina, in the magnificent house of Cordero, which occupies the site of the once famous convent of San Felipe el Real, on the Calle Mayor, there may be found excellent society for those who speak French or Spanish, and a modified nationality of diet which has carried comfort to the bosom of many a wayfarer. Of restaurants, there are of course many, some of them indifferent, but the greater part very bad. The *café* of L'Hardi, immortalized by Dumas for its "*nourriture honorable*," still nourishes as honorably as in the days of the royal nuptials, and the Fonda de San Luis, in the Calle de la Montera, may almost be said to herald the day when, as in the land of its saintly patron, cookery will be a fine art and keep a Muse of its own!

Quiet people, who propose residing at Madrid for any length of time, and prefer having things more under their control than the *restaurant* or the *table d'hôte* will allow, may do so satisfactorily now, without much trouble. Excellent apartments, with comfortable fire-places and all other desirable appointments, are beginning to be offered for rent in the most agreeable and convenient quarters of the city. With a good servant, commanded at his peril to overlook the household and keep vigils over your flesh-pots as a knight over his virgin armor, you may live and prosper, at one of these establishments, as well as a man need hope to do away from home. My first experience was at the corner of the Calle Mayor and the Calle del Correo, with a range of five balconies looking upon the Puerta del Sol, and in the very heart of all that was lively and bright to be heard and seen. Not a pageant but passed that way,—not a gallant regiment that went to post or to parade, but favored me with the sound of its trumpets and the glitter of its arms. Work and sleep, however, are sometimes as needful as hearing and seeing, and in such a locality I found it somewhat difficult to pay proper attention to either. The noises of the day were by no means careful to close their accounts at midnight, and it was painfully early, indeed, when the bells of the goats and the clatter of the milk-vendors in the street below me would begin to insist that it was morning. There were other good reasons too for change, more potent than even distraction and unrest. In the sketches of my former experience in Spain, I endeavored to contribute something towards removing the popular prejudice that the garlic-crop is the chief staple of the Peninsula. I even went so far as to say, that the esculent in question had never once crossed my own particular path, during a three months' excursion of no very limited range. In sack-cloth and ashes I must now confess, that, having gone farther, I fared worse; and that, although my original observation was correct, so far as the customs of the better classes are concerned and the general experience of a traveller who frequents the best inns in the best towns, there is, nevertheless, garlic to be found within even the sacred precincts of the court! The amiable Dolores, in whose balconies I gloried, did vow and plight her Andalusian faith that she despised the aromatic poison, and would not suffer it to pass her threshold; but there are certain of the senses which sometimes overpower even faith, and I shall ever believe that, had Dolores been Pandora, *tocino y ajo*, bacon and garlic, would have been found at the bottom of her box. I changed my quarters accordingly to No. 1 of the Calle de Pontejos, in the same vast building, and there, on the first floor, fronting on a quiet street, with all the sunshine that I needed, excellent apartments, a good landlord, and a most desirable location, I spent a pleasant winter and some portion of a bright and cheerful spring. If Don Jose, the *prendero* of the Calle del Correo, should be living when the reader arrives at Madrid, let him be sent for straightways, and if there be room in his house let the reader install himself at once, and ask questions afterwards, if he has a mind.

There is no lack of good servants, or at all events of good material for servants, anywhere in Spain. Honesty, fidelity, and that best of courtesies which springs from self-respect and gives dignity to the humblest station, are characteristics which mark them, as a class, to an extent of which I believe no other country furnishes an example. As a consequence,—perhaps, in some degree, a cause,—in no country is the relation of servants and their employers made so agreeable by respectful and affectionate familiarity. This remark applies to all ranks, without exception, and there is something in the innate and peculiar politeness and high tone belonging to the national character, among even the humblest and least educated, which prevents the usual ill effects of that sort of freedom elsewhere.

Madrid is too much of a capital to be without the proper supply of thieving valets. Intriguing masters are abundant, and "like master, like man." Nevertheless, good servants may be found there readily, and at moderate wages, provided the traveller be able to speak to them in their own language. Those who possess any familiarity with foreign tongues are very few, and of course command higher salaries. Of English scarce any of them know any thing. Out of Madrid and the commercial cities, it is extremely difficult, indeed, to find attendants whose acquirements go beyond the Castilian and their native dialect, and this must be added to the thousand other reasons which continually thrust themselves upon a traveller of any intelligence, to convince him, that, without at least a fair acquaintance with the language of the country, it is utterly impossible for any one to visit it, with any prospect of comprehending or enjoying it, except in the most superficial and unsatisfactory manner. I am more firmly impressed than ever, since my second visit to Spain, with the conviction that ignorance in this particular is the chief source of the thousand ridiculous and romantic misrepresentations, of which that country has been made the victim, more frequently than any other; and upon which foreign—especially English and American—opinion in regard to her customs and laws, her morals and religion, is so largely and erroneously founded. " What say you, then," says Nerissa, " to Faulconbridge, the young baron of England?" " You know," replies Portia, " I say nothing to him, for he understands not me, nor I him; he hath neither Latin, French, nor Italian; and you will come into the court and swear that I have a poor pennyworth in the English." To this passage the learned Warburton, with characteristic acuteness, appends a note, informing us that it is "a satire on the ignorance of young English travellers in our author's time." Alas! Shakspeare wrote for all times, and there are Faulconbridges who never saw England!

III.

FOUNDATION, LOCALITY, CLIMATE, DRESS, HEALTH, &c. OF MADRID.

IT is not easy to fathom the reasons of kings or women,—at least so says an ancient, if not wise, saw. To express any opinion upon the latter branch of the subject would be altogether extrajudicial and unnecessary here; but the selection, or rather the creation, of Madrid as the capital of Spain, may be taken as a fair argument to support the anti-royal phase of the proverb. Some say that Charles the Fifth laid the foundation of its greatness, from a fondness he contracted for it during a residence which cured him of the ague. If so, posterity has certainly paid dear for what would now be accomplished, probably, by a three days' course of quinine. Philip the Second, whose exquisite taste in such matters is further exemplified by the charming site of the Escorial, inherited, it is likely, the imperial liver and predilections, for he fixed his court at Madrid, in 1560. Forty years later, Philip the Third translated the royal residence to Valladolid, but weighty interests and influences were so wielded as to compel his return after a five years' absence. From that time to the present Madrid has been, emphatically, *la Corte*, the Court, and nothing else. For its elevation to that dignity there is not, nor has there ever been given, that I am aware, one plausible reason, except that its position is, to a certain degree, central. Undoubtedly this would be the best of reasons, if the centrality were any thing but a matter of measurement,—if the location, in reference to industry, commerce, or agriculture, exercised any centripetal or other favorable influence whatever. The top of a mountain in the midst of a fertile plain would be eminently central, and the Grand Lama might like it for a sacred residence; yet it would be an up-hill sort of business, to prove that it ought to be chosen, for its centrality, as the site of a metropolis.

Madrid has no commerce, nor the means of any. Its inhabitants must eat and wear clothing, and the materials therefor must pass the walls, within which they must set in motion, well or ill, certain departments of necessary industry. Beyond this, no trade enters or abides, and there is none at all that passes out. The Manzanares, which trickles by the city, has scarce water enough to furnish even a court poet with materials for any thing exceeding the limits of an epigram. The surrounding country is barren and arid, sparsely populated, and without attraction of any sort; so that, on the whole, whatever there is in Madrid of population, wealth, industry, or power is altogether factitious. It is the capital, because it was made so, and it is only populous, wealthy, industrious, or powerful, because it is the capital. If it be four thousand and nineteen years old, as we have the official authority of the *Guia de Forasteros* of 1850 for saying, we must admit that few places have profited as little by age; and if all the Chaldeans and Phœnicians, Hebrews, Greeks, and Romans, whom the antiquaries suppose to have busied themselves with its name, gave half as much attention to its education, it has certainly a sad account to settle for neglected opportunities. The advantages which it has enjoyed, within the range of authentic chronology, would have made of fair Seville an imperial city such as Europe scarcely knows, or have built up again at Córdova the magnificence of Abderrahman's proudest day.

I have said, that when we entered Madrid it was enveloped in a thick fog. This was considered extraordinary, and especially so because it lasted about a week, during which one might have imagined himself in London, but for the fact that the Madrid mists appeared to be legitimately derived from pure water; whereas the corresponding commodity in the British capital has, to an unfamiliar eye, the appearance and density of highly vaporized molasses. Whatever defects there may be in the winter atmosphere of Madrid, humidity and obscurity form generally no part of them. I have nowhere seen, except in the United States, and there only during the prevalence of the coldest winds from the northwest, any thing to equal the pervading clearness and splendor of the Madrid sky, and the transparency of its air. As a general thing, it lacks, like ours, the soft and genial tints of the Italian heavens, yet often, when the sun was going down, I have stood in the gay avenues of the Retiro, or on the high grounds near the gate of Alcalá, and have seen the many cross-crowned spires and towers of the city bathed in a light so golden, with a background of such deep and various purple, roseate, and crimson, that I have almost doubted whether even Naples could boast of any thing more gorgeous.

It would be well if as much could be said in favor of the climate as of the sky. When Spain is spoken of with us, most people, without any particular reflection, have an idea immediately presented to them of a far southern country, with clustering vines and perfumed orange-groves. I was frequently congratulated, before I left home, upon the delightful opportunity I should have of spending my winter in so mild a climate as that of Madrid. A pleasant fancy, truly!

The Spanish capital is in a latitude two degrees or thereabouts higher than that of Washington, and stands upon the Platform of Castile, at an elevation (Madoz tells us) of two thousand four hundred and fifty feet above the sea. The rarity of the atmosphere produced by this latter cause would be quite sufficient of itself, under ordinary circumstances, to make new, if not unpleasant, impressions upon unfamiliar lungs and nerves. I thought—though it may have been fancy—that at all times I perceived a tenuity and pungency about it to which I was unaccustomed. But this is not the worst by a great deal. From any unobstructed point of view within the city or about it, you notice that the horizon towards the north and west is encircled by the high and snowy mountains of Somosierra and Guadarrama. To the blasts which roll down from these latter hills, and even more to the still and subtile influence of their cold proximity, is the fatal insalubrity of the situation to be chiefly traced. When the wind blows from that quarter, every one is in terror, and no man is deemed prudent who ventures into the street without covering his chest and throat, and especially his mouth, with the *embozo* of his cloak. You may walk for squares without seeing any more of the human face divine, than a sort of zone, bounded on the north at the eyebrows by a hat-brim, and on the south by a horizontal strip of velvet cloak-facing, running perpendicular to the bridge of the nose. I very early satisfied myself—whether justly or not I will not dogmatically say—that the frequent *pulmonias* (or pneumonias), which were so fatal at such times, might be the result, in a great measure, of this practice, by means of which the lungs were accustomed only to the obstructed inhalation of warm air, and rendered sensible, in a tenfold degree, to any accidental or necessary exposure. That, without any particular robustness of health, and certainly without having especially avoided opening my mouth in any wind or weather, I am now alive and storytelling, may go, as a fact, for what it is worth, to sustain my notion. Fashion, I think, is fast working a practical revolution in the habits of the people on this point, which could not be produced, one might safely swear, by a century of mere medical disquisition or other manner of preaching. Cloaks are going rapidly out of vogue, and the *beau monde* generally have handed themselves over to the undraped dominion of the French overcoat. On windy days, when the *pulmonia* is supposed to be whistling around every corner and dancing in the deserted *plazas*, the more daringly elegant attempt a compromise between their love of Paris and their fear of death, by the use of a large, separate fur collar, covering the whole neck and jaws, and giving a most top-heavy and ludicrous appearance to the scanty and skirt-denied *paletot*. Here and there, one of fashion's most reckless desperadoes may be seen without even this bungling and ungraceful protection, so that I think the days of the *embozo's* popularity as a life-preserver may be fairly said to be numbered. Unless, however, the police of the city be improved in sundry unsavory particulars, to which every traveller's reminiscences will point him at once, the popularity of the *embozo* may still be prolonged, by transferring its protecting folds from the mouth, which needs them not, to the nose, which needs them greatly.

But it is the still, small voice from the mountains, and not the loud breath of the tempest, which bears the fatal message oftenest. Bright and apparently bland as the weather may be, during the winter or the spring, you have but to remove yourself for a moment from the direct influence of the sun's rays, to experience the most marked and unwholesome difference of temperature. Sunshine and shade, town and country, day and night, seem to belong, severally, to different climates. The clothing which oppresses you on your way to the Prado, an hour before sunset, is too light for comfort when you return in the dusk; and as you enter the sheltered portal of one of the huge houses which are now so numerous, you long, at midday, for the cloak which would have nearly stifled you upon the street.

Almost every one has heard of the proverb, which says that "the air of Madrid will kill a man, but not put out a candle." Many of the Madrileños think that there is something in the composition of their atmosphere, independently of its rarity and temperature, which entitles it to this bad name; but the same reproach, it strikes me, would apply, with greater or less force, to the air of any city so closely fenced about by snowy mountains. I remember to have noticed precisely the same characteristics—to a diminished degree, perhaps—in the climate of Florence. It was like a voyage from Indus to the Pole, to pass from the glowing sunshine of the early spring, upon the Cascine or the Lungo l'Arno, to the cold, still, collapsing influence of the narrow,

3

unsunned streets. No doubt the memories of older and better travellers will shiver over similar experiences. But whether Madrid be peculiar or not in the quality of its air, there can be no doubt about the insalubrity of its climate. The young die very young, and numerously; the vigorous years of life are in great peril, always, from every variety of inflammatory disease; and age comes on with rapid pace, and many ills, to the most of those who linger. Nervous disorders are a staple commodity. Apoplexies were of more frequent occurrence, it seemed to me, than in any bills of mortality I had ever seen. Even when the thermometer indicated but a moderate winter temperature,—the freezing point or thereabouts,—there was something so penetrating in the air,—so searching within doors and without,—that it seemed far colder than a temperature many degrees lower anywhere else. The *pulmonia* then walked alike at noonday and in darkness; nor were its arrows aimed at humanity alone. The horse-guards at the palace, whose fine appointments and gallant chargers attracted so much attention, were dispensed with in midwinter,—their horses dying almost nightly from this terrible and rapid scourge. Late in the spring, when I visited the royal stables, a beautiful stallion was shivering with the death-agony, and they told me his disease was *pulmonia.*

If I am asked how it is possible that king, minister, and noble can so far overcome the inborn mortal dread of dissolution, as to live thus ever in the valley of its shadow, I do not know that I can give a more satisfactory reply than the stereotyped Spanish extinguisher upon impertinent or inconvenient curiosity,—*Quien sabe?* Who knows? In the superb apartments of one of the most luxurious palaces of Europe,—

surrounded by every guard and fence which human skill and care can build up against fleshly ills,—it is perhaps not difficult to understand how royalty can bring itself to bear the risks, of which it knows and feels comparatively little. While winter is still lingering in Madrid, their Majesties can seek the early fragrance of an almost Andalusian spring, among the groves and fountains of beautiful Aranjuez. When summer burns the blood of all sojourners in the capital, their Majesties find health and vigor in the mountain freshness of La Granja. To those who have not such resources, the honors and profits of their several pursuits supply some compensation, I suppose, for perils such as they encounter. "Where the king is," says the Castilian proverb, "there is the court." Where there is grain to be trodden out, and in a somewhat unmuzzled manner besides, the oxen are apt to congregate. So long as Madrid shall be the fountain and reservoir of favor, the *pulmonías fulminantes* will thunder in vain, as they have thundered long, to keep the thirsty from going up to drink. And who can think it strange? A residence in Paris will extinguish a race in three generations, and yet numberless families go there and become extinct. Half a generation will usually answer the same purpose, quite as effectually, among the golden Golgothas of California, and yet we have not heard, for all that, that the Golgothas are lacking skulls!

IV.

PUERTA DEL SOL.—PUBLIC HABITS OF THE MADRILEÑOS.—THE PRADO.
—EQUIPAGES.—HORSEMEN.—ATOCHA WALK.—WOMEN OF MADRID.

WHOSOEVER desires to know any thing of Madrid, or the people that live in it, must make himself acquainted, at once, with La Puerta del Sol,—the Gate of the Sun. It is not worth while to be at all mythological on the subject, for the Puerta is itself no gate, nor has it any appurtenance whatever to remind you of Aurora's rosy fingers. It is neither more nor less than a central, open *plaza*,—not very large nor elegant,—into which nine or ten of the chief streets discharge their crowds. A congress of cab-horses are the only representatives of Apollo's radiant steeds, and the beautiful Hours have for their sole abiding-place the dial of a large clock, in the church front of Nuestra Señora del Buen Suceso. The graceless, though fashionable, temple to which the clock belongs, and the tall, stilted façade of the Casa de Correos, are the only and poor substitutes for the "*flammantia moenia mundi.*" The sun, however,—out of gratitude, I suppose, for the complimentary use of his name,—shines with peculiar good-will upon his Puerta, and there is no knowing the amount of fire-wood, or rather of charcoal, which is thus saved to the gossips of Madrid. The Prado, though a beautiful and genial walk, is too far out of town for lounging or midday access, and too extensive for that cosy contact which your genuine tattler loves. The Plaza de Oriente, down by the palace, is also too far from the centre, and receives, besides, in rather too direct a manner, the breezes from the Guadarrama Mountains, whose grand white summits furnish it with so superb a prospect. But the Puerta del Sol is as accessible as it is warm, and no true Madrileño can he be, who does not bask away, within its teeming precincts, the largest portion of his daylight life. Even when the sun has gone down, and there is no moon to take up the wondrous tales which are always being told there, the tall gas-lamp, in the centre of the *plaza*, holds a cloak-wrapped court of its own; so that to have passed through the Puerta del Sol when there was no one about it to speak or to listen, a man must have kept later hours than her Majesty's watchmen, and more faithful vigils, by far. There must, of necessity, be a great deal of gossip in every capital, where there is nothing to do but to govern, to intrigue, and be amused. Madrid being of that class of capitals, preëminently, is as full of scandal as the sewing society of a village in a highly moral neighborhood. The Puerta is the great condenser of all its small-talk,—its *mentidero general*, or general lie-factory,—and cannot, with such functions, afford to be, for many moments, empty or disengaged.

I have taken other occasion to touch upon the fondness of the Spaniards for out-door life. Madrid exhibits this, as it does the most of their peculiarities, in a very extreme point of view. The inhabitants—the *gente fina*, at all events—are no very early risers. It lacks but little of noon when the most of them have broken their fast and are ready for their daily occupations, if they have any. If you call familiarly upon a gentleman, about twelve, it is probable his servant will tell you,—not that he has gone to his business, or indeed anywhere in particular,—but that " *ha ido su merced á la calle,*"— his worship has gone into the street! The particularity of this information reminds you, at first, of the testamentary liberality of the Irish gentleman, who left his son a million, and the wide world to make it in, but a short experience teaches you that it is little less than a specific direction to the Puerta del Sol. There, from an early hour, laborers in search of hire have been watching for customers,—venders of all manner of pet dogs and small wares have been clattering and chaffering,—newsmen have been crying their tidings, and selling to all who have been fools enough to buy. There, too, there are a hundred chances to one that you find your friend, in the midst of a group, at the foot of the Calle de la Montera, puffing with enthusiastic energy at his cigar, while he devours, or pours into ears as greedy as his own, the last rumors of a ministerial catastrophe or the freshest developments of social transgression. The length of time that he will pass where you find him will depend entirely upon the amount of gossip to be had. His daily labors, be they what they may, and especially if he be an *empleado*,—a placeman,— as almost every body is, are matters of but little concern, and indefinite susceptibility of postponement. As, however, the Puerta is not precisely fashionable until somewhat later in the afternoon, it is probable he will proceed, after a moderate instalment of discourse, to refresh the place of his business with the light of his countenance. How much of his time, if he be in a public office, will be spent in lighting and relighting his accustomed succession of *cigarritos*, and increasing his own and the official stock of exciting information, the initiated can tell, and may, if they choose. Not many hours, however, will have elapsed, before the foot of the Montera shall see him again, in the midst of still shorter *paletóts* and yellower gloves than those that were visible in the less consecrated moments of his morning visit.

As the time for the parade upon the Prado comes on,—an hour at least before the setting of the sun, when the weather is moderate enough to permit it,—the Puerta del Sol begins to give up its gayest and most gallant loungers. The church of Buen Suceso occupies the extremity of the acute angle formed by the streets of Alcalá and San Gerónimo, both of which, issuing from the Puerta, strike the Prado at different points. The larger portion of the crowd passes up the Alcalá, which is one of the stateliest and most noble avenues I have seen,—wide at its commencement, and increasing in width and beauty, until, crossing the Prado and passing alongside the Retiro gardens, it reaches the city walls, at the superb triumphal arch known as the Gate of Alcalá. The Carrera de San Gerónimo, however, is the line of march for the more choice and exclusive spirits, who linger for a moment, in passing, at the *café* of L'Hardi, to derange their digestion with dear confectionary, and fortify themselves, by a glass of muscatel, against the toils of the walk and the perilous onslaught of unmerciful bright eyes.

The Prado has been often described, and I shall only say of it, that it extends along the whole eastern side of the city, from the Gate of Recoletos, up to the Gate and Convent of Atocho. In that part of it, called the Salon, which lies between the streets of Alcalá and San Gerónimo, directly facing the monument to the heroes of the *Dos de Mayo* (May 2d, 1808), it was fashionable for all the world to congregate, during the earlier weeks of the season. I have often seen it so full, of a bright afternoon, that

"Those navigators must be able seamen"

who could find a channel through it. While the pedestrians, thus packed at such close quarters, went through the pedetentous performance which is called "walking," in Spain, the long broad avenue which runs through the whole Prado was lined with gay equipages and equestrians. One would think, from Mr. Ford's description of the "antediluvian carriages, with ridiculous coachmen and grotesque footmen to match," that Madrid was a sort of Pompeii of coaches, under whose crust of lava or ashes there was nothing to be found, in the way of a conveyance, of much later date than Pliny the elder. The learned licenciate, Don Pedro Fernandez Navarrete, in his *Conservacion de Monarquías*, expressed his fears to the council of Philip the Third, that the kingdom might share the fate of the house of Jacob, according to the prophet Isaiah, "because the land was full of horses, neither was there any end of the chariots." I should fully concur with Mr. Ford in thinking, that to scourge the Peninsula generally for excessive luxury in coaches would be a mysterious, and, to human eyes, a rather severe dispensation. But I am bound to say, on the other hand, that in the capital I think the manifestation of elegance and good taste in equipages was general and striking. A few days after my arrival, I witnessed the funeral of the Conde de Oñate, a grandee of Spain, which took place from his palace in the Calle Mayor, nearly opposite my lodgings. The display of coaches, horses, and liveries was most ample and magnificent; quite as much so, I am sure, as any similar occasion would have elicited in London or Paris. It is no great compliment, perhaps, to the Madrileños to say this, for nearly all their finest carriages are of English or French manufacture, principally the latter; but be that as it may, the fact is as I state it. Such, indeed, is now the rage for coaches in Madrid, that sorrowful is the dame of note who does not own one. They appear to think, as the good Navarrete and his voucher, Trogus Pompeius, allege, that "not to ride about and be seen is to confess themselves ill-favored." A friend, who had certainly no wish to slander his native land, informed me, that there were persons, to his knowledge, in Madrid, who reduced themselves to the extremity of hiring their table and bed linen, in order to keep coaches for the evening ride upon the Prado! Pride and poverty, alas! are companions, it seems, everywhere.

But whatever may be said of the vehicles, I do not wonder that an Englishman should be in peril of his life from laughing at the horsemen. The horses, for the most part, though often pretty, are under-sized, and it seems to be taken for granted that, if they are fat and sleek, there is nothing more required, unless it can be managed that they be spotted or piebald, like the charger of Mr. Briggs, in Punch, which had been taught to take a seat when he heard music. Their natural paces are completely destroyed by vicious education, and every ribbon-tailed little fellow of them will canter, in magnificent attitudes, such as a horse was never made to assume, except by the Spanish *picadores*—and the illustrious

David, when he painted Napoleon on the Alps. Indeed no class of animals, that I know of, has greater reason than the Spanish riding-horses to feel under personal obligations to the attraction of gravitation. But for that potent check, there would be no visible reason why, between the horizontal impetus communicated from behind and the perpendicular motion they are taught to give to the fore legs, they should not pass off, on the diagonal of forces, to meet the renowned Clavileño among the Pleiades.

As the spring came on, and with it more genial weather, the Salon gradually lost its popularity, and the walk between the Gate and Convent of Atocha became the rendezvous of all that was elegant and attractive in Madrid. There is nothing very remarkable in that part of the Prado. On the left, as you face the convent, there is a long, bold hill, which, though surmounted by a pretty little astronomical observatory, is barren and repulsive, like all the hills along the Manzanares. On the right extends the city wall, which is as graceless in appearance as it would be insignificant for any serious purpose of defence. The right was the fashionable side for pedestrians. Under the shadow of the wall some little grass had been able to keep itself alive, and the proprietors of chairs had taken advantage of the green carpet to make the public comfortable there at a *cuarto* apiece. After walking till you were tired, you would take a seat for a while. A charity match-bearer, from the poor-house of San Bernardino, would immediately present himself, with his badge upon his hat to show you his authority, and his box at his belt to receive your contribution. It is the privilege, perhaps the monopoly, of the poor old fellows, to light cigars upon the public walks, and it does not enter into their imaginations to conceive that you can sit down for five minutes without needing their services.

When you are comfortably arranged, either with or without your *cigarrito*, you must be hard to please, if you do not find blessed occupation for your eyes, as long as the daylight lasts. In their handsome open carriages—moving at the slowest, most convenient pace for observation, or walking, slowly, in bright groups, before you, or sitting in groups just as bright around you—are as many of Eve's fairest daughters as in the longest day of the year you ever saw before, or are likely again to see. In other parts of Spain the women, beautiful as they may be, have their peculiar, unvarying, provincial type. In Madrid, though the "dark side" of loveliness is that which you most generally see, there is, nevertheless, in that, extreme variety. Bernardin de Saint Pierre gave up in despair the description of the strawberry-plant in his window, because he found that at least seven-and-thirty different species of gorgeous butterflies made it their beautiful pleasure-ground. The Prado, with the fair spirits which are its ministers, must remain unchronicled in loveliness, by me, for reasons quite as plentiful. I may be permitted only to say, by way of qualification, that I do not think beauty has a much longer span in Madrid than other vitalities. At a moderately middle age, there is a sad tendency towards the robustious in figure; and a young maiden at all prudential should carefully keep her mother in the background, lest hopeful swains might be deterred from uttering obligatory vows, by the dread of avoirdupois weight to come!

V.

CONSTITUTIONAL HISTORY AND EPOCHS.—CONSTITUTIONS.—FERDINAND THE SEVENTH.—DUC D'ANGOULÊME.—CRISTINA.—DON CARLOS.—ESTATUTO REAL.—HISTORY OF PARTIES.—ESPARTERO.—NARVAEZ.

THE Spanish government is called "a constitutional monarchy," and there is no doubt that it is entitled to the appellation, if the number of organic laws that have ruled it be taken as evidence. I had the pleasure of examining the original of the first of these, the constitution of 1812, which was reproclaimed in 1820 and 1836. It is magnificently engrossed and bound, and has the interesting signatures of many patriotic and illustrious men, who devoted themselves during the struggle with Napoleon, and the gloomy period which followed it, to the glorious work of their country's political regeneration. It has been the fashion of late days, in some quarters, to undervalue the efforts of these men, and to reproach them with failures and follies which were but the unavoidable results of political inexperience and the most untoward circumstances. My occupations in Madrid made it necessary for me often to recur to the proceedings of the constituent and legislative Cortes of 1812–20, &c., and it would be unjust for me to conceal how much my admiration was excited by the deliberative eloquence and the political philosophy which they displayed. That in the midst of revolution, uncertainty, and novelty,—with prejudices the most inveterate to overcome, and ignorance and apathy to enlighten and stimulate,—there should have been many things evolved which were ephemeral and puerile, can surely be no matter of surprise. But that in a country where political discussion of every sort had been unknown for centuries,—where free thought and a free press had never existed,—where education had been imperfect or perverted, and oratory had never stepped beyond the precincts of the pulpit and a restricted forum,—there should have sprung at a moment's warning, from an oppressed and exhausted people, men equal to the labors which the Constitutionalist leaders of those days did unquestionably perform,—is a phenomenon well worth the notice of those who believe that "benighted" and "barbarous" are the only epithets to which the Spaniards are entitled.

Side by side with the first constitution, in the archives of the Chamber of Deputies, is its successor of 1837, even more gorgeous in vellum, velvet, and chirography. It was shown to me, with just and manly pride, by a distinguished member of the *Progresista* party who had a conspicuous share in its formation, and could not avoid sighing over the departure of its authority. In the same archives is the original of the constitution now in force, which was promulgated in 1845. It does not appear to have been considered as of any great dignity, if one may judge from the fact that it exists only in printed form, and that its garniture is by no means luxurious,—a significant thing in Spain. It is probably adorned, however, quite as well as it is sometimes observed,—if it be not treason to say so.

Every one who is familiar with the recent history of the Peninsula will remember that the constitution of 1812 was framed during the absence of Ferdinand the Seventh in captivity in France, by the men who had been most active and earnest in devoting themselves and their fortunes to the maintenance of the national independence. Loyal, as well as patriotic, they had taken no advantage of their king's long absence, to weaken his legitimate authority or sap the foundation of his throne. They had done nothing without his declared and apparently sincere approbation, and when, at last, he was about to resume the sceptre of his ancestors, it was the pride of the good and brave men who had preserved it for him, that they had made him and his descendants secure in it, by linking the dignity and power of the monarch with the freedom and happiness of the people. The defects of the constitution were probably many. It was not easy to ingraft a representative system—in the sense in which such systems are now understood—upon the habits and traditions of the most eminently monarchical country of Europe. But the Constitutionalists of 1812—be their errors what they may—kept constantly before them the one great principle of making the throne subordinate to the law. The Cortes were intrusted, to all intents and purposes, with the government of the realm, in subjection to the constitution. The personal inviolability of the monarch was neutralized, so far as was proper, by the direct responsibility of his ministers; and there were guards and checks which secured the rights of all classes from the encroachments of prerogative and power.

During the short period of their sway, the Cortes reformed many abuses, and established much that was wise, liberal, and of hopeful promise. The first act, however, of the restored king was to avail himself of the enthusiasm produced by his return to overthrow the constitution, forswear the oath he had voluntarily taken to support it, and repudiate and denounce whatever had been done in its name. To the faithful servants who had devoted themselves, through blood and fire, to their country and to him, but had been guilty of the sin of constitutionalism, dungeons and chains were the mildest testimonials of his gratitude. All that was wise and eloquent, and liberal and good, in the land, was sent into exile, poverty, and sorrow. Despotism became more despotic than ever, for it was the despotism of a treacherous and unprincipled reaction. In 1820 the constitutional system was revived, and there was a brief, brave struggle to maintain it; but the suffering saint of San Ildefonso called aloud to his once suffering brother of St. Cloud, who hearkened mercifully to his voice. In the face of all the world, and especially of constitutional England,—by whose teachings the patriots had been led, and on whose succor they relied in vain,—the Duc d'Angoulême, in 1823, marched from the Bidasoa to Cadiz, trampling down every vestige and hope of rational freedom. Unhappily for Spain, those were the days, in Europe, of sovereign congresses and Holy Alliances, and the United States had not as yet been enlightened on the subject of intervention by any Hungarian revelations as to the meaning of the Washingtonian policy. Riego was hanged without let or hindrance of Turk or Christian, and Quiroga, escaping as best he might, had not a single speech made to him by a major-general or other functionary, legislative, judicial, or executive.

From that period down to the death of Ferdinand, in 1833, the picture is all shadow. It is hard to say whether folly or iniquity was the predominant characteristic of that very wicked and foolish man. His only objects in life were power, vengeance, and the gratification of his appetites. His policy had but two departments,—force and fraud. His only address was falsehood, and when it was not necessary to him as an instrument, he sported with it as an accomplishment, or revelled in it as a luxury. He hated constitutions, because they trammelled him. He hated reform, even when it did him no harm, because the Constitutionalists were reformers, and had befriended him, and he hated them. Having no idea of government except as the exercise of his own will, he found the ancient traditions and institutions of the kingdom as objectionable as the new lights, and he loved them all the less because he understood none of them. Religion—though he professed it sturdily, went through its forms ostentatiously, and clung to it like a bad coward when death terrified him—he practically valued only as a lever of government. Education and literature he discouraged, because he knew nothing about them, and had an indefinite idea that they were not to be trusted. Men of learning and talent he drove as far away from him as possible, "being as much afraid of them," to use a phrase of Lord Chesterfield's, "as a woman is of a gun, which, she thinks, may go off of itself, and do her a mischief." He had, in fine, no sympathy with the feelings of his people, because he had no heart, and none with their intellectual yearnings, because he had no head. The only good thing he ever did was to die; and he did that as slowly and as unsatisfactorily as possible, having never learned, in all his vicissitudes, to submit with grace to necessity, and being opposed, on principle, to gratifying his subjects, as long as he could in any way avoid it. As a rebel poet said of his grandsire, Charles the Third,—a far better and wiser man,—

"Murió de mandar harto,"—

he died of a surfeit of power. We may pardon power many of its enormities, for having ultimately become his executioner.

Upon the death of Ferdinand, his widow Cristina, the Regent, would have willingly adhered to the simple despotism which he had taken so much trouble to establish; but Don Carlos, the brother of the late king, declared himself at once the legitimate heir to the crown, and the Regent was compelled to make friends, as well as she could, for her infant daughter, who had been proclaimed Queen under the title of Isabella the Second. Don Carlos, being a narrow-minded bigot, whose chronology of ideas came down no lower than the fifteenth century, rallied around him, of course, the most influential politicians of the stationary and retrograde schools. There was no alternative, therefore, left to Cristina, but to throw herself and her daughter's cause into the arms of the liberal party. It was an alliance of interest, not of love, so far as the Queen Regent was concerned, and the smiles of Heaven were never upon it. The first pledge of it which appeared was the *Estatuto Real,* or Royal Statute, a poor apology for a liberal system, establishing the semblance of popular representation, but in reality only adding that attractive and ostensible machinery to the usual conveniences of absolute rule. It created a Chamber of *Proceres,* or Peers, who of course were to be the creatures of the government, and placed the election of the popular branch substantially under the same control. Such a contrivance could not please or last. The liberal party had devoted themselves with undeviating faith to the throne of Isabella; but they were too wise not to know the folly of relying upon royal generosity or justice. They had just come home from the banishment into which kingly treachery had sent them, and they were aware that Cristina was of the house of Naples. The *Estatuto Real*, therefore, could not satisfy them. The Regent, being a Bourbon, was of course fated to be deaf to reason and experience, and the result was, that in 1836 she found herself compelled, amid the bayonets of a rebellious soldiery at La Granja, to sign a decree for the promulgation, once again, of the constitution of 1812–20. This was but a prelude to the meeting of a constituent Cortes,—or, as we should call it, a constitutional convention,—whose labors were crowned, in June, 1837, by the adoption of yet another fundamental law.

When the constitutional system was overthrown, in 1823, the liberal party had been long enough in power to be broken into factions. Many of its divisions had a merely personal foundation, but the absorbing question was one of principle. It was the same which divides all popular parties,—the question as to where progress should end, and conservatism begin. Ten years of sorrow and persecution seemed but to have confirmed the advocates of each set of doctrines in their original convictions, and when the necessities of the Queen Regent recalled them all to the responsibilities of government, it was but a signal for the revival of old discords. The conservative liberals had become more than ever satisfied, that they could only escape the dangers of the past by centralizing the administration, strengthening constitutionally the hands of the executive, and appealing to loyal and conservative traditions. The men of progress, on the other hand, were quite as thoroughly convinced, that too many concessions had been already made to the monarchical idea, and they believed that they could see in those concessions the true secret of the downfall of former free institutions. The Regent, being a queen, of course followed but her instinct, in assuming that conservative liberalism was a lesser evil than the same iniquity, rampant with the spirit of change. She therefore, without hesitation, united her fortunes with those of the *Moderados*, between whom and the *Progresistas* the breach was of course made wider daily, by personal struggles for power.

Party names, like all other words which typify practical opinions, mean much or little, according to the latitude. Most things, indeed, owe a great deal of their signification to the eyes with which we look at them, and the light in which we see them. A *Progresista*, who would be deemed quite a rabid and dangerous radical in Spain, would be but a pale and twinkling light beside even the most subdued exhibition of those democratical pyrotechnics, which, here in America, we have grown to consider quite harmless at their brightest. An unenterprising *Moderado*, on the other hand, whom our Kossuthian disciples might consider altogether unrepublican, and bad enough to be under "Austrian influence," would perhaps be taken for quite a revolutionist in Spain, when placed in contrast with those orthodox *Realistas* who adhered to Don Carlos and the *jus divinum*, and would have gloried in reëstablishing for church and state the maxims and practices of Philip the Second and Antonio Perez, without a spark of the intellect and energy which gave dignity and respectability to that grand, though gloomy despotism. The two fractions of the liberal party, therefore, were not as far apart as they might seem, and although, by dwelling upon their peculiar points of difference,—each to defend and fortify its own,—each grew more absolute and more exclusive,—the *Moderado* more moderate, and the *Progresista* more progressive,—they were near enough together still, in 1837, to find some terms of compromise. The *Progresistas* had the Cortes of that year entirely at their command, but, to the lasting credit of their intelligence and patriotism, they magnanimously made concessions to the vanquished, even in the flush of victory.

The constitution of 1812, instead of being merely an organic law, had more the appearance of a code or an elementary treatise, in the multitude and particularity of its details. This violation of the unity and brevity so essential in such instruments arose in a great degree from the pressure of peculiar circumstances. The Cortes of 1837 corrected this error, and, by giving to the executive the power of convoking and dissolving the Cortes, under proper limitations, as well as a substantial participation in making of the laws, removed some of the most serious objections which the advocates of prerogative had upheld against the former system. The legislature itself, which had consisted of a single body under the constitution of 1812, was separated into two. Of the wisdom of such a change, few, it is supposed, could now be found to doubt. The experience of the French Republic has made conspicuous what the experience of the Cortes had demonstrated long before in Spain,—that a single chamber, having no battles to fight with one of its own kind, is always ready, at a moment's warning, either to serve under the banner of the executive or to usurp its powers. It is invariably either subservient or contumacious. An executive or a legislative tyranny is thus its inevitable result, unless peculiar circumstances so equalize the strength of the contending departments, that they neutralize each other, and render all government impossible. At the same time that the Cortes of 1837 applied the remedy to this evil, and added one more enlightened conservative element to their system, they developed the peculiar principles of the *Progresista* majority in a more liberal and simple electoral machinery, an increase in the number of representatives, and a series of other important popular guaranties. The new constitution was thus made acceptable to both parties, and there seemed to be in prospect, for a while, one of those political millenniums, which are so often prophesied, but never happen, even in communities where political augury ought to be a more demonstrative science than in Spain.

The famous *convenio*, or settlement, made at Vergara, in August, 1839, between Espartero and the Carlist general Maroto, virtually put an end to the bloody and protracted civil war, and the pretensions of Don Carlos. The defeat and emigration of Cabrera, his ablest general, in the following year, left nothing further even for his hopes. The victorious leader of the national armies, Espartero, of course became— as from his many high qualities and eminent services he certainly deserved to be—a person of much weight in public affairs. Being at the head of the *Progresistas*, he naturally availed himself of his influence to elevate and strengthen the position of his party, which at that moment was much depressed. A *Moderado* majority in the Cortes had just adopted a law adverse to the system of *ayuntamientos*, or municipal corporations, which the liberal party had always vigorously upheld, as the chief protection of provincial and popular rights against the absorbing centralization to which the *Moderado* doctrines tended. To procure from the Queen Regent a veto upon the obnoxious measure, and a dissolution of the Cortes which had passed it, was the object of Espartero's solicitude. Cristina refused to yield, and the result was a popular outbreak, which was followed, in the autumn of 1840, by her renunciation of the regency and immediate departure for France. Espartero succeeded her, as was to have been expected. Agustin Arguëlles, the distinguished author of the preliminary discourse to the constitution of 1812, and an orator so graceful and impressive that he had the surname of "the divine," was appointed "tutor" to the royal children. The *Progresistas* then, for a little while, had everything in their own hands.

In Calderon's beautiful drama of the *Cisma de Inglaterra*, the melancholy Catherine of Aragon, in the depth of her desertion and disgrace, calls on her maidens for a song, wherein she asks the very flowers to learn from her how all things fleet and fade:—

> "Aprended, flores, de mí,
> Lo que va de ayer á hoy:
> Que ayer maravilla fuí,
> Y hoy, sombra mia no soy!"

The chances and changes of Spanish politics might give quite as serious instruction to the leaves and grass, as the vicissitudes of Henry's victim. In the summer of 1843, Espartero,

Duke of Victory, Regent and Saviour of the Realm, found himself a fugitive on board an English steamer in the Bay of Cadiz, stripped of his titles, and stigmatized in a ministerial decree as "bearing the mark of public execration!" With Espartero fell the friends who had clung to him, and the doctrines they had espoused. In the face of the constitution,—which expressly provided that fourteen years should be the term of the royal minority,—the Queen, a child not quite thirteen, was declared to be of full age, and invested with the symbols of dominion. Then commenced the predominant influence of Narvaez, Duke of Valencia, who from that time to the period of my visit had, with occasional interruptions, been the ruling spirit of the Peninsula. Much, of both good and evil, has been said of this remarkable man, to whose position and character I shall have occasion hereafter to allude. Those who praise him may perhaps do him more than justice,—those who denounce him, less; but it were folly to deny that he has permanently and honorably linked his name with the repression of civil discord and the revival of his country's prosperity in the nineteenth century.

It was under the auspices of Narvaez and the *Moderado* party, that the constitution of 1845 was adopted, which, down to the last steamer's dates from Madrid, continued to be preached from as the fundamental text. It is not likely to be soon changed, for all parties seem to have adopted the idea, made illustrious among ourselves not long ago, of administering constitutions "as they understand them." In such case, one form answers about as well as another.

VI.

CONSTITUTION OF 1845.—ITS PROVISIONS AND CHARACTER.—THE CORTES.
—ELECTIONS.—PAY OF MEMBERS.—EXECUTIVE INFLUENCE.—ITS
BENEFITS.—REPUBLICAN PROPAGANDISM.

THE fanciful theorist who thought the concoction of popular songs a far more important source of power than the making of laws, might, if he had lived in these days, have applied his remark *a fortiori* to constitutions. The Marseillaise has been generally found equal to the overthrow of any organic establishment against which it has been pitted, and I greatly doubt whether, if a popular question were made between Yankee-Doodle and the best of our State constitutions, there would not be large odds, and perhaps a convention, in favor of the ditty. The truth is, that, where there is any decided and predominant governing element in a nation, experience shows that paper regulations are far more apt to subserve than to thwart it. It is easy, at the worst, for those who make to unmake if they please; but the science of interpretation has of late been carried to such a pitch of perfection, as almost entirely to supersede the older and clumsier methods of change. We certainly are not without our own examples of new constitutional readings, made orthodox at once by the very popularity of the novelty or the expounder; and we cannot fairly express any surprise that the few who have the power elsewhere should wield it, in their own way, like the many who possess it here. The knowledge of this mutability in fundamental laws, and of the trifling resistance which they practically make to real power, has destroyed a great deal of that sacredness with which people used to invest such things, when society and politics were in a more reverent and pastoral state. It is not worth while to inquire whether such a falling-off in respect for what ought to be most respectable is not a sad and serious evil. It is a fact, let it be what else it may. Men may differ a little as to the sort and number of masters they would prefer, if they could have their choice; and most men prefer being among the masters themselves; but it is now pretty generally understood, that those who have the mastery will use it, be they few or many, and that paper obstructions are not likely to prevent them.

The Spanish constitution of 1845 does not surround the exercise of absolute dominion by the powers that be with any insurmountable barriers. It is very full, no doubt, of patriotic and liberal generalities, and many of its theories and guaranties are ostensibly as popular as need be. Yet while almost every right is seemingly secured to the citizen, there is attached to each of the provisions on which that security depends a significant clause, which has the real effect of setting the whole matter, to all intents and purposes, at sea. Thus, for example, by "Art. 2. All Spaniards may print and publish their ideas freely, without previous censorship, *but with subjection to the laws.*" By "Art. 3. Every Spaniard has the right to direct written petitions to the Cortes and the king, *as the laws may direct."* By "Art. 7. No Spaniard shall be detained or imprisoned, or kept from his domicile, nor shall his house be forced, *except in those cases and in that manner which the laws may prescribe."* And by "Art. 8. If the security of the state should require, under extraordinary circumstances, the temporary suspension, in the whole or in any part of the kingdom, of the provisions of the preceding article, *it shall be so determined by law."*

It will be very obvious that the protection which the citizen is to derive from these and similar provisions must depend altogether upon the constitution and temper of the law-making department. If, by the fundamental law, the legislature can, without hindrance, be made what the people will, then the constitution secures, or may be made to secure, the popular immunities, and the nation will be well or ill governed according to the popular capacity and disposition to govern. If the throne, on the contrary, can make or manage the law-givers, then there is nothing but a circumlocution and a slight complication of machinery in the way of its being, to a degree, absolute. This last seems to be frequently the practical working of the Spanish system at present.

The Cortes are composed of two chambers, the Senate and the Congress of Deputies. The Senators hold office for life, and—with the exception of the sons of the reigning monarch and of the immediate heir to the throne, who are members of the Senate, as of course, on attaining the age of twenty-five,— they derive their appointments exclusively from the crown. Their number is unlimited, so that a ministry can always create a majority at need. To secure their conservatism, they are required to have a considerable fixed income, or to pay

a specified amount of taxes. That their sympathies may be
upon the side of power, they can only, now, be chosen from
among the nobility, the higher clergy, and such individuals
as may have filled certain distinguished positions in the public
service. Lest, however, it should be important for the government, hereafter, in an exigency, to go beyond the enumerated
classes in search of friends, it is provided that the sphere of
selection may at any time be enlarged by law. So far, then,
as the control of affairs by legislation is concerned, it must be
a rare ministry which cannot, with such facilities, protect
itself against the happening of any thing inconvenient or
disagreeable. But the functions of the senators go farther.
The creatures of the throne, they are yet the constitutional
judges of all alleged offences against the state and the person
or dignity of the monarch. Dependent upon the ministry for
the very dignities which make them eligible, or for the senatorial dignity itself, they have yet exclusive jurisdiction over
impeachments of ministers. It must be no small relief to a
statesman, in his sense of official responsibility, to know that
he has a check on the laws which are to govern him, and can
legitimately pack the tribunal which alone can try him!

The Congress of Deputies is, to all appearance, a mere
popular body, though not always so in fact, as the system
works. Its members are chosen for five years and are indefinitely reëligible. They need not reside in their respective
districts, and may, therefore, be lawfully selected, as they
often are, from among the hack politicians and the courtiers
who trade in place, at Madrid. They must be laymen, above
the age of twenty-five, and chosen in the proportion of at
least one to every fifty thousand souls. The mode of election,

and the pecuniary and other qualifications required, are prescribed, under the constitution, by the electoral laws of 1846 and 1849,—chiefly by that of 1846. A representative, under those laws, is given to every district containing thirty-five thousand inhabitants. The colonies, however, have no share in this distribution, having lost, since 1837, the right of representation in the Cortes, which they enjoyed under the constitution of 1812–20. They are now governed by special enactments, which, be they as wise as they may, can never be welcome, altogether, to a people who have no voice in their making.

A Deputy is required to have an annual income of at least six hundred dollars from real property, or to pay fifty dollars yearly in direct taxes. Captains-general, and certain other specified functionaries, are declared to be ineligible, unless their official duties should require their presence in Madrid; so that, if any obnoxious officer of the kind should be chosen, the government has but to render his duties engrossing somewhere else, and there is an end of his legislative pretensions. As many of the most able and influential men are likely to hold the offices enumerated, this provision in an important spring in the ministerial man-trap.

To vote for deputies, the elector must be at least twenty-five years old, and pay, at the lowest, twenty dollars of direct taxes annually. Lawyers, physicians, academicians, parish priests, and persons of similar category, are allowed the right of suffrage upon paying half that amount. The extent to which even this moderate qualification sometimes diminishes the number of electors may be inferred from an article of the law, which provides for those districts in which they may be fewer than one hundred and fifty. The *Jefes Políticos* (political chiefs of the provinces, who have since been superseded by provincial governors) are required to make out the electoral lists once in two years. From any error of omission or commission upon their part, an appeal is provided to the *Audiencia*, or court of superior jurisdiction for the province. As, however, the *Jefes Políticos* were, as their successors, the governors, continue to be, subject to removal at discretion, and as judicial officers of all kinds may, under the constitution, be suspended at any time for trial, by a simple royal order, it needs no sorcery to divine the probable complexion of the electoral list, whenever the government chooses to take sides. So well, indeed, is the matter understood, that, in most of the special elections, the successful candidate can always be named at Madrid before the votes have been counted. Some idea may be formed of the thorough manner in which the thing can be done, even in a general canvass, from the fact that, in the election which first took place after my return, two hundred and thirty ministerial deputies were chosen, to fourteen *Progresistas!*

The coolness with which such results are canvassed, by men of both parties, is quite amusing. If I had found the influence of government only complained of by the unsuccessful side and denied by the victors, I should have supposed that what I heard was to be taken with the usual and proper allowance for partisan facts. Nobody, however, thinks of disputing the matter or expressing surprise at it. I was talking one day to a friend, in regard to a prominent member of the opposition, a man of distinguished abilities, who had favored me with some degree of intimacy and in whose success as a candidate for the next Cortes I felt much interest. He was about to offer himself for his native district in Andalusia. "I am very sorry," said the gentleman whom I addressed, "very sorry, indeed. My brother-in-law is *Jefe Político* there, and will have to defeat your friend or lose his place!" Upon another occasion, a senator, deep in the secrets of the ruling powers, was discussing the practical operation of the constitution with me. "*Es un embuste,*" said he, "*y un embuste muy caro, el sistema representativo!*—The representative system is a humbug, and a very dear one! It costs the government, and of course the country, enormously, to get the right sort of people elected, and when they are in, it costs a great deal more to keep them from doing mischief. Every man of them must have something for himself, his children, or his friends, and unless he can get what he wants, he takes advantage of a critical opportunity and goes over to the opposition!" A striking evidence that my companion made no mistake in this, is furnished by a test vote which took place on the 3d of January, 1850, upon a proposition which the government exerted itself to defeat. Of one hundred and thirty deputies who maintained the ministerial side of the question, the *Clamor Público*, one of the *Progresista* organs, enumerated, by name and station, one hundred and eighteen who had places, and five who were believed to have them! There was, no doubt, some little of partisan exaggeration in the statement, but the ministerial papers did not succeed in correcting it very materially. The *Clamor* promised to prepare a subsequent table of the salaries which the gentlemen of the majority were enjoying. It would have been very edifying, no doubt, but I do not remember that it appeared.

It was in view of such things and their results that Gonzalez Bravo, a prominent member of the *Moderado* section of the opposition, expressed himself thus, one day, in debate :—

"I can understand the system of force, which closes the door against discussion,—the absolute system which is represented by Russia. I can comprehend that system, on the other hand, which lives with and applies the spirit of the age,—which deals out prudent concessions, and does justice to the national necessities,—the system, in fine, of England. But what I cannot understand, and what signifies nothing to be understood, is the bastard system, which is neither the one thing nor the other,—which is not constitutional, because it does not rest upon an honest administration of constitutional principles, and is not absolute, because it lacks the dignity and power of monarchical traditions!"

Señor Bravo is an able man, no doubt, but it was hardly reasonable for him to complain that the government of her Majesty was not absolute enough to be comprehended as such. The Duke of Valencia and his colleagues certainly did all that lay in their power to prevent themselves from being justly liable to animadversion on that score. Indeed, the Duke did not scruple to take the orator to task, upon that very occasion, for the tone of his remarks, in a style which I will not say was Russian altogether, but which would have created some astonishment in the House of Commons, and would certainly have elicited some elegant allusions to "here and elsewhere" in either branch of our national legislature.

Neither the senators nor deputies receive any direct compensation, nor is the Spanish language so fortunate as to possess any word corresponding to "mileage,"—that pleasant invention of the American genius, whereby honorable gentlemen are so often enabled to illustrate the proverb, that "the longest way round is the shortest way home." The Peninsular legislators are supposed, in theory, to be amply compensated by the honor of the station, the pleasure of serving their country, and the felicity of making speeches. The real *quid pro quo*, however, consists in the opportunity just alluded to, of securing profitable places for themselves and their friends, by the use of a little diplomacy and the advantages of position. An acquaintance of mine, who had been all the winter in Madrid, *pretendiendo*, as they call it,—office-hunting, in the homely American vernacular,—called, late in the season, to take leave of me. He was a worthy person, and I expressed my hope that he had been able to handle his cards successfully. "Not at all," he answered, "and I am tired of playing the beggar. I am going home to have myself returned, if possible, to the next Cortes. If I can succeed in that, I think I shall be able to make my own terms!"

It has often been a question whether the system of direct compensation to members of the legislature is a wise one. That it places the honors of the republic equally within the reach of the wealthy and the poor, is deemed with us an unanswerable argument in its favor. It is supposed, besides, to secure legislative independence. If a *per diem* would in truth prevent the members of the Cortes from surrendering themselves to that subserviency which no place-hunter can escape, it would certainly be both wise and economical to let them name their own stipend. Unfortunately, however, it is by no means absolutely certain that the result would be so happy. It might be asserted, as a fact quite susceptible of proof in our own beloved country, that members of Congress have been found,—circumnavigatory to the last degree in their demands for mileage,—scrupulous, to the extent of good conscience, in the exaction of their pay,—and yet feeling themselves in no way precluded thereby from asking and taking every scrap of official preferment to be had. Perhaps the best remedy for this evil would be to make members of the legislature incapable of filling any but elective offices, within at least five years from the expiration of their legislative terms. But even then there would be uncles and cousins to provide for, besides lineal descendants and influential constituents, so that, on the whole, it is greatly to be feared there is but poor chance of any sure reform in the matter, until some plan be devised for remodelling human nature.

It must not be supposed, from the tone of this chapter, that I regard the decided influence of the Spanish executive over the legislature as by any means an unmixed evil, in the present state of the Peninsula. I shall have occasion hereafter to consider that point, in a more general connection. There are, no doubt, those by whom it will be held marvellous that a republican should entertain any question whatever on the subject; but I think it the duty of every candid man, upon proper occasion, to set his face against the folly so prevalent with us, of striving to fit all the world with governments according to our own measure. An American, who returns from European travel without an increased sense of the value to us of the institutions under which we were born, and a profounder feeling of gratitude to the good Providence whose beneficence made them our birthright, must be as mad as the most "undevout astronomer," or too silly to reach the dignity of madness. But, on the other hand, his intellect must be very narrow, and his prejudices most absurd, if he has not been able to rid himself of the superstition, that our system is the best for all nations, all times, all circumstances, and all stages of intelligence, merely because it happens so to be for us and ours. He must be made of impenetrable stuff indeed, if observation abroad has not convinced him—as sanity and reflection at home might surely do—that no government under popular auspices is likely to answer its true purposes, unless it tally, not merely with the abstract convictions and theoretical demonstrations of constitution-tinkers, but with the actual necessities, the ingrained habits, sentiments, and traditions, the very prejudices and weaknesses, of the people whose welfare it concerns.

It is easy enough to create institutions. Mr. Burke's inventory of what was to be found in the pigeon-holes of the Abbé Sieyès, is but a trifle compared with the stock in the market at present. All popular government, nevertheless, must be a form and a folly, unless it be the shadow of the true, predominating national character,—the projection, as it were, of the national mind and temper. Men are not to be dealt with as right-angled triangles; and he is a sad statesman, be he ever so much a philosopher, who acts upon the notion that human nature is one of the exact sciences. The best constitution in the world will be but a source of perpetual discord, misrule, or no rule at all, unless there be the adequate amount of good sense and good feeling among the people, to get them practically out of the theoretical difficulties against which no foresight can entirely provide. A very bad constitution, on the other hand, with popular intelligence and purity, and a compromising spirit to remedy its defects and relieve it when in straits, will make a people prosperous and happy for many generations,—or, to speak, perhaps, more logically, will interpose no serious obstacle to their making themselves so. In England they get along very well with a system which would set all Yankeedom at loggerheads in a month. Here we seem to have a passion for making ourselves uncomfortable, under a constitution which ought to secure the peace and felicity of any people out of Bedlam. Nowhere in the world have wiser or more eloquent expositions of the true principles of government been heard, than in the late French Assembly, and yet they probably afford a less substantial indication of rational republicanism to come, than would be furnished by the existence of a single thorough-bred French Quaker,—drab, broad-brimmed, earnest, and orthodox. One such fixed human fact would show the possibility of self-control among a people who as yet have given no proofs of it,—just as the finding of a solitary fossil man or monkey would settle for ever one of the problems of geology. Without that self-control, who shall pretend that the legitimacy of La Rochejacquelin and Montalembert, or the *coup d'état* of Louis Napoleon, is of less promise for good than the drunken Utopia of socialism?

The art of good government may find more profitable analogies in medicine than mathematics. The man who is only weak needs but a staff; the cripple requires his crutches; he of the fractured limb must have it bandaged, splintered, and put at rest. The surgeon should be hanged, without benefit of clergy, who would prescribe gymnastics to them all, because their neighbors, who were not halt, could dance and be glad at a merry-making. We have quacks enough among us, notwithstanding, who are always prescribing to other people, in the way of government, something quite as innocent and sensible. Now the fact is,—let the newspapers and stump-orators say what they please,—that the sun of civilization neither rises nor sets within our national limits, ample though they be. The moon of Athens was no finer moon than that of Corinth, though there were Athenian patriots, in Plutarch's tale, who would have fought to prove it so. With a good deal of political philosophy, and extraordinary political sagacity, we yet have no monopoly of either. We are not, like the friends of holy Job, "the only men," nor is there any danger that "wisdom will die with" us. A fair appreciation of these truths would greatly enlighten some of our public men and popular oracles, who seem to be entirely unaware that there is a breathing, thinking world outside the happy valley which surrounds their tripods. It would save us (a wise economy!) Heaven knows how much of cant and fustian, which now pass, unhappily, with many, as the only language of patriotism and the genuine evangely of the rights of man. It would, upon occasions of national solemnity or rejoicing, make teachers and counsellors of our statesmen, instead of flatterers merely, as, for the most part, now they are. It would have spared us the recent triumphal march of Hungarian propagandism over our national dignity and self-respect.

VII.

The Executive and Judiciary.—Juries and the Trial by Jury.

IN view of the substantial influence which the Spanish executive has been shown to possess and exercise over the legislature, and through it over all the details of government, it would seem hardly worth while to analyse the functions which, on the face of the constitution, legitimately belong to the monarch. These, nevertheless, in themselves, are quite as extensive and various as would seem compatible with the notion of a limited monarchy.

The Queen is irresponsible, and her person is inviolable. The royal dignity is hereditary in her line. She is the fountain of justice, which is administered in her name. She has the power to convoke the Cortes, suspend and close their sessions, and dissolve the Chamber of Deputies at will,—subject only to the obligation, in the last case, of calling together a new legislature within three months after such dissolution. Through her ministers, she may introduce projects of laws for the consideration of the Cortes, and she may not only refuse her sanction to a law, but thereby prevent its revival during the session of the legislature in which it may have arisen. This last result, however, can be equally well attained by the dissent of either house from a law originating in the other, so that the Senate may relieve her Majesty, if need be, from the necessity of interposing her prerogative in cases where it would be unpopular or impolitic. The promulgation and execution of all the laws are her especial duties, and in the performance of the latter she has the right to issue such orders, decrees, and instructions as may seem meet to her. In practice, this enables her to explain, modify, amplify, or nullify, very much at discretion. She is the arbiter of war and peace, and distributes and disposes of the army at her will. She directs and regulates commercial and diplomatic relations; coins money; pardons criminals; and has the uncontrolled disposition of all officers and honors. She needs the assent of the Cortes, however, to any alienation of the national territory, and she cannot, without their permission, admit foreign troops into the kingdom, ratify commercial treaties or offensive alliances, make any stipulations for the payment of subsidies, or abdicate the crown in favor of her immediate successor.

The amount of the royal income is fixed by the Cortes at the beginning of each reign. Her present Majesty has certainly no reason to complain of her loyal people in that particular, since her annual endowment is thirty-four millions of reals, equal to one million seven hundred thousand dollars, over and above the royal patrimony, which is immense, and with which the legislature has nothing to do. The King Consort, whose majesty is merely titular, and who has no concern whatever with the government, has a yearly stipend of one hundred and twenty thousand dollars. That of the Queen Mother is one hundred and fifty thousand dollars, in addition to the immense private fortune which she has acquired through her connection with the Spanish throne. The rest of the royal family, embracing the Duchess of Montpensier and the remoter collateral branches, have three hundred and twenty-five thousand dollars per annum among them, making two million two hundred and ninety-five thousand dollars, in all, according to the official *presupuesto,* or budget, for 1850, which is lying before me.

The judicial department, by its constitutional organization, is not likely to be much of a clog to the prerogatives, direct and indirect, which the monarch is so liberally paid for exercising. The judges are appointed by the crown, their number and functions being regulated by law. Except in extraordinary and enumerated cases, the determination of causes, civil and criminal, is committed to the *Alcaldes;* the judges of *Primera Instancia,* or primary jurisdiction; the territorial *Audiencias;* and the Supreme Tribunal of Justice. An appeal lies, generally speaking, from the court in which proceedings are instituted, to that which stands next above it, in the order in which I have enumerated them. In some suits, if the litigants please and can live long enough, they may chase justice through the covers and preserves of the whole judicial establishment. Ecclesiastics, in many cases, and those engaged in the military and naval services, have their separate tribunals and *fueros,* or privileges. Commercial causes are also heard by special courts, whose jurisdiction and decisions are prescribed and regulated by a separate code. Besides these, there are many exceptional jurisdictions and privileges of forum, which are annexed to particular stations and classes, so that, if legal tribunals be, as Carlyle has said, but "chimneys for the deviltry and contention of men to escape by," Madrid ought certainly to smoke like Birmingham. By the official report, published at the beginning of 1850, there were seven hundred and twenty-seven lawyers in the capital, of whom five hundred and seven were candidates for practice. The population of the city being but little over two hundred thousand, there is every reason to believe that the chimneys will not suffer for want of fuel or tending.

The constitution provides that no judicial officer shall be removed, except by sentence of a competent tribunal, or suspended, unless by due judicial action, or a royal order alleging sufficient cause, with a view to prosecution. As before observed, this suspensory prerogative in the monarch is a complete negation of all real independence; but when it is added, that the offences committed by a judge, in his official capacity, are to be tried by his next superior,—save in the case of the supreme tribunal, where the offender is judged by his fellows,—and that the arbiter, like the accused, is the appointee of the crown, and liable to similar suspension and prosecution, it cannot but be obvious that the whole judiciary is, for all needful purposes, under stringent executive control. The noted case of Diaz Martinez, which was tried during my visit, furnished very satisfactory evidence that the ermine could be made to take an exceedingly ministerial hue. The prisoner was charged with having addressed General Narvaez, by letter, in a style which was interpreted to signify a challenge. That eminent functionary cannot easily be made afraid, and has, as a general thing, no particular objection to the handling of deadly weapons, if it occurs to him; but as he was altogether "*ego et rex meus,*" it fell little short of lese-majesty to compass or contrive his bodily peril or discomfort, against his will,—and the unhappy Martinez was dealt with accordingly. His defence was conducted with characteristic manliness and ability, by Don Joaquin Francisco Pacheco, a very eminent jurist and advocate, and there was but little difference of opinion, as far as I could collect, among professional men of all parties, in regard to the utter illegality and anomalism of the proceeding. The *Juez de Primera Instancia*, however, who heard the cause, had no difficulty in arriving at a judgment of conviction. I read his opinion, which certainly bore both obsequiousness and absurdity upon its face. As the sentence involved serious pains and penalties, the case was taken to a higher tribunal; but it, of course, is not easy to foretell the result, where the ways of justice are so much in the depths of the sea.

The trial by jury has never been thoroughly incorporated into the judicial administration of the Peninsula. Some antiquarians have persuaded themselves that they have discovered its germ in the ancient constitutions of Aragon, as well as in some of the older codes and charters of Castile. Distinct evidences of its existence are said to appear, particularly, in the *Fuero Juzgo* of the Visigoths. It will be found, however, upon examination, that the provisions which are relied on as in point do not approach much nearer to establishing the theory as now understood and practised on, than the initials of the "lang ladle" at Monkbarns to an inscription of Agricola's. Better proof of their insufficiency could hardly be found than the very language used in the *Fuero Juzgo*, where it directs ten assistants to be chosen as the Alcalde's coadjutors in certain cases, "*ex optimis, et nobilissimis, et sapientissimis.*" Such epithets, it is clear, could never have been gravely intended to designate jurymen, even in those days of primitive jurisprudence and mediæval Latinity. But let the antiquarians be right or wrong, as they may, certain it is, that within the memory of modern men nothing like the trial by jury has existed in Spain, except very lately, partially, and for a brief period. The constitution of 1812 provided for its future introduction, in case it should be deemed advisable, but it was not practically adopted until 1822, and then only for the trial of cases arising under the laws which regulated the press. Having disappeared in 1823, with the press and the constitutional system, it was revived with them in 1836, and was again recognized by the constitution of 1837, though still confined to the same class of cases. The law of 1844, which modified the freedom of the press according to the notions of the *Moderados*, provided a hybridous sort of jury, with innumerable requisites and all manner of embarrassing paraphernalia, which must have made it unavailable as a working thing and were probably intended to do so. The constitution of 1845 has no jury clause whatever, and by the legislation of that year all the lingering traces of the "Palladium" were finally swept away.

Whatever may be the course hereafter in Spain of that political amelioration which is certainly going on, it is not likely, for many reasons, that the jury system will ever become ingrafted upon theirs, as an institution of general scope. We, whose notions have been formed by the study or by our experience of the common law of England, are apt to consider the trial of facts by laymen as absolutely essential to the beneficial operation of every popular or liberal form of government, and there can be no doubt that we generally state our doctrine on the subject a great deal too exclusively and broadly. It of course must be conceded, that, for the trial of criminal causes, the jury, on the whole, is the most satisfactory contrivance which the ingenuity of men has thus far been able to devise. Without reference, moreover, to the subjects of its action, the introduction of so popular an element into the administration of justice must necessarily tend to diffuse among the community, from whose ranks the jurors are indiscriminately taken, a higher degree of confidence in the tribunals of the law, and a heartier disposition to respect and uphold their judgments. Nothing, of course, can contribute more than such a result to the stability of society and the sure enjoyment of the rights which lie at its foundation.

It is not to be questioned, on the other hand, that immediate and frequent contact with the system, as it works, has the effect of notably diminishing our reverence for it as a mode of arriving at the truth. It doubtless affords admirable scope for the dexterous playing of that uncertain game, the law, and hence must always command many eloquent suffrages from the professional players. But, with a good cause and no other object but the enforcement of right, I greatly doubt whether any candid man, among those who know the jury system best, would hesitate about selecting, in preference to it, the intervention of a well-trained and well-educated judge. Where the object is to put the right and wrong upon a level, and to take the chances of their confusion, I grant that the choice would probably be different; but such cases surely afford no test. Experience has taught that courts of equity are altogether capable of dealing, justly and wisely, with the greatest complications of fact,—so that issues are sent from them to juries in but few and peculiar cases. There are, it may be safely said, no tribunals in our country whose decisions are more uniformly just, or more universally approved, than those of the federal courts sitting in admiralty without juries. In those States of the Union, too, where the judges are empowered to try issues of fact with the consent of parties, the large number of cases, both civil and criminal, in which juries are willingly dispensed with, may be taken as the best evidence of a public and practical conviction greatly differing from the theory about which there is so much declamation. Nor is it at all wonderful, that such a conviction should exist. As juries are selected and constituted generally, both in England and this country, their verdicts in nine cases out of ten are but the results of voting by ballot or "striking an average"; and it is by no means an easy matter to determine how often a wilful appetite, and an anxious desire to leave the unprofitable adjustment of other men's business for the more advantageous pursuit of their own, may cause the majority of the imprisoned twelve to select the promptest conclusion as the best.

Perfect or imperfect, however, as the institution may be in its present shape and operation, it is with us, to some extent, a sacred thing. It is surrounded by so many of the holiest associations, and has fought so many of the best battles of freedom, that it is destined long to remain a sign of that popular security to which it is no longer necessary as an element or a guaranty. With the Spaniards, however, it has no such prestige, and as it has never been a household god to them, there seems no particular reason why they should give it a place in their inner worship, as we do in ours. The very familiar and accurate knowledge of the laws and customs of

England, which many of their most intelligent and influential statesmen have acquired during long years of exile in that land of European asylum, will most probably secure, in time, the introduction of the trial by jury, to such an extent and in such cases as may accord with the best features of their own venerable jurisprudence. They may be enabled thus to strike the happy medium between the subserviency of judges to power and wealth, and that dread of public passion and deference to popular opinion, which too often make the jury-room but an echo of the press and of the voices that cry aloud in the streets.

VIII.

Jurisprudence.—Codes.—Colonial System.—Administration of Justice.—Escribanos.—Judges.—The Legal Profession.

NOTWITHSTANDING the very formidable expansion which is frequently ascribed to the Spanish jurisprudence, it is really condensed within limits which appear extremely moderate, to one who is familiar with the ordinary copiousness of popular legislation. The codes into which it has been shaped are, it is true, voluminous enough, but those of them which are of common and practical application can easily be mastered, with reasonable industry. Let other evils be what they may, the judges are not reduced to the necessity of toiling through innumerable reports and the varying opinions of judicial legislators and expounders,—sages sometimes, dolts and doubters often,—in order to excogitate what they can from prior cogitations, which are not the less authoritative because they are in great part contradictory. It is reserved for the freest and most enlightened of the nations to rejoice in such judicial precision and philosophy as that amounts to, and gravely to set it up for men to worship, as " the perfection of reason." Since the Goddess of Reason, in the French Revolution, there has not probably existed a deity bearing the name with a less reputable character or more flimsy pretensions.

The *Novísima Recopilacion*, published by Charles the Fourth in 1806, is the most recent digest of the Spanish law, and is binding in all cases not affected by subsequent legislation. It had for a nucleus the *Nueva Recopilacion* of Philip the Second, (sometimes called the *Recopilacion*, simply,) and may, perhaps, be more properly considered as but the latest edition of that great code, with the intermediate enactments and judicial expositions incorporated. The more ancient jurisprudence of Castile is, however, the basis of these later works, and the antique codes have therefore some authority still,—not merely as illustrating the modern text, but as operative, of themselves, in cases not otherwise provided for. The *Novísima Recopilacion*, by a special provision, determines the order in which the codes shall bind,—giving preference, among the more ancient, to the *Fuero Real*, which was promulgated in 1255 by Alfonso the Wise; next admitting the *Fueros Municipales*, or municipal charters of right, from time to time recognized or granted by Saint Ferdinand and his more immediate successors; and resting finally upon the *Siete Partidas*, which, though prepared under the supervision of Alfonso the Wise, were not published till long after his death, during the reign of Alfonso the Eleventh.

Since the promulgation of the *Novísima Recopilacion*, there has been no collection of the laws printed, which approximates or pretends to completeness. The decrees of Ferdinand the Seventh and of the different Cortes are, it is true, readily accessible in print; but many radical changes have been wrought, by special orders, resolutions, and interpretations, which lie buried for the most part so deeply in the executive archives, that, for all purposes of general information, they had as well been affixed to the top of the old tyrant's column. Indeed, the whole system of administration has undergone so many shocks and revolutions during the present century, that it is not always easy to determine the precise location even of the archives themselves, through which the course of any particular legislation is to be traced. So many councils have been modified, abolished, and recreated with new functions, and the duties of all and each have been so often altered and transferred, that, even after ascertaining the date and origin of a decree or order, it is next to impossible, often, to discover in what vortex of the documentary chaos the authoritative original may be revolving. Fortunately, the cases in which this uncertainty and difficulty exist are for the most part administrative or merely political, so that the ordinary course of public justice is not often obstructed or obscured thereby.

So large a portion of territory on this continent, belonging once to Spain, has now become attached to the American Union, that it may not be altogether out of place in this connection to notice briefly the Spanish colonial jurisprudence. The laws governing "the Indies"—by which title all the discoveries in both hemispheres are comprehended—were always wholly separate from the main body of domestic legislation. In 1511 Ferdinand the Catholic created the Supreme Council of the Indies, to which he gave, under the royal supervision only, the entire control of the colonies, in all matters, legislative, executive, ecclesiastical, and judicial. Charles the Fifth, in 1524, in some degree modified the form of this almost sovereign body, but the ordinances for its regulation were not given to the world, with any completeness, until 1636, during the reign of Philip the Fourth. In 1658 a small number of its decrees and acts were published. In 1680 Charles the Second had the glory of promulgating the gigantic work called the *Recopilacion de las Leyes de Indias*,—a complete body of jurisprudence, which, although modified from time to time, and not always wisely, is still the main depository of colonial right. Where, by chance, it may be silent or have become inoperative, the vigorous old legislation of Castile fills up the chasm.

Those who judge of the merits of the *Recopilacion de Indias* solely from the results of the civilization which it was intended to direct, will do but poor justice to the most complete and comprehensive scheme of colonial government which the world has ever known. Although, no doubt, greatly defective in many particulars, and tinctured most prejudicially with the errors in political economy which were peculiar to the times, the *Recopilacion* bears all about it evidences of the most far-seeing wisdom, the most laborious and comprehensive investigation and management of details, and a spirit of enlightened humanity not easily to be exceeded. That, with these characteristics, it should have been practically so complete a failure, seems at first sight somewhat paradoxical, but historians have given many good reasons for it, which are obvious enough, though it would be foreign to my purpose to repeat them. There was one fundamental error,—an error rather of the system than of the code,—which would suffice, of itself, to account for all the consequences that have ensued; I mean the idea that colonies could be nursed into great nations and yet preserved as colonies. It was upon this impossibility that the *Recopilacion* was stranded. Its municipal regulations, its laws controlling territorial acquisition and descent, its whole commercial plan and political economy, had but the single purpose of building up empires, to be yet dependent upon the mother country. The prosperity of the colonies, even as colonies, was thus rendered impossible. If they took a step forward, it was with a chain and a clog on their feet. They were kept for a long time, it is true, from being independent, but they were prevented, during all the time, from growing vigorous or great. When they became free, at last, it was through the weakness of the metropolis, and not through their own strength. They escaped from being governed by others, but they did not know, nor have they yet learned, how to govern themselves. If it had been the order of Providence that children should be children always, the Spanish system had certainly been successful, for it was wise to that end. As Providence has otherwise ordained the nature of men and nations, the introduction of so unnatural a basis made all its wisdom folly.

Of the decrees and other enactments which have been passed and promulgated since the *Recopilacion de Indias*, there is no collection whatever extant, and the most learned of the colonial jurisconsults are only familiar or unfamiliar with them by comparison. In the enlightened reign of Charles the Third, an attempt was made to digest a new code out of all the then existing materials; but although the work was prosecuted nearly to its conclusion in the following reigns, and was in 1819 ready for the press, to which it was on the point of being given, it disappeared altogether during the subsequent revolutions, and there is now no trace whatever of the digest itself, or of the multitudinous and valuable documents collected for its preparation. It may be lying, for aught that the best lawyer in Madrid can tell, among the rubbish in the garret of a neglected *archivo*, or have been sold by the *arroba* to the proprietor of a book-stall, to be retailed at a *real* or a dollar the volume, according to the vender's theory of the purchaser's curiosity and pocket.

Under the ministry of the Marquis of Sonora, in 1786, there was a collection of ordinances published, for the establishment and regulation of Intendancies in New Spain. These were in time extended to the rest of the colonies, so far as they were applicable. The general ordinance for the government of colonial Intendants, which saw the light in 1803, and was the result of much labor and ability, was, by a strange caprice, revoked almost entirely in 1804, and is now but partially operative in any particular. The Council of Indies was abolished by the Cortes of 1812. It was too princely an establishment, as it stood, for a limited monarchy. It was, however, reëstablished by Ferdinand the Seventh in 1814, but fell again in 1820, upon the re-proclamation of the constitution, was restored in 1823, and finally suppressed in 1834. Its functions are now distributed among the several executive departments. Those who are best informed do not hesitate to say, that, properly modified, the Council would have been an invaluable administrative agent under any system, and that its destruction has put an end for the present to that politic and comprehensive unity, without which there cannot be much scope or efficacy in any scheme of colonial government.

Of the administration of justice in Spain, a great deal has been said by writers of all classes, foreign and domestic; but nothing particularly complimentary, that I have ever seen. How far the evils of the system continue to be oppressive at the present time, I had no opportunity of knowing, except from hearsay, which did not leave any favorable impressions. The *escribano*, the clerk or notary,—a sort of judicial go-between,—is, on all hands, conceded to be the chief nuisance in the details of the system. Every picture that is painted of the law's delay and of the costly injustice for which men curse it, has for its chief figure

"el escribano,
Con semblante infernal y pluma en mano."

The suitor who unhappily is forced to seek the aid of Themis employs a *procurador*, a sort of inferior attorney, to prepare a statement of his grievance. This passes to an *escribano*, through whose hands it goes to the tribunal having jurisdiction; and when it has received the proper attention there, it returns to the *escribano*, who gives the needful direction of process or notice to the adverse party. The defendant's reply passes up to the bench, through the *escribano*, and finds its way by the same channel to the plaintiff,—whose replication, in its turn, performs the same voyage. Thus the matter proceeds, until each party has alleged all that he has to say,—the *escribano* of course taking toll every time that he opens the gate, or allows either party to look over the fence within which he keeps justice impounded. All the testimony goes up in the shape of declarations made before the *escribano*, and reduced by him to writing. Every document of record is copied by some *escribano* from his archives. Indeed, there is nothing which concerns the case, in law or in fact, of which the *escribano* is not the conductor, from the judge to the parties and from the parties to the judge and to each other. How completely all are dependent upon his good faith, and how conveniently he can make a fortune,—not merely out of his honest perquisites, but by an advantageous use of his good will and opportunities,—the least ingenious of the sons of men may readily imagine.

In further illustration of the extent to which the rights of the community depend upon the honesty and pleasure of these scribes, it is but necessary to state that they are the depositaries of all testamentary records, and of all deeds and contracts whatever which are required to be in writing. A man desirous of making his will gives his instructions to any *escribano* he may select, who prepares the instrument, which the testator executes before him with all the formalities. The *escribano* retains the original, which of course he is bound to keep secret during the life of the testator. Whether he observes that obligation or not depends upon his integrity, and the liberality of the parties who may desire to penetrate the mysteries of the future. If he chooses to play false, he need never be found out. With deeds and contracts the same mode of preparation and registry is observed,—the parties being furnished at the time with copies if they require them; the originals remaining with the *escribano*, until his death or disqualification, and passing then to his successor. Each *escribano* is, by law, required to remit to the *Audiencia* of his district, once in each year, a copy of the index to his records made during that period. The *oficio de hipotecas*, or mortgage office, in each district, is likewise annually furnished with abstracts of all encumbrances affecting real property. No doubt some check is thus provided upon the perpetration of gross fraud, and yet the suppression of an occasional document, in both index and abstract, could be so easily managed and might be so profitable, that there can scarcely be said to exist any real security, while the muniments of title are in so many hands, and secrecy and divided responsibility afford so much opportunity and temptation.

Nor must it be supposed that in any case a man can enter a public or notarial *archivo* and search the records himself. Profane hands cannot be allowed to violate the sanctity of the official books or bundles, and the party who institutes an inquiry is compelled to be satisfied with the accuracy and fidelity of the *escribanos* in making the searches, and their candor in communicating the result. When you have ascertained at last the existence and location of a document with which it interests you to become better acquainted, the *escribano* will permit you to read it or not, according to his politeness and your persuasiveness. If you desire a copy, you must present a petition therefor to a *Juez de Primera Instancia,* through another *escribano,* and when you have procured an order,—which you cannot always do without notice to other parties in interest, and perhaps a contest with them of indefinite duration,—you serve it on your original *escribano,* and are gratified. If the record be that of a will, the *juez* will not allow you to have a copy or an extract, unless you are an heir at law or a devisee. If you are fortunate enough to fill either of these characters, you are allowed a copy of the clause which affects you, preceded with due solemnity by the formal exordium, wherein the testator makes profession of faith, tells the names and genealogy of his father and mother, and disposes of his soul and his body. The whole instrument you will not be permitted to have transcribed except under extraordinary circumstances. You cannot need such a transcript, they suppose, except for hostile purposes, and for such they feel under no obligation to afford you facilities. This system, doubtless, has many evils, but it has at least the good result, that the "upsetting" of wills is not very frequent in Spain, and a testator is not often declared *non compos*, because he happens to have had some notions as to the disposition of his own property differing from those of his neighbors and his heirs at law.

The *escribano* gives his certificate under his hand and sign, "*signo*," instead of a seal. The *signo* is the apex of an immense and elaborate flourish, or *rubrica*, which terminates as to its upper parts in a cross made with the pen;—that sacred "sign" giving solemnity to the authentication. Each notary, on his appointment, writes the *rubrica* and *signo* which he intends to adopt, and leaves them with the "college" to which he belongs. From the specimen of his penmanship thus adopted he never varies, and it is really curious to see how the identity of the hieroglyphic is preserved, from the firm, bold draft of it in youth, to the trembling fac-simile in that old age, which notaries, like all place-holders, are sure, under Providence, to reach. When any instrument, with the certificate of an *escribano*, requires to be formally proved, three notaries of the "college," under their hands and signs and the seal of the corporation, authenticate the signature and sign of their brother. A *Juez de Primera Instancia* authenticates the certificate of the three notaries; the Regent of the *Audiencia* certifies to the *Juez;* the Minister of Grace and Justice, who is the chief notary of the realm, authenticates the Regent; the Secretary of Foreign Affairs indorses the Minister, if the copy is to be used in evidence abroad, and the diplomatic representative of the nation for which it is intended puts the last stone on the house that Jack built. By the time that the fees of the certifiers, and the *procurador* who obtained the certificates, have been paid, the evidence may, it is true, be worth nothing, but it will be sure to have cost enough.

Report says that judges in Spain are not altogether deaf to those convincing arguments which have the ring of metal in them, but I have no doubt that there is a great deal of exaggeration in all such stories. Where a man cannot give judgment in favor of both parties, he must needs displease one, who naturally enough takes him to be in some sort a fool or a knave; and as the amount and nature of a judge's folly are not quite so comprehensible to the unlearned as knavery is, the latter is made to bear the principal burden of the supposed injustice. The publicity of all proceedings under the common law, and the hourly challenge which the judgments of courts receive from those who are competent to give it, are a barrier, in a great degree, to such suspicions, and certainly tend to prevent there being much cause for them. The comparative secrecy and silence through which men walk to judgment in Spain, leaves room, on the other hand, for much questioning of motive, and as surely increases the possibility and consequent likelihood of its being just. Certain it is, that the Spanish judges do not hold themselves aloof, as with us judicial delicacy prompts, from the personal influence and private suggestions of parties. A well-timed present, and the judicious application of that personal courtesy and attention, which go farther with a Spaniard than with any other man, are not considered as by any means unwelcome or out of place. When I was in Seville, in 1847, one of my pleasantest companions was an old gentleman from Granada, who had come down, he told me, to superintend a *pleito*, or lawsuit, of a friend of his, which was then about to be decided. He was not a professional man, and his errand had nothing to do with the conduct of the case, except as to the extra-forensic part of it. Every morning, after breakfast, he would make his appearance, *muy peripuesto*, well brushed, shaven, and accoutred, for a visit to the judges. "Of course," I said, "you never mention the suit to them?" "*Ave Maria purísima!*" was the reply, "are you dreaming? Do you think I came all the way from Granada, *para hacer cortesias*, to make bows?" He then told me that, of course, he presented his views to their honors very much at large. "But do you present any thing else?" "*Quien sabe?* who knows?" was the satisfactory reply. If my friend's opponents were as attentive and practical as he, the judges may well be suspected of having been like the false lawyer in the "Dance of the Dead,"—

> "Don falso Abogado, prevalicador,
> Que de amas las partes levastes salario!"

Of the members of the legal profession it would be altogether unfair to judge by the current scandal, for every one knows how sadly men's sorry wits have made havoc with that devoted and exemplary class, in all ages and countries. It is singular, too, by the way, how popular such attacks have always been. The traveller who has visited Rome will of course remember the depository of the dead which rises on a little hill beside the Appian Way, and is called the Columbarium of Hylas and Vitalina. It is in perfect preservation or restoration, and the urns and vases are probably in the same state and positions in which they were placed, when each tenant of the spot went to his home. Over each little niche is the name of the proprietor, engraven on a simple slab of white marble, with sometimes a posy or brief sentiment. I was struck with one epitaph, which I have never seen alluded to in print. It ran thus:—

"CÆSARIS LUSOR.
MUTUS ARGUTUS. IMITATOR. TIBERI CÆSARIS AUGUSTI.
QUI PRIMUM INVENIT CAUSIDICOS IMITARI."

As it was a professional relic I copied it. The fellow, who would otherwise in all probability have had his ashes funnelled into a small and nameless vase, for a mere king's fool as he was, was handed down to immortality because he was the first "who invented imitating lawyers." Peace be to his manes, notwithstanding! There have been greater fools, since his day, who have found their way into niches of their liking, by turning into a text of popular morality and profitable denunciation what Mutus Argutus treated as a joke!

The members of the Spanish bar with whom I was brought into personal contact were certainly for the most part men of high intelligence, learning, and accomplishments. The majority of them, it is true, were devoted to political pursuits,—indeed almost all the high political positions were occupied either by lawyers or military men; but the practice of the profession is conducted in a manner which gives more leisure —not merely for professional accomplishment, but for general cultivation and the pursuit of reputation in other walks—than an American lawyer can readily conceive. All the written pleadings and their conduct are the work of the *procuradores*, or attorneys, who only trouble counsel for advice, relieving them from all the drudgery and mechanical details of litigation, and enabling them thus to devote their attention to those branches which are purely intellectual. Among us, as is well known, without great reputation and an exceedingly elevated position, few are able to select for themselves any exclusive walk of the profession. A man is expected to be attorney, solicitor, proctor, counsel, barrister, and conveyancer, as well as property-agent and general accountant, too happy if it be not his inevitable destiny to edit a newspaper, or preside over a bank or a railroad company. As, in addition to all this, every American, from the tendency of his nature and of our "peculiar institutions," must be a member of Congress, a governor, or a foreign minister, at some time of his life; and as lawyers, from the tendency of their pursuits, have these other tendencies in an aggravated degree, it follows that the professional "mission" has its best advantages and triumphs darkly mingled with painful and oppressive toil, and all the evils which are sure to follow such criminal overtasking of the body and the mind. Welcome be the civilization which shall change these things,—yea, even if it come from Spain!

IX.

The Press.—Newspapers.—Sartorius.—The Puritans.—Pacheco.—Party Organs.

THE freedom of the press, in Spain, is guarantied, as has been seen, by an express provision of the constitution, which ordains that it shall suffer no restrictions but those to be imposed by law. It is a singular fact, and very illustrative of constitutional habits in the Peninsula, that, in the face of so direct and unequivocal a clause, the rights of the citizen and the powers of the government in 1850 were regulated, in the premises, by a succession of decrees, which had from time to time been promulgated by the executive, without the shadow of legitimate authority. So bold, indeed, was this assumption of legislative functions considered upon all hands, that Sartorius, Count of San Luis, then Minister of the Interior, by way of concession to public opinion, had introduced a bill into the Cortes, during the session of 1848, which professed to carry out the spirit of the fundamental law. I did not see the *projet*, but I was credibly informed that it abounded in excellent sentiments, and extended unlimited freedom to all publications in which there might be no discussion of religion or morals, politics, manners, or legislation. Bad or imperfect as the scheme was held to be, it was, nevertheless, but a tub to the whale. The Minister spoke well of it on all occasions, and referred to it as an evidence of his *zelo y patriotismo*, but was careful to give some good reason always to the *Progresista* opposition for refusing to let them make it the order of the day. The Cortes were dissolved in 1850, without its having been submitted to their action, and the members had hardly, it seems, returned to their constituents, when an edict more stringent than any which had gone before appeared in the columns of the official *Gaceta*. A still more arbitrary one has since followed.

While I was in Madrid it was a frequent occurrence for the whole daily edition of an opposition paper to be seized by the police, as it was upon the point of distribution,—some disagreeable expressions in an editorial article, perhaps, being the offence alleged. During Holy Week, when there were fierce rumors of dissensions at the palace and an impending ministerial crisis, four or five papers were "*recogidos por orden de la autoridad*," as it was politely called, in the course of a single day. Nobody seemed to think it at all remarkable, and I will do the parties who suffered the justice to say, that they did not permit it to diminish the boldness and pertinacity with which they maintained and circulated their opinions. These encroachments on the privileges of the fourth estate were made, in due course, through the Department of the Interior. Sartorius was the last man in Spain, perhaps, who could, consistently, perform such functions. He had been a journalist himself not long before, and had gloried in the name of *periodista*. He owed in a great measure to that profession his elevation to the power which he so abused against it. During his continuance in the ministry, it was believed that he still retained a fondness for his former calling, and there was a rumor, perhaps scandalous, but certainly very current, that those articles of the *Heraldo* which were most gracious to his own measures and his parliamentary displays had a striking resemblance to his well-known style.

Sartorius is certainly a man of considerable cleverness and resource,—adroit, ready, and not troubled with many scruples. In the Cortes, though he was too painfully dressed and buttoned, and wore gloves too tight and yellow for oratorical grace, he was still a bold and efficient debater, full of point and personality, and generally carrying the war into the enemy's country. The haughty and magisterial tone which he assumed was ill tolerated in one who was still a young man, and had but recently won his nobility and station, but it gave a certain force and weight to what he said, and made it seeming wise, if not in fact so. Being a party man, in the strict and even the offensive sense of the term, his hand was against every one who did not belong to his fold; and the consequence was, that there was no member of the cabinet in regard to whom I heard expressions of such general and deep ill-feeling. This was perhaps attributable somewhat to the fact that his Department, among the other internal affairs of the realm, was charged with the management of the elections; and as the modes by which the return of the government candidates was procured were often not of the choicest or most scrupulous, the Minister was necessarily associated with many things in the public mind which could not add to his dignity or popularity. He had a great hold, however, upon the confidence of Narvaez, who no doubt found him a useful colleague, fruitful in expedients, and asking few questions. To his credit be it said, that, since the dissolution of the Narvaez cabinet and the disfavor of the Duke, Sartorius has ever been the foremost to defend his patron, and that, too, with a zeal which he could not have surpassed, had the Duke been still dispenser, as of old, of place and honors. The gossips of the Puerta del Sol insisted, while I was among them, that the Count had grown very rich from his political opportunities, and as Becky Sharp thought she could be a good woman if she had five thousand a year, perhaps he feels that, under the circumstances, he can afford to be magnanimous,—especially as Spanish ministers in Coventry are not like the "*vox missa,*" which "*nescit reverti,*" and there is no knowing the day nor the hour when the Duke of Valencia may have his own again,—and that of a good many other people besides. It is hardly fair, however, to deny to Sartorius—until time shall prove it undeserved—the consideration which is due to that rare virtue among politicians,—shall I say among men?—fidelity to a fallen and absent benefactor.

The lively author of a late agreeable English work on Spain[1] deals rather harshly, I think, with the newspaper press of Madrid. He laughs, justly enough, at the French arrangement, type, and taste, which all the journals there display, even to the ridiculous extent of devoting the bottom of every sheet to a "*folletin,*" usually crammed with a translation or a paraphrase of some prurient Parisian romance. But it is hardly fair, upon the other hand, to condemn the Spaniards

---

[1] *Gazpacho: or Summer Months in Spain.*

by the wholesale, because they do not rival the *Times* of
London or the Paris *Presse*,—or to judge of their standard of
intelligence by such mistakes as Mr. Clarke selects from the
letters of their foreign correspondents. If accuracy in the
details of foreign news were the criterion of newspaper excellence, I am not sure that the English or French leaders, any
more than those of our own country, would have much to
boast of. I know few things more amusing, than to read
some of the French and English paragraphs on American
politics, unless perhaps it be to take up an occasional American commentary on similar matters in the Old World.

It would be a great end gained by the Peace Congresses, if
they could persuade the editorial corps of all nations to learn
and know some little about other countries, before venturing
to disseminate those crude opinions—so often harsh because
adopted ignorantly—which are the cause of so much prejudice,
bad blood, and error. I do not really think that the Spanish
newspapers need a lesson a whit more than their contemporaries elsewhere. Except in one particular, which I shall have
occasion hereafter to mention, I found their errors generally
more amusing than serious, so far as allusions to the United
States were concerned. Those of us, for instance, who were
anxious to learn the result of the long and discreditable ballot-
ing for Speaker which occupied the House of Representatives
in 1849, were greatly surprised one day by the following
announcement in the *Clamor Publico:*—" Estados Unidos. Se
disputaban la Presidencia de la Cámara de Diputados MM.
VVintrop, VVhig, Mr. Crabbe, radical, y Mr. Scattering, del
tercer partido." This, being interpreted, signifies that " In
the United States, the Presidency of the Chamber of Deputies

was in dispute between Messrs. VVintrop, VVhig, Mr. Crobbe, radical, and Mr. Scattering, of the third party!" The same paper likewise informed us, not long after, that there was prevailing in California a frightful degree of misery, —so great, indeed, that the crews of the American ships of war were deserting daily, "throwing their officers overboard before they left!"

Penny-a-line trifles of this sort,—of which I could repeat many, were it worth the pains,—the reader will concur with me in thinking, I am sure, no conclusive proof of degeneracy in the press, especially where, as at Madrid, less space is given to them than in the journals of any other country. In the political department of many of the Madrid papers, the very best abilities of the nation are enlisted, and the prominent articles in the leading party organs are often the work of men whose literature, learning, and statesmanship are beyond peradventure. I had occasion to know that the most distinguished members of the Cortes were frequently contributors to the papers which advocated their particular opinions, and with all allowance for the advantages under which even commonplace may appear in their gorgeous language, I do not, I am sure, exaggerate in saying, that there were frequent articles which for eloquence, boldness, and largeness of views would have done honor to the columns of any newspaper in Europe or America.

When Mr. Mackenzie was in Madrid, in 1826, to write his "Year in Spain," he found but two papers, the *Diario* and the *Gaceta*. The former was a daily small quarto sheet, which contained, he says, "all the commercial intelligence of the Spanish capital;" to wit, the names of the saints of the day, with those of the churches where there would be masses; advertisements of Bayonne hams and Flanders butter; with the names and residence of wet-nurses fresh from the Asturias. The *Gaceta* was a tri-weekly, and embraced "all the literary, scientific, and political intelligence of the whole empire." It was printed on a piece of paper "somewhat larger than a sheet of foolscap," and its contents were limited to an account of the health and occupations of their Majesties, extracts from foreign papers selected and modified for the meridian, lists (no very long ones) of state bonds to be paid, statutes about tithes, and edicts punishing and damning free-masons! The reader may make up his own mind as to the fairness of supposing that the intelligence and literature of the nation were properly represented by the organs of a despotism, which treated every demonstration of either as a crime; but it is very certain, that Mr. Mackenzie has hardly caricatured the journals which monopolized the capital in those days. It fell within the range of my duties to examine the files of those which were published about the close of the constitutional dynasty in 1823, when the leaders of the liberal party had carried king and Cortes to Seville and Cadiz, and it is due to history to say, that in regard to the quantity and quality of their matter, and the style of their typography, it would be hard to fall on an expression which would not be complimentary. Down to the death of Ferdinand, in 1833, there was, of course, no change possible for the better, and the protracted and uncertain civil war, which lasted for ten years from that happy epoch, naturally enough prevented the embarkation of capital in so novel and precarious an enterprise as journalism. The *Heraldo*, the oldest of the present political papers, was not established until

1842, and it will, I think, be justly deemed an evidence of no small progress in the nation, that, in February, 1850, there were thirteen daily papers in circulation in Madrid, the most of them receiving such encouragement as justified their continuance. Their daily issue, in all, was about thirty-five thousand copies, according to an estimate which went the rounds during my visit; and when it is considered that Madrid is, as has been seen, entirely without commerce, and that the advertising support, and the subscriptions consequent thereon, must necessarily be very limited, the state of things cannot be regarded as other than extremely satisfactory and promising. The rate of subscription to the most expensive sheets is very moderate, in view of their almost exclusive dependence upon it. Twelve reals, or sixty cents, per month, is the maximum, and there is no interruption of the issue on Sundays. The non-subscribing public are tempted in the Plaza Mayor, the Puerta del Sol, and all other places of resort, by news-venders as noisy as could be desired, though perhaps not as industrious. Their long and marvellous stories of the wonders they are selling awaken strange echoes in places where, so short a while ago, it was a sin to think without permission, and printing without the censorship was held to be in some sort a machination of the Devil.

The ministerial organ in 1850 was the *Heraldo*. It was edited by Señor Mora, the son of a distinguished writer, then a member of the Cortes from one of the Alicante districts, and an under secretary, besides, in the Department of the Interior. He was believed to be the author of the principal articles, but it was generally understood that they breathed the inspiration and often knew the hand of his chief. Being the mouthpiece of the government, the *Heraldo* could not of course be expected to do otherwise than approve and defend its measures; but although this was often done with plausibility and force, the general tone of the editorials was so intensely and enthusiastically laudatory, as to destroy, in a great degree, the effect that otherwise they might have had on the opinion of the nation. I do not remember to have read any thing more nauseously servile than some of them. The principles which they invoked and enforced were of the most retrograde and illiberal character, tending studiously always, under the cover of monarchical reverence, towards the establishment of a ministerial despotism, at the expense of the crown's security and dignity, and the constitutional rights of the people. It was really curious to see how the organ of an administration—every member of which had sprung immediately and recently from the people, and every guaranty of whose ministerial power and independence had been hard won by popular suffering and perseverance—could, over and over, every day, devote itself to the most unlimited denunciation of popular doctrines, and the most fanatical advocacy of the sacred rights of prescription. It was curious, I say, but not astonishing; for I had just come from France, where the president of a republic which had sprung from the blood of a revolution had newspapers in pay to denounce revolutions, and himself rode out among his fellow-citizens protected by an escort such as even Louis Philippe—so often shot at—had never supposed himself to need. So true it is, that every man in power is a conservative, and that he whose interest it is to keep is the natural and necessary enemy of him whose effort is to take!

The *Epoca*, an afternoon paper, in the interests of the government, was hardly more than an echo of the *Heraldo's* morning jubilations.

The chief opponents of the administration—as indeed of the whole *Moderado* system and dynasty—were the *Progresista* organs, the *Clamor Público* and the *Nacion*,—the former perhaps the more orthodox; the latter representing more especially the peculiar opinions of those members of the Cortes who were called *Progresistas Moderados*, or moderate *Progresistas*. I saw the *Clamor* more frequently, and read it more carefully, than any other of the opposition prints. Its reputed conductors were Galvez Cañero, a deputy from one of the Malaga districts, and Corradia, who had considerable repute as a writer. The more authoritative articles were believed to be the work of the former, but the leaders generally were extremely creditable, not only in style and taste, but for their boldness, information, and manly good sense. The *Moderados* professed, as well as their opponents, a desire for the maintenance of the constitutional monarchy, but they regarded it always from the monarchical or conservative, as opposed to the constitutional or progressive, point of view. The *Clamor*, on the contrary, without falling into the subversive doctrines of the radical party, was the steady advocate of the constitutional side of the question, and inculcated the rigid enforcement of constitutional restrictions and responsibilities, and the development, in a constitutional way, of the more popular elements of the state. Its tone was invariably respectful to the person and legitimate prerogatives of royalty, and courteous towards the individuals in power, but its spirit was perfectly independent under all circumstances, and nothing that it was proper to say ever lost force in its columns for want of being said both fearlessly and plainly. When, as would sometimes happen, an unguarded paragraph would cause the suppression of the morning's edition, the publishers would set themselves to work to get out another forthwith, and the subscribers would find on their tables, only a few hours later, the usual supply of good doctrine, made a little more piquant, perhaps, by an allusion to the "law's delay," which would probably occupy, in prominent type, the place of the confiscated article. Thus the government rarely gained any thing by its usurpations but the opportunity of uselessly asserting its power, losing ten times as much, of course, from the moral effect of opposition so indomitable and successful.

The *Patria*, of which the author of "Gazpacho" speaks most favorably, was an opposition print, which was started by some members of the *Puritano* or puritan party. These gentlemen, it will be readily imagined, did not take their party name from any religious notions, such as the word suggests to us. They originally belonged to the *Moderado* division, but, finding that their associates were fast becoming absolutists in principle, and did little practically except to keep themselves in place,—finding too, perhaps, that those associates were in power, and they themselves were unlikely to attain it, except upon a different basis,—they "pronounced" for a return to the older and genuine *Moderado* doctrine of constitutional conservatism. This assumption of an especial purity of doctrine gave them their title.

The *Puritanos* have some eminent persons among them, and their leader, Sr. Pacheco, is one of the first men in Spain.

I have referred to him as the counsel of Diaz Martinez, and recur to him in this place because he was in private life when I was in Madrid, and his name will hardly arise in any but the present connection. He was in power in 1847 for a short time during my first visit to the Peninsula, but his administration, though from many causes practically a failure, has not diminished his reputation as a man of integrity and thought. A distinguished foreign diplomatist—whose opportunities of knowledge had been ample, and whose ability to judge would be immediately conceded, were I to name him—informed me that he considered many of Pacheco's despatches, which had passed specially under his observation, as equal to the best of M. Guizot's. In his profession of the law, Sr. Pacheco stands with but few rivals in Madrid. He had published several works upon subjects connected with it, which are of acknowledged authority. In politer letters he is also distinguished,—being a prominent member of the Academy, and a poet of vigor, tenderness, and great purity and accuracy of versification. His prose style is grave and stately, like his elocution, which is very impressive. He had published a portion of a History of the Regency of Maria Cristina (the present Queen Mother), which was regarded as a work of great impartiality and merit; but his principal reputation as a prose-writer grew out of his written discourses and his contributions to the periodical press. His inaugural address, upon his introduction to the Academy, was on the subject of journalism, and a good many years of his life were devoted in some degree to that profession. It was thus that he became concerned with the *Patria*, in conjunction with Benavides, a member of the Cortes, of whom I shall have occasion to speak hereafter. Pacheco, however, had retired from his connection with the paper before I reached Madrid, and, as I have said, was pursuing his avocations as a private citizen when I had the good fortune to be admitted to the circle which his many accomplishments rendered so attractive. He proposed being a candidate for Ecija, his native town, in Andalusia, at the election for Cortes which succeeded my departure. Whether he undertook the canvass, I have no means of knowing; but I regard it as a misfortune to the nation that he was not on the list of those who were returned. After the dissolution which followed the downfall of Narvaez in 1851, he was a successful candidate, and is now one of the leaders of the Chamber of Deputies.

It would be hardly worth while to trace, through the different periodicals which represented them, the varieties of political opinion which circumstances and the ambition of individuals and cliques had made so numerous in Madrid. The *Moderado* opposition, who were in opposition because they were out of place and wanted to get in, by making themselves worth bidding for, had administered *de bonis non* on the political estate of the defunct *Puritano* influence, and had thus obtained possession of the *Patria*. The Marquis of Pidal, who was Minister of State, had his personal views and those of his brother-in-law, the noted finance minister, Sr. Mon, put forth in the *Pais*. The *Epoca* was another *Moderado* press, under the sway of Sr. Olivan, a deputy of many hopes. Queen Cristina, too, kept herself before the public, with her usual adroitness, in the pensioned columns of the *España*. The *Pueblo* was democratic and rampant, though edited by a Marquis. The *Esperanza*, on the other hand, was the echo of the high tories, and the organ of Carlism and every thing else reactionary. That the Carlist organ had one of the largest subscription lists, would have been startling and significant under other circumstances. But the *Esperanza's* impunity was no doubt principally due to the fact, that the throne had but little to fear from that quarter, and the rulers of the day were very willing to hear conservatism preached, when Carlism bore the burden of its obnoxiousness, and the *Moderados* reaped the benefit.

X.

CUBA AND THE UNITED STATES.—THE CRÓNICA NEWSPAPER.—PARTIES IN CUBA.—PUBLIC SENTIMENT THERE.—ABUSES AND THEIR REMEDY.—ANNEXATION.

I HAVE said that, in one particular, the comments of the Madrid press upon American affairs were not directed always by the best informed or kindest spirit. In this I had reference to the Cuba question,—the proposed annexation of that island, and the piratical enterprises in contemplation against it,—one of which, but a short time previously, had been frustrated by the vigilant good faith of General Taylor's administration. Although I had full occasion to experience, in the facilities afforded me for the discharge of my own duties, the cordiality with which the course of the President and his cabinet had inspired the Spanish government, it was impossible not to see that there were circumstances surrounding the question, which of necessity created, in both ministers and people, an uneasiness, and indeed distrust, as to the future. The obligation of the nations to observe their treaties incontestably and obviously involves the duty of enacting laws which shall compel that observance, to the letter, on the part of their own citizens. When, therefore, a people who are peremptory in exacting the strictest performance of treaty stipulations from others, set up the nature of their own institutions as a reason for their inability to keep as strictly the faith which they have as positively pledged, they have no right to marvel if their honesty be brought in question. Nations treat as equals. In their internal government, they may be what they please,—in their external aspect they are nations merely, with all the faculties and duties of such. Sovereignty which is responsible enough to contract and thereby obtain benefits, cannot be allowed to disclaim responsibility in the matter of keeping promises. It may be strong enough to disregard the consequences of so doing,—bold enough to challenge them,—but it must submit to be called unprincipled, or at all events to be considered so. If a nation's institutions unfit it for keeping treaties, it ought not to make them. It either has a government, or it has not. If it has not, it ought not to make pretence that it has; if it has, that government should govern. The logic of the matter is as clear as its honesty; and false pretences are as criminal under the public law as under the municipal.

It must be confessed, that, in reference to the Cuba question, appearances were not very favorable to our national fair-dealing. That in a civilized country, in the nineteenth century, it should have been seriously proposed, and openly, as a scheme of public policy, to acquire, by actual or moral force, the territory of a friendly nation,—believed to be a weak one,—for no other reason and with no other pretext than, simply, that the party proposing to take thought proper to covet,—was quite enough to startle those plain people, all the world over, who had been taught to consider good faith as sacred, and rapine a crime. But when such a scheme was advocated, boldly and constantly, in the public journals of the aggressive nation, without provoking a universal, nay, even a general expression of indignation and shame,—when, in the ports of that nation, expeditions were set on foot and men and munitions of war were got together for the purpose of invading the coveted territory, and either seizing it, or revolutionizing its population, with a view to its ultimate acquisition,—it is hardly to be wondered that the civilized world should have poured forth unanimous denunciations. The people of the outraged nation had certainly a reasonable apology, if they forgot the soft words and the forbearance which became them as Christians. The Spaniards have a national endowment of fortitude, which is remarkable. San Lorenzo, whose gridiron is immortalized in the Escorial, is said to have suggested, when they were broiling him, that they had better turn him on the other side, as that nearest the coals was, he thought, sufficiently cooked. His descendants, upon the present occasion, behaved as well as it was reasonable to anticipate from even such an example. But there are limits even to the spirit of martyrdom, and it is not in human nature that men should be altogether patient and philosophical, when they witness a systematic and deliberate organization for the robbery and murder of their brethren. Nor is their equanimity at all likely to be increased, by the fact that national insult is added to private injury, and that men who are carrying out, and presses which are glorifying, the principles and practices of the Norse freebooters, should be thanking God they are free and enlightened, and not like the "ignorant, uncivilized race" which they are about to plunder and slay.

While, then, it was generally conceded in Madrid, that the United States executive government had done its best, in view of its limited powers, it was equally clear that those powers were more than necessarily circumscribed,—at all events practically,—and there was enough in the demonstrations of the American press,—enough, with shame and sorrow be it said, in occasional expressions which disgraced the American Congress,—to satisfy the Spaniards that there was danger before them from the possible action of our people and the weakness and imperfection of our laws. Their ideas were, besides, affected further by their own notions and habits of government. Accustomed to the *surveillance*, and the rapid, secret, and unscrupulous action of a detective police, they could not comprehend the tardy and imperfect operation of that popular, free system, which leaves so much undiscovered and unpunished, least any should, perchance, be unduly suspected or oppressed. They could not understand how a warlike expedition could be set on foot, in any country, without its being known, immediately, to the government; and it was inconceivable to them that a suspected person could be left at large, without connivance on the part of some of the authorities. They felt and knew that their own government had the means of preventing the preparation for such outrages in its ports, and that its powers would be exercised, immediately and effectually, to suppress and punish. They had some difficulty, therefore, in being persuaded that they had not a right to expect what they felt themselves bound and were always ready to render, and what the United States, upon at least one memorable occasion, had exacted from them at the point of the bayonet.

There was another cause of irritation and anxiety, which, though unfortunate, was natural. Very few American newspapers reach the Peninsula, and the information as to American affairs which is derived from the European journals is generally meagre and partial. The principal details which were received and reproduced by the Madrid press were furnished by the *Crónica*, a newspaper published at New York, in the Spanish language, and commonly asserted, in Madrid, to be supported by the Cuban government. It would be impossible for any thing to be more elaborately and systematically unjust, than the mass of that paper's editorial observations upon the character and sentiments of the people of the United States, —an injustice which it is difficult not to pronounce wilful, in view of the general intelligence which pervades the journal, and precludes the imputation of ignorance. At the time referred to, the good faith of the American government was constantly impeached in the *Crónica*, and the integrity and sincerity of the Cabinet officers were systematically assailed. The wholesome and honest public feeling and opinion which pervaded so large a portion of the American community and found such frequent utterance in the columns of its influential journals, were studiously ignored, or broadly denied to exist. It seemed, in fine, the whole, unscrupulous effort of the paper to create and strengthen the impression that our government was without faith, or power for good, and our people destitute alike of truth and honesty. The tenor of my own views, as already expressed, will, I think, be some guaranty to the reader, that I have no sympathy—not the most remote—with the perpetrators of the outrages in question, nor any national supersensibility, which would lead me into an overstatement of the misrepresentations to which I am referring.

Facts and circumstances, such as the *Crónica*, in the spirit I have spoken of, took pains to promulgate, were published for truth, as the testimony of eyewitnesses, in the newspapers of Madrid. "*Se lee en un periódico de Nueva York*," they would say,—" We read in a New York paper the following," &c., &c.; and the public, not familiar with the mysteries of journalism, took for granted that the "thrilling narratives" with which they were regaled were the concurrent testimonials of the indigenous press of New York, and thought it astonishing that the *pueblo Norte-Americano* should not only be so full of villany, but so barefaced in pleading guilty to it. It is but proper to admit that the commentaries of the Madrid papers were extremely moderate, in view of the facts which they believed to be thus in their possession. A supposed determination on the part of England to annex California would, I am sure, condense more hard names and indignant eloquence into the editorials of any one of our village newspapers, than the whole Madrid press gave vent to, under similar circumstances. But it will, nevertheless, be readily imagined, that such things could not fail to awaken suspicion and apprehension, even in those who did not credit them altogether, and that, most naturally, there existed much question of our motives and action, even among those whose political principles led them to admire our institutions, and take pleasure in our prosperity and greatness. It cannot be denied that they had in fact much solid reason to think ill of us, and plausible grounds for doing so even to a far greater extent than we really deserved.

I had fortunate opportunities of meeting in Madrid with many gentlemen from Cuba, of intelligence and influence, and of all shades of political opinion. The unreserved expression of their views, and the details of fact with which many of them favored me, enabled me to form perhaps as accurate an idea of the politics of the island, as even a visit there would ordinarily afford a stranger. Parties, I was told, were, in the main, but three. Among them, the uncompromising friends of the existing state of things occupied the first place in political power and ostensible influence. To this class belonged, of course, all the government officials, with their friends and dependents,—all the military men,—many of the wealthier Creoles and the numerous resident Spaniards, engaged in private pursuits. These last are principally Catalans or Basques,—mostly the former,—with the courage and energy characteristic of their respective provinces. Considering themselves still as citizens of the Peninsula, and looking forward to an old age of competence, at home, from the fruits of their temporary exile, they naturally incline towards maintaining the predominance of the mother country against the immunities which the Cubans, as naturally, covet. They are most of them wealthy; almost all in promising or prosperous business. If taxes are high, they thrive notwithstanding. If government is arbitrary and exacting, it still leaves them the means of getting rich and escaping in comfort. Their acquisitions and prospects, therefore, are things far too serious and substantial to be put upon the hazard of any revolution, and they consequently form a conservative phalanx, which it will be found extremely difficult at any time to break. They will be ready, in any crisis, to place at the disposal of the government a large portion of their wealth, for the preservation of the rest, and they themselves will form no trifling accession to the military strength of the island,—the civil broils of latter years in Spain having unfortunately left few from the northern provinces unaccustomed to bearing arms, or ignorant of military discipline.

The extreme party on the other side—that alone to which immediate or forcible annexation would be tolerable—is, I was told, and as subsequent events have shown, quite insignificant in influence, character, extent, and true patriotism. It of course embraces, as all parties of extreme opinion do, some few sincere enthusiasts; but its principal recruits are from the ranks of those who have nothing to lose, and those who, having fallen under the ban of the government, have fortunes to redeem or injuries to revenge. Its members are chiefly Creoles, or strangers who have no other livelihood than opening nine Ancient Pistol's oyster. In a country with different political and social habits and organization, the many grievances which really irritate and seriously oppress would render desperate adventurers like these a possible nucleus of dangerous agitation. But political abstractions melt away under that burning sun, and the population is neither large nor concentrated enough, nor sufficiently accustomed to political discussion, to be easily moved by the ordinary appeals which have so much force in popular governments and colder climates. The Cubans, besides, are of too lax a fibre, and too fond of pleasure, for any of those doings with which "fierce democratics" are wont to thunderstrike old systems. Pine-apples and cigars,—the opera, the *paseo*, and the sea-breeze,—are far pleasanter things, even under a Captain-General, than the dust and blood (besides the trouble) of a doubtful revolution. The enervating influences which have made the stalwart language of Castile a lisping bastard on the Creole's lips, have emasculated his character also, and destroyed within him the virile independence and proud fortitude which centuries of oppression have not taken from the old Castilian heart. The spirit of the radical party, therefore, is of as little practical consideration as its numbers.

The third division—if parties and principles have any thing reasonable in them—should be, and I was told it was, by far the most numerous, as it is certainly the most patriotic of the three. It is composed, mainly, of the Cubans themselves, but embraces the best elements of intelligence, enterprise, and virtue to be found among them. Its members have simply in view the interests of the island and its inhabitants. They are wedded to no particular scheme or system, and are willing to support any which will secure to them a rational freedom, and an exemption from oppressive and unjust burdens. They have no preference for independence, except as a means of securing these benefits, and regarding it, under the circumstances, as a perilous, and most doubtful experiment, they are many of them anxious, and almost all of them content, to continue the colonial relation. Other things being equal, or, indeed, approximating equality,—it would never occur to them to imagine a transfer of their dependence from the mother country to the United States. All their national peculiarities—the sympathy of race, a common language, historical associations, family ties, and national customs and tastes—incline them irresistibly towards the land of their origin. The Spaniards are not of a blood that readily amalgamates, and least of all with the Saxon or any mixture of it. But the predilection of the intelligent Cubans for the Spanish connection, though a strong one, is, nevertheless, not blind. They complain of bad government, and are earnest in insisting, so far as they lawfully may, upon having their grievances redressed. This is not the place to inquire how far their complaints are well founded. That the evils which produce them have been greatly overstated, both as to number and aggravation, I have no doubt. This has been particularly the case in the many absurd publications which have been made in the United States, with a view to stimulate and keep up the annexation and invasion excitements, and which have misled so many to suffering and death. But, on the other hand, it is only just to say, that, among the many intelligent Cubans I have met, I do not remember one—no matter what may have been his politics—who has not spoken, in strong language, of grievous abuses as existing. Such unanimity cannot certainly be without cause. That the government of the island is neither more nor less than a military despotism, all the world knows. Its responsible and lucrative offices are, almost exclusively, in the hands of *empleados* from the mother country, where, indeed, Cuba is held, as Mistress Page was by her enamored knight, to be "all gold and bounty." Politicians who have rendered services which the coffers of the Peninsula are too empty to compensate conveniently, and aspirants to place at home who are needy and dangerous, are rewarded habitually, or propitiated, as the case may be, by a chance of picking the colony. The administration of justice is admitted, on all hands, to be tardy, costly, and corrupt. Nowhere, I was told, does the *escribano* system, with all its consequences,— "insani præmia scribæ,"—flourish half so gloriously. Taxation, if not so exorbitant as is sometimes pretended, is unquestionably unequal and needlessly oppressive. The restraint on commerce, and the subserviency of its regulations to Peninsular interests, contribute to render that oppressiveness still more unwelcome,—while the fact, that all the impositions which weigh so heavily upon the colonists go to the support of an administration of strangers, or the maintenance of a government across the ocean, suffices, of itself, to throw on the colonial relation a certain shade of inevitable odium.

It is not to be concealed, that the pressure of these things is made more galling, even to the most loyal of the Cubans, by the proximity of this republic. They cannot avoid feeling that the palpable contrast between our relative prosperity and progress and theirs is mainly attributable to the difference in political institutions and their administration. Every unsuccessful application to the home government for measures of redress of course heightens the effect of that contrast, and proportionally inclines them to turn from a system which perpetuates misrule, to one which furnishes such practical demonstration of its efficiency for good. If, therefore, all the freebooters who disgrace our shores were driven from them,— if the few shameless presses were silenced which proclaim as honorable and patriotic the breach of our treaty faith and the total abandonment of national honor,—the Cuban government itself alone might give efficiency, and weight, and final success to the project of annexation. A very interesting pamphlet, presenting this view of the subject, was published in Madrid while I was there, by Don José Antonio Saco, a distinguished Cuban, who, although an anti-annexationist, was then reaping in banishment, at Calais, the reward of his honest but too candid zeal. The liberal newspapers adopted and advocated his ideas, with a great deal of freedom and force, while the government organs, of course, denounced them as treasonable and absurd. The columns of the latter journals were filled, meanwhile, with letters from Havana, which gave magnificent accounts of public displays, operatic *fiestas*, and balls and banquets enthusiastically attended, at the palace of the Captain-General,—all obviously got up as proof conclusive of the splendor, happiness, and plenty which flourish under the existing system. For men mad enough to think that such things can long disguise the evils or retard the overthrow of a bad government, there is no hellebore except the fate which they invoke. Nor can that fate, in its good season, fail to overtake them, if they so continue to deserve it. Now, it will be comparatively easy for the Spanish government, in the patriotic reaction after the defeat of Lopez,—the loyal rallying of all parties and classes around the throne,—to put an end to discontent and danger. The most moderate reforms,—the mere foreshadowing of something better,—anything that may give or seem to give, an earnest of a more liberal system to come,—will suffice to revive hopes and quicken and confirm allegiance. Every year of delay will render the task more difficult and the result more problematic.

It requires, one would think, but ordinary forecast and familiarity with human nature to perceive all this; but men in power, and especially in Spain, seem cursed with the fatality of thinking that the present is all of time. The pleasure and pride of governing and getting rich by it appear to absorb all other considerations, even with men whose capacity and experience of public affairs ought to teach them that duty is worth discharging, as a matter of policy and reputation at all events, to say nothing of principle. Causes, however, will not cease to operate, because politicians choose to disregard them. The flood-tide of the ocean had small care for Canute. Unless there be a change, and a most decided one, in the attitude of Spain towards her chief colony, there must, sooner or later, but inevitably, be a repetition of the memorable lesson, *"C'est trop tard!"*

But let it not for a moment be inferred from this, that there is or can be any real sympathy, on the part of the inhabitants of Cuba, with the expeditions of the buccaneers who have given so much trouble to them, and brought so much discredit on us, of late. Results have been demonstrative enough on this point. What the Cubans desire is improvement, not revolution,—protection to property, and personal security, under a better government and better laws. If they cannot obtain these things from the mother country, they may be forced or tempted to seek them in the last resort, as I have said, under the auspices of a powerful and freer nation. But this will be in the last resort only, and peacefully, if possible. Revolt would, at the best, involve consequences which it is horrible to contemplate. The Spanish government has announced its inflexible determination, that the island shall continue Spanish or be made African. *"Cuba ha de ser Española ó Africana."* The hour in which the standard of revolt should be successfully reared, would see the slaves let loose upon their masters. The rapine, murder, and incendiarism of a single day of servile triumph could never be repaired, to the present inhabitants of the island. Others might come after them and prosper,—the island itself might become rich and great in time, under other institutions,—but the men of this day and the things that are theirs would disappear in the conflict. The power of the Union might conquer,—it could not save. If, then, the Cubans would have so much reason to dread the drawing of the sword, with all the force of this republic on their side, it presupposes madness in them to imagine that they can seriously countenance revolt, with no other reliance than the Falstaff regiments of our steamboat "patriots." There is double reason for their shrinking from the struggle in that shape. Success would be as bad as defeat. The motives and hopes of such adventurers as would seek their shores under such banners could only be based on plunder. Of necessity they would be in search of better fortunes. Whence would the plunder—whence would the fortunes—come? All the generals and colonels, all the governors and other miscellaneous functionaries and heroes who might lead or follow the liberating chivalry, would of course expect a pound of pay to every ounce of glory. They would take leave to dictate their own rewards, and to apportion them, if there were need, at the point of the bayonet. Unhappy Cuba would have cause to sigh, amid the seven devils that had come to her, for the single one she had been so anxious to cast out. It cannot be that the Cubans are blind to all this; and the hopes and calculations which rest on the existence of such blindness must be frustrated. Even among the Antilles there are people who have heard of Æsop, and remember the fable of the horse who submitted to the rein that he might take vengeance on his enemy, and was ridden and driven for ever after,—the drudge and victim of his friend! They must have read our history but little and ill, not to have learned that "annexation" is equivalent to absorption, and that the "proud bird" in which we glory so much has claws and a beak for his own edification, as well as benignant wings for the protection of dependent poultry.

XI.

THE CHAMBER OF DEPUTIES.—TEATRO DE ORIENTE.—MINISTERS AND OPPOSITION.—COUNCIL OF MINISTERS.—SEATS OF MINISTERS IN THE LEGISLATURE.

ALTHOUGH legislative bodies, even under the most liberal system of suffrage, do not universally (with deference be it said) represent the best phases of the national spirit, intelligence, or taste, they are nevertheless sufficiently characteristic, always, in their deliberations, to interest a stranger greatly. This is particularly true of the more popular branch, where there are two. The Congress of Deputies in Madrid was accordingly one of my favorite places of resort. The new Palace, which the Deputies now occupy, at the head of the Carrera de San Gerónimo, near the Prado, was not finished or dedicated to its legislative uses until some months after my return home. It is a large and costly building, but very badly situated, it seems to me, for effect, and, although rendered somewhat imposing by its size and classical pretensions, is wanting in dignity and taste. Théophile Gautier says that he doubts whether good laws can possibly be made under such architecture; but a traveller from the United States must needs be more hopeful, in view of the excellent legislation which has now and then emanated from our own Capitol, in spite of its dome and the statuary on its portico and in its neighborhood.

The Congress held its sessions, during my stay, in the saloon of the Teatro (theatre) de Oriente, an immense building, then still unfinished, but since converted, at the expense of the government, into perhaps the most superb opera-house in Europe. It lies at the foot of the Calle del Arenal, the street which runs directly from the Puerta del Sol to the Royal Palace, and obstructs, with its huge, unsightly pile of bricks, the thoroughfare and view from the Puerta to the beautiful Plaza de Oriente. The French, during their occupation of Madrid, determined, with their usual good taste in such matters, that the avenue between the Puerta and the Palace should be direct and uninterrupted. As it cost them nothing to gratify their fancy, they caused the interposing buildings to be demolished accordingly. Ferdinand the Seventh, with his proverbial want of taste, and his recklessness in making all things bend to it, resolved, on his return, not to remedy the private wrong which the destruction of property had inflicted, but to throw away for his private amusement the public good which had been purchased by the sacrifice. It occurred to him, that he would like to have a theatre within a stone's throw of the palace, so that he might step into it by a covered way, after dinner, without danger of the *pulmonia* or prejudice to his digestion. Straightway, therefore, arose the Teatro de Oriente, in the very course of the Arenal and the very line of view from the Palace and the Puerta. In order to render the exploit as acceptable as might be to his people, he caused the massive foundations and ridiculously heavy walls of the structure to be laid with an utter contempt of cost, and provided the necessary funds by *arbitrios* upon the fruits of Malaga, and other equally rational impositions. "*Dios nos libre del despotismo!*—May God deliver us from despotism!"—was the fervent ejaculation, at this stage of his story, of the worthy *Progresista* who called my attention to these details. But Ferdinand did not live to consummate the triumph of his caprice over popular convenience, the beauty of the capital, and common propriety and sense. The political troubles which followed his exit were two engrossing to permit even theatres to be thought of or paid for, and the lumbering mass lay almost as he left it, until 1850, when Sartorius resolved to complete it under the auspices of his Department, so that the prestige of the *Moderado* dynasty might be strengthened, by the popularity of Alboni the singer and Fuoco the dancer. In the meantime, however, what had been meant for the amusement Ferdinand most loved (among those which were harmless) was applied to the purposes he most hated,—those of popular legislation. The saloon, a beautiful and commodious chamber, was finished and elegantly fitted up, in 1841, for the Congress of Deputies. All the necessary apartments for offices, committee-rooms, library and archives, were easily provided, without taxing half the capabilities of the enormous edifice, and—except for the name of the thing—Spain might have been spared, for at least another of her constitutional cycles, the cost of yet another palace. Surely, in the state of her finances, Señor Conde de San Luis! she might have managed to dispense with a government opera-house.

At the head of the saloon, towards the north, upon a lofty platform, was the throne, magnificent in drapery and gilding, guarded by couchant lions, gilded also. In front of this was the chair of the President, before whom the secretaries sat at their table. On each side was a sort of tribune or pulpit, whence orators might speak, if they chose, and from which the ministers read royal edicts on occasions of great state. Along the walls, upon the platform, were the diplomatic and other privileged galleries. The seats to which the public were admitted were at the lower extremity of the chamber. The benches of the members were placed in ascending grades, parallel with the length of the saloon, down the centre of which there was an open passage to where the halberdiers, in antique dresses, stood at the foot. None but the ministers were supplied with desks. Little slips or leaves of mahogany, attached to the backs of the benches, and so arranged that they could be raised and used by those sitting behind, for the convenience of taking notes, seemed to answer all necessary purposes. The ministers sat together, on the first front bench to the right, at the foot of the presidential platform. Immediately behind them were the seats of some of their most prominent supporters, and a little lower down, on the same side, were several of the leaders of the *Moderado* opposition. The *Progresistas* were principally grouped directly in front of the ministers on the opposite side of the central passage. The appearance of the body was, on the whole, dignified and prepossessing, and although it numbered three hundred and fifty members, there was, even in the most excited debates, a general observance of personal and parliamentary decorum, which illustrated the proverbial good-breeding of the nation.

The President of the Deputies seems to exercise a much more arbitrary jurisdiction than the corresponding functionary with us. His control over the hours of meeting and adjournment appears to be discretionary, and his decision, upon questions of order and parliamentary privilege, to carry the force of law. If authority so large may sometimes (as it must) be abused,—especially where the influence of government is so marked, and where the Presidency must generally be within its gift,—there is, on the other hand, no doubt that time and disorder are greatly economized by it, and that a vast amount of empty and profitless debate is superseded. Nor, indeed, am I sure that the power of a partisan majority over freedom of speech is not less likely to be unscrupulously used by a single and solely responsible individual,—who, although elected by that majority, has yet his personal integrity and intelligence directly and conspicuously at stake,—than by the majority itself, in whose action responsibility is divided, and individual scruples are swept off their feet by the rush of the crowd.

The ministers of the crown are not *ex officio* members of the Cortes, but, if they belong to either of the legislative bodies, they may take part in the discussions of both, though without the right of voting except in that of which they are members. The administration is distributed into seven Departments, each of which has its Secretary. The Minister of State discharges the usual duties of such a functionary. The Minister of Grace and Justice is charged with the superintendence of the legal and judicial system,—the control of ecclesiastical affairs, patents of nobility, pardons, privileges, and legal dispensations,—the custody and authentication of the laws of the realm,—and a thousand collateral branches of duty and patronage such as must necessarily belong to so comprehensive a Department. The Minister of *Gobernacion* (or of the Interior), has the control of police and taxes,—the post-office and the conscription,—the internal government of the provinces, so far as that belongs to the central authority,—the management of theatres and bull-fights, the press and the prisons. His jurisdiction embraces the colonies, and his duties therefore are complicated and almost incalculable. The Minister of Commerce, Instruction, and Public Works, and the Secretaries of Finance, War, and the Navy, exercise respectively their obvious functions. The seven Secretaries form what is called the Council of Ministers, which is presided over by one of their number, or by an eighth minister designated by the crown, in its discretion, and without any particular administrative duties. Narvacz, like a sensible man, chose to be President of the Council, and nothing more in name or duty, though every thing in power. He was rarely absent from the sessions of the Congress, and although he of course left to his colleagues the labor of discussing those measures which involved their particular Departments and the details of the administration, he was always on the alert, like a skilful general and brave soldier, watching the changes of the fight, and ready to throw himself, sword in hand, wherever the enemy pressed fiercely.

I may say in this connection, that I could not avoid being frequently struck, in the Cortes, with the great advantage, in many points of view, of giving seats in the legislature to the chief counsellors of the executive. I do not, of course, speak with regard to the convenience of the members of the Cabinet themselves,—though there is no reason why that should not be consulted,—but in view of the many and great facilities which the system gives, for the transaction of public business. A thousand unimportant inquiries, gravely instituted by the House of Representatives of the United States, and entailing upon the heads of Departments the most wearisome and unnecessary waste of that time, which, when most faithfully and economically used, scarce suffices for the thorough discharge of their indispensable duties, might be satisfied, in a few moments, or altogether superseded, by a timely word or two of oral question and explanation. The gross and unbecoming personal attacks which have, of late, so unfortunately tended to make our executive dignities comparatively unattractive to those who could wear them most worthily, would not be half so frequent, I am sure, were the assailants confronted with the ability and character, which, at a distance and under so many disadvantages, may now be outraged with impunity. Suggestions, which the experience of a Secretary and his superior knowledge of details might enable him constantly and most advantageously to throw out, for the perfection of measures concerning his Department, now only, in most cases, reach the legislature indirectly, and often through the medium of committees whose adverse views hardly transmit them fairly, and never fully.

Nor is there any evil very apparent which diminishes the force of these considerations. The fear of executive influence is a sorry bugbear,—for, if the executive is not present to speak for itself, it must needs, in the best way it can, procure others, among the legislators themselves, to speak for it,—and it is not very likely that corruption will be decreased by increasing the necessity for its application. Equally unfounded, too, is the notion that the presence of those who dispense patronage will be a restraint on legislative independence. The yeas and nays are far more tyrannical than any browbeating. Where every man's vote is known to his neighbor, or may be, those who vote to be profited will find no compulsion more stringent and domineering than that applied by their interests. If people are superstitious on the subject of keeping the legislative and executive functions distinctly apart,—a very singular superstition, by the by, under a constitution which embodies the veto power,—let them give the Secretaries the right to participate in the debates, but not to vote. Let each—if scrupulosity in the premises be deemed a virtue—be confined to the discussion of what involves his particular branch of the service, or at all events let none of them have a wider range than over matters purely executive. I do not, myself, see the necessity of any such restrictions. I think that what is called the "one-man power" is only dangerous in the newspapers. The legislature, within its constitutional province, is quite able to take care of itself, and in its customary practice of "platform" and President making has an additional element of mastery, which renders it almost omnipotent. The introduction of the change I have commented on, instead of diminishing the legitimate or increasing the illegitimate sway of Congress, would, I am sure, have a contrary effect. It would make executive responsibility more certain, by rendering it more direct and unavoidable, and would, on the other hand, give to ability, candor, eloquence, and patriotism the opportunity of preventing misrepresentation and injustice, by being their own immediate interpreters.

XII.

GENERAL NARVAEZ.—MINISTERIAL PROFITS.—MARQUIS OF PIDAL.—ASTURIAN NOBILITY.—SR. MON.—PROHIBITIVE DUTIES AND THE CATALANS.

I HAVE already spoken of the Duke of Valencia,—better known as General Narvaez,—with the respect which I think his ability deserves, in spite of many things, in his political system and practices, which it is impossible not to condemn. The controlling position which he occupied, for some years, in his native country, and the remarkable energy and wisdom with which he managed to carry his government in peace through the stormy times which succeeded the last French revolution, have attracted much attention to him from the European world. Upon the Continent, his reputation, as a statesman and ruler, is very high. In England—particularly since his dismissal of Sir Henry Bulwer—there has been a disposition shown to treat him as a mere soldier of fortune, to whose greatness accident has stood godfather, and who could only be eminent, *inter minora sidera*, in Spain. As the most of what we know, in reference to Continental matters, comes to us from the British press, it is natural that British opinions should, in the main, be the basis of ours, and it thus happens that the little which is said and thought of

Narvaez, in the United States, is tinctured with the injustice prevailing at the source from which it comes.

Entering the diplomatic gallery of the Salon de Oriente, you found yourself not very far from the bench occupied by the ministers. At its head there sat—or frequently stood, receiving the salutations of the members as they passed—a man apparently a little over fifty years of age, and rather below the middle size. He was scrupulously well dressed,—sometimes almost too elaborately,—his figure erect and well proportioned, his bearing somewhat haughty, yet full of studious courtesy. But that he had place and power, which ladies love, it would not have been easy to conceive what had made him so proverbial a favorite with the fair daughters of his country; for his features, though striking, were hard and weather-worn, and the best Paris *perruquier* had not been able to make art as ornamental as nature. Sometimes he wore a ribbon at his buttonhole, but often he was without any decoration, and, save the aspect of the man himself and the deference which almost insensibly waited on his presence, there was nothing of outward sign to tell a stranger that the absolute ruler of Spain and its dependencies was before him.

If you waited, however, until the order of the day was called, and the discussion happened to be one of moment, it soon became perceptible that the leader of the ministerial phalanx was, by all odds and on all accounts, the leader of the Congress. Although, as I have said, he left to his associates the consideration of details, he assumed absolute control over the spirit of the debate on his side of the question. Upon all points involving the dignity of the monarch and the integrity of his own administration,—upon all personal questions,—all occasions where there was play for that wisdom which comes of will, and, more than all things else, despotically sways assemblages of men,—his mastery was instantly manifest. It is true that his position, and the deference of the President and the majority of the Deputies, would have given great advantages to even an ordinary man; but there was that in the glancing of his fierce gray eye, in his condensed and pointed thought and his impassioned utterance, which made the parliamentary predominance of Narvaez obviously his own. Sometimes he was overbearing in speech, as he undoubtedly is in temper, but he would almost invariably make generous atonement,—often, indeed, so chivalrously, as to render his very trespass an element of sympathy. Occasionally he would fling out a stinging epigram, conceived in the very happiest spirit of popular oratory. "The honorable gentleman," he said one day in reply to Cortina, one of the leading *Progresistas*,—" the honorable gentleman will have it, Sir, that the administration is indebted, for its failures, to itself,—for its successes, to Chance! I give Chance joy, Sir, of so eminent a votary as the gentleman! I congratulate the honorable gentleman himself upon the happy accident which, when he tossed into the air the seven-and-twenty letters of the alphabet, brought down the graceful combinations of his eloquent discourse!"

I was informed by a distinguished member of the opposition, that Narvaez lacked fluency except in passionate appeals, and that his argumentative efforts were always carefully prepared, even to the extent of being written as they were delivered. If this be correct, the Spanish statesman does only what the greatest masters of parliamentary art have done, and wisely; but I can scarcely reconcile it with his impulsive nature and fervent elocution. His graver speeches were generally reserved to close the debate,—a course which he was particularly justified in pursuing, as well by the force of his character and influence, as by his power of analysis and condensation. He was never very long upon the floor, for he is a man of few words. His mind seemed to direct itself, instinctively, towards the heart of the controversy,—avoiding all things collateral and extraneous. He presented the strong points of his own case in the most compact, impressive way, and attacked the strong points of his adversaries with a directness and a gallantry which were always effective, and often triumphant. When he had finished his argument, his speech was finished too; and although men of finer elocution, more attractive fancy, more philosophical and copious thought, might, with their best ability, have gone before him, his summing up seemed always to have left the question at the very point whence you could see it best and judge of it most justly.

What I have said of the parliamentary efforts of Narvaez is perfectly consistent with the fact that he is not a highly educated or intellectually cultivated man. Although of noble connection, he spent the earlier portion of his life among the mountains of Andalusia, in narrow circumstances, without much chance of converse with men or books. Many of his first speeches, it is said, gave decided evidence of the defects which so limited a career necessarily induced, and now his best efforts are but little indebted for their success to literary taste, historical illustration, or other men's theories and thoughts. His rapid perceptions, however, and rare memory, have made the brilliant opportunities of his later years stand practically in stead of the advantages of youth, and while, even in the midst of a life of action and excitement, he has been able proportionally to widen the sphere and multiply the variety of his acquirements, his extraordinary tact has converted him into as consummate a man of the world, as one with so impetuous and proud a spirit well can be. In the most polished circles of Madrid, surrounded by distinguished foreigners and the *élite* of his own countrymen, he would be selected at a glance for what he is, by any careful observer of men; nor would a nearer view disclose a single point, in which he would appear to fall below the high social standard by which his position exposes him to be tested. His accent and forms of speech are decidedly Andalusian, and his familiar conversation has, from this, a freshness and frankness rendering it at times exceedingly attractive. On the whole, however, his manners are more kingly than genial; and were it not that he is loyal and abiding in his friendship,—remembering benefits always, and rewarding services at every hazard,—he would seem more likely to command respect than win a warmer feeling. Nevertheless, there were many around him, at that day, whose devotion scarce knew bounds. His present political adversity will afford him an unhappy opportunity of testing their sincerity and constancy.

Rumor says that Narvaez has acquired large wealth by his political career. It would be strange if there were not some truth in this, for what Gongora said of his own generation has not gone out of fashion:—

"La corte vende su gala,
 La guerra su valentía."

Rare is the public servant, now-a-days, who does not hive enough honey, from a summer in the gardens of the state, to sweeten the remainder of his days! I remember calling upon a venerable gentleman, who had filled for several years, with rare ability and punctuality, the post of Finance Minister under Ferdinand the Seventh. The modest simplicity of his household arrangements attracted the attention of my companion, a practised courtier, who exclaimed as the door closed on us, "How unobtrusively that old man lives! Yet he was minister ten years! One who is minister for ten days, now, is considered simple if his fortune be not made!" I could not help recalling the bitterness of an apostrophe, which I had just read in a contemporary sketch of an eminent person, who, like our host, had passed without reproach through a life of temptation and opportunity. "Console not thyself," said the biographer, "with the anticipation that generations yet to come will bless thy memory, or name thee as a model of propriety and honor! In the unhappy country where thou dwellest, and in the glorious times which thou and we have fallen on, though he who steals is called a thief, he who steals not is reckoned but a fool!"

An anecdote, related to me, unreservedly, by one of the parties, will show, that, although the passage just cited may have slightly exaggerated the evil for the sake of the antithesis, it does no great injustice to the political habits of the capital. That the anecdote should be true, as I am sure it is, seems strange enough. That it should have been told, without hesitation, is stranger, but makes it the more characteristic, as a picture of public and private morals.

"I am about to form a ministry," said a prominent Deputy to a still more prominent Senator,—"will you join it?"

"No,—I am too old, and, besides, it will not last."

"*Vaya hombre! Está vmd. loco?* Are you mad? You are surely old enough to be wiser. Take a secretaryship, and pocket all you can get hold of. When you are tired, or have enough, you can join issue with the administration, on the popular side of some exciting question, and go out with your gains, in patriotic disgust. Nobody will interfere with you, if you keep quiet. You will have no rivals, because you will be in nobody's way, and the people at large will venerate you too much, as a martyr, to think of molesting you or your money."

"*Y era sabio el consejo!*—It was good advice too!" said the Senator; "but I am too old for intrigues, now: and besides, I didn't like his programme!"

If Narvaez has, indeed, been frail enough to yield to the temptations of his class and generation, he is, nevertheless, entitled to the credit of having done good work for good wages,—which is saying a good deal, as the ways of politicians are ordered in our day. An Aristides or a Washington is, of course, the best model for a statesman, but as that style is not prevalent just now,—except, perhaps, among candidates for the Presidency of the United States,—nations (in the Old World at least) ought to be satisfied, if they can compromise for ability, firmness, and nationality in their rulers, without looking too closely into their accounts. The *Heraldo* of Madrid administered, one day, a most indignant and virtuous rebuke to some *curioso impertinente* in the *Patria*, who dared to suggest that the *Corregidor* of Madrid received a larger salary than he was worth. "To sift such matters too closely," said the ministerial organ,—taking the bull by the horns, in gallant style, like a true Spaniard,—"is to trifle with the proper importance of the authorities, and to take away from them the *prestige* and moral force, without which they will not be respected!" Narvaez, even if he be grasping, is, at all events, not sordid,—having all the good qualities of a soldier, though he may have some of the faults which too generally follow military men into the exercise of civil power. In exile, as in prosperity, his generous impulses have never halted at personal sacrifice. In the capital, as Prime Minister, he dispensed a liberal and magnificent hospitality, which must have scattered his harvest almost as rapidly as it was gathered. In this particular, his practice was perhaps the more remarkable, from its contrast with that of his colleagues, into whose houses no one was ever known to penetrate, except an occasional burglar or a man with a present.

A conversation which took place before me—and to which I am not precluded from referring, by its tenor or the circumstances under which I heard it—gives so fair an idea of the principles of action by which Narvaez has raised himself to power, that I may very properly close with it this incidental review of his most salient traits. A remark was made, by one of the company, in regard to the large number of robberies which the newspapers had recently reported. Narvaez replied, that he had no doubt there was much exaggeration in them. "I have been hearing of such things, all my life," he added, "and I suppose a great deal that I have heard has been true. Yet I have travelled, alone, in every part of Spain,—over plains and mountains,—by night and by day,—on foot and in the saddle,—often without arms, and sometimes with a very full purse,—without having once met a highwayman, to my knowledge,—certainly without ever having been robbed. I cannot, therefore, help thinking that I have a right to my doubts, and that the reputation of the country is entitled to the benefit of them." "Your Excellency's experience scarcely furnishes any basis for a general rule," was the reply. "Some men's fortunes (*la suerte de algunos*) are proof against all contingencies, and those of your Excellency were not fashioned for mishaps." "I beg your pardon," said the Duke, I have no faith in any luck, except that which arises from foresight and care (*prevision y cuidado*). Luck would run equal and even to all men, in a year, on the doctrine of chances, and one who wants more of it than other men must make it for himself." It was natural enough that the winner of such heavy stakes should be unwilling to let the cards have all the credit of his game. As a loser, perhaps, he might have had no objection to throw the responsibility on *la suerte*. His life, however, has been an active illustration of his sincerity in what he said, and no one can doubt the wisdom of his conclusions.

Next to the President of the Council, on the ministerial bench, sat the Secretary of State, the Marquis of Pidal. Like the other members of the Cabinet, he was among the *nobleza nueva*, or new nobility, having been formerly plain Don Pedro Pidal, without any marquisate, and having come, report said, from a very humble origin. The Asturians, however, of whom he is one, are all *nobles* in a certain sense, nobility having been gratefully and royally bestowed, by the wholesale and in advance, upon all who might be born within the Province, as a reward for the glorious and patriotic efforts of their fathers, who fought with Don Pelayo. The distinction is, no doubt, a very gratifying one, though its principal practical benefit, I believe, consists in giving them certain honorable privileges, should they happen to find themselves under the band of the penal law. Before the abolition of hanging, by Ferdinand the Seventh, the Asturians were exempt from the degradation of that uncomfortable mode of dismission. They were entitled to be *garrote*-d, in preference,—which was always held far more satisfactory and creditable. Not only that, but the law made further distinctions in their behalf. The *garrote* is either *vil* or *noble*,—vile or noble. The *garrote vil* does a gentleman to death upon a bare platform of planks, without luxuries or appliances of any sort. The *garrote noble* refreshes his eyes and consoles his feet with such carpeting as he and his friends may find suitable to their taste and fortunes. The Asturians were exempt from the *garrote vil*, except only when convicted of leze-majesty. For all other offences, they had the right to the *garrote noble*, and went to their reward, like gentlefolk as they were, according to the statute in such case made and provided. I take it for granted that the suppression of the hangman has not impaired this inestimable and inalienable privilege. Indeed, to allow them still their proper and equitable rank, they ought to be entitled to such an improvement in their furniture, on such occasions, as would give to the Asturian the precise degree of superiority over the vulgar *garrote*, which the *garrote* itself, in its totality, once enjoyed over the gallows.

But I am wrong in saying that the privilege which I have mentioned is the chief benefit the Asturians derive from their provincial patent of nobility. They drive a brisk trade, it is said, in *entroncamientos*, or family-trees, which they sell to the *nouveaux riches* from other provinces, who, like the Niger, have no source. You can purchase the very best commodities of that sort, in the Asturian pedigree-market, at a very reasonable rate,—a fact which may not be altogether uninteresting to those of our republican countrymen who are in the habit of seeking their ancestral arms at the British Herald's Office. To have come down from a hero who wore sheepskin breeches in the days of Don Pelayo, is quite as respectable as to have descended from

"An outridere who loved venerie,"

in the times of the red-headed William, and, *cæteris paribus*, cheapness ought to be a guide of a commercial people, even in the matter of purchasing blue blood.

The Marquis of Pidal—who (with the reader) must pardon this digression to his Province—is a large and rather heavy-looking man. He might readily be taken for the grave, laborious student of the legal antiquities of his country which he is,—but one would hardly have imagined him to be the best debater, as he was, among the *Moderados*. According to the character I had of him, he is, by natural inclination, a conservative, somewhat in the extreme,—so that he carried to the discussions in the Cortes a sincerity of conviction which many of his fellow-partisans could hardly have the gravity to claim. Although a lawyer of eminent attainments in the more recondite learning of his profession, he had not acquired, by any large devotion to its practical duties, that unfitness for parliamentary debate, which so many of his brethren, in other countries, have illustrated by conspicuous failure. Nor had he gone sufficiently beyond those fields of literature and history which lie near his own peculiar domain of legal antiquarianism, to embarrass himself with the broad views and theoretical difficulties which sometimes render philosophical statesmen as unready at the tribune as Athelstane in the tourney. He had tact and logical adroitness,—was bold and confident,— denounced the recreant, and whipped in the lagging,—asserted dogmatically what he could not prove, and indignantly denied what could not be proven against him. If need were, he could be sarcastic; if pleasant satire suited better, he was no mean master of the weapon. Generally grave, however, he managed to surround his speeches and himself with an atmosphere and earnestness and authority, which made what was true the more effective, and kept the most of his opponents from laying hands profane on even what was false. All who know any thing of popular assemblies and the oratory which impresses and controls them, will see the wisdom of the choice which made Pidal, with such abilities, one of the official defenders of the Ministry.

As Secretary of State, the Marquis was less of an acquisition. His general attainments were said to be limited, and he was particularly narrow, it was reported, in his knowledge of foreign countries, and his views of foreign policy. His habits of business were so extremely sluggish, that they had passed into a proverb. The verb *pidalear*, framed by a witty journalist upon his name, was held to signify the utmost effort of possible dilly-dallying and procrastination. The influences which had made him prominent were not, in the main, his own; for his manners—which do much in Spain—had somewhat of the rustic savor that his mountain education naturally gave, and his temper was by no means of the plastic sort.

He had, however, married the sister of the former Finance Secretary, Don Alejandro Mon, whose superior advantages and real ability, with an excellent talent for intrigue, had given him access to the springs of power. The alliance made Pidal's fortune, and doubtless Mon found in him a useful yoke-fellow. They went generally by the name of "the brothers-in-law," and their friendship was supposed to be that of Damon and Pythias, rendered additionally durable and affectionate by an identity of interests. They were both Queen Cristina's men, and were supposed, like her Majesty, to have no very sincere regard for Narvaez, who had an unpleasant will of his own, and obstinately refused to be governed by that of any body else. It was for this reason that, as I have said, they considered it prudent to have their own particular interests and opinions advocated by the *Pais*, instead of making common cause with the Ministry, and trusting to its formal organ.

Mon, some time before, had left his place in the Cabinet, probably not from choice; and he was believed, when I was in Madrid, to be upon such equivocal terms with the Administration, as to render it probable he would be advised to visit London for his health. The fiscal policy of his successor being, however, but a continuation of his own, he came forward to defend it in the Cortes during the debate on the budget. His speech was announced some days beforehand, and, as it was looked for with much interest, the floor was surrendered to him at his discretion. I was present at its delivery; but it was one so purely of detail, that I found myself without the information (or, as the Spaniards say, *los antecedentes*, the antecedents) necessary to a proper appreciation of its quality. I have no hesitation, however, in saying that, as a piece of elocution, it was worthy of the worst possible cause. The speaker's voice was thin and weak, his appearance not striking, his gesture hasty and ungraceful, and his articulation exactly what might have been expected from Demosthenes, during his first experiments with the pebbles. All parties, nevertheless, seemed to agree that the discourse was an able one, and it certainly was bold, explicit, and manly. I was glad to have heard it, if only to have learned what the orator authoritatively declared, that the Ministry intended to continue the modifications of the tariff which he had begun. They had resolved, he said, to remove the shackles from commerce and production, and not to protect the one to the destruction of the other. The Catalan Deputies of course cried aloud, in anguish of spirit, at the announcement, but it was received with great approbation by all who were not manufacturers themselves, and had no constituents to whom the abuses existing gave profits of two hundred per cent.

There is no doubt that, if the muleteers were represented, as a class, in the Cortes, there would be great indignation on the part of their Deputies at the mention of a railroad, or the most delicate suggestion of a turnpike. The Asturian water-carriers, too,—through their honorable representatives, if they had such,—would probably be vehement in their denunciation of any change in the system of hydraulics, now so picturesquely carried out by themselves with donkeys and jars. But neither these good people nor the Catalonian monopolists have any right to suppose that the onerous absurdities and clumsy customs of the past will continue for ever for their benefit, or that Spain will be satisfied to lie still, like a leaf in an eddy by the shore, while the mighty stream of civilization and development sweeps the rest of the world along.

XIII.

Sr. Arrazola.—Bravo Murillo.—The Budget.—Ministerial Movement.—The Senate.—Moderado Principles.—Bravo Murillo's Speech.

THE parliamentary pretensions of the Count of San Luis have been already referred to. Don Lorenzo Arrazola, the Minister of Grace and Justice, had but little reputation as an orator, although he was regarded as a sharp and subtle disputant. He was said to be particularly adroit in the defence of a bad cause, and as the government, his client, had many such, his services were proportionably valuable. Although he had not practised his profession to any great extent, he certainly displayed the characteristics of a ready, clever advocate, full of resource, cunning of fence, and, like many of that class, not over scrupulous,—at all events, in his logic. His manner was not impressive, for, though full of plausibility, he seemed to want conviction. In fact, the special pleading which he was frequently driven to, and for which he seemed to have a natural fondness and turn, impaired the substantial strength of his speeches,—as indeed it necessarily must, without a miracle, destroy the vigor of any mind. Don Lorenzo's aptness at finding excuses must have been of singular avail to him in his particular Department,—the enormous patronage of which, unless managed with great adroitness, was as likely to make enemies as friends. I was often interested and amused, in his antechamber, watching the countenances of the numerous *pretendientes* to whom he gave audience,—almost all of whom came out with smiling faces,—many of them no doubt for the hundredth time. His enemies, political and personal, of whom he had many, insisted that he was *muy falso*, marvellously insincere; but that was perhaps more in the trade and the circumstances than the man. In early life he was reported to have been a *sacristan*, and afterwards a schoolmaster, both which callings, the light wits of the opposition used to say, were conspicuous in his manners and conversation. Be that as it may, however, he was, when I knew him, as he had for some time been, a very notable person. He has since been transferred to a distinguished judicial position, which I have no doubt he fills with great respectability.

In his Department, Sr. Arrazola was a model of industry. His duties, as has been said, were of the most various and complicated kind, but his activity and energy kept pace with their requirements. No one, it is true, knew better than he the virtues of that "masterly inactivity," by which Spanish officials put an end, without tangible offence, to solicitations which they cannot directly refuse to entertain. Yet when he intended to be punctual, or found it necessary, no one could be more prompt and business-like. His audiences began at an earlier hour, and lasted longer, than those of any of his colleagues. His personal participation in the labors of his bureau was greater by far than was customary among personages of his grade, and yet, even during the sessions of the

Cortes, which occupied him several hours daily, he found leisure to contribute regularly to an encyclopædia of political and civil law, which was then published periodically in the capital, with the highest approbation of the profession. When it is borne in mind, that the ministerial departments in Spain are very paradises of the *dolce far niente*,—where labor is so comfortably distributed, that its stages are counted by the *cigarritos* which young gentlemen of spirit can demolish between a very late breakfast and an early dinner or earlier *paseo*,—it will not be wondered that a man of Arrazola's habits and capacity for affairs should have climbed with moderate luck to the high places of the state. A genius for intrigue is no doubt an excellent item of capital for a politician; charlatanism, too, has frequently its miraculous uses, and a fortunate hit or a happy accident will often achieve, in a moment, what a lifetime of merit and toil will end in vain search of. In the main, nevertheless,—though the notion may seem a strange one,—the surest method of attaining station is to be, in some sort, fit for it. Half the pains men sometimes take to pass themselves off for what they are not, would suffice, in many instances, to make them what they ought to be. It must, upon the whole, be a more costly and laborious process to win by cheating, than to lose with unsoiled hands. Whether Sr. Arrazola embodied the cardinal virtues or not, can make no difference in the truth of these reflections.

Don Juan Bravo Murillo, the Minister of Finance, was oftener heard in the Cortes than any of his colleagues. In truth, he had no sinecure; for money, which is only the root of all evil elsewhere, has in Spanish politics possession of the whole tree, and, to be safely intrusted with its cultivation and the gathering and keeping of its golden apples, a man must be of long suffering, as of sharp eyes and busy hands. It is an occupation which no doubt pays well, when fairly understood and wisely exercised, but it has its manifold tribulations, notwithstanding, like all other the good things of earth. Every one knows that the Spanish treasury has long been free from any symptoms of plethora. Sr. Bravo Murillo consequently found himself, like many of his predecessors, in a quadruple quandary. He had to pay expenses, and if he did not keep himself in funds, the mouths which he left empty had no other occupation than to cry aloud and spare him not. If he talked of increasing the taxes, the voices of those who were to pay them, and of all the economists and calculators in the Cortes, were lifted up, in chorus, against him. If, by way of compromising matters, he made promises,—to the hungry, to feed them when he could get the means,—and to the tax-payers, to devise some scheme of raising money without taxation,—he was of course called on to redeem both promises at once, which he could not find other than inconvenient. If, in his despair, he dared to name the only possible mode of salvation,—the suppression of fiscal abuses, the abolition of useless offices, the reduction of overgrown salaries, the introduction of strict, manly, prudent economy into all branches of the public service,—the sting of every drone in the hive pierced him at once,—the present and the future were in arms against him,—those who had and those who hoped to have. What was he to do, then? His estimates fell below his necessities, and his collections were sure to fall below his estimates. He had no alternative left, but to keep his temper, and make speeches,—which taxed nothing but the public patience. The *Progresistas* besieged him in front, and he returned their fire with his best battery. Sr. Gonzalez Bravo, an enemy from the *Moderado* camp, gave him a shot from the rear, and Sr. Bermudez de Castro, Sr. Moron, and others of the same political fellowship, planted guns on his flanks. He threw them back ball for ball, and shell for shell. His foes— and especially those of the *Moderado* opposition—were not satisfied with attacking his views, which were surely vulnerable enough, but must needs set up theories and schemes of their own, which were perhaps more so. Like a prudent man, he immediately turned on the offensive, and if he did not succeed in demolishing the projects of the adversary, he at least withdrew attention from his own, which was quite as well.

It seems to me, that I rarely, during any of my visits to the Chamber of Deputies, escaped finding Sr. Murillo, at some time or other, and for a long time, on his feet. His voice and manner were so exceedingly monotonous and invariable, that he appeared to be always saying the same thing in the same way,—and, indeed, I am hardly, to this day, sure that he was not. Lord Castlereagh and Moore's pump seemed to be his models of elocution, and the "cheerful, voluntary air" and virtuous expression with which he took and gave his blows, must have been studied from Elia's portrait of the happy borrower. On one occasion, however, when he had the game in his own hands, I heard him speak out, boldly, aggressively, and without reserve. The occasion and his sentiments will illustrate the reverence with which constitutional forms and liberal principles were treated by the *Moderados*, when they chose to give themselves the rein.

The constitution requires that the *presupuestos,* or financial estimates, shall be presented to the Cortes, in due course, with the plan and rates of taxation proposed, for consideration and discussion. The government, under various pretexts, had postponed the discharge of this disagreeable duty until the latest possible day; but the budget had, at the time I am about to refer to, been for some short period in the possession of the legislature. Several of the Deputies had given notice of their intention to submit views and reports upon various interesting points, and the whole policy of the administration, financial and of all other sorts, had already begun to undergo able and critical examination. In point of parliamentary ability, the opposition had, unequivocally, the advantage, besides having the right, as well as the popular, side of the principal questions in controversy. The government, it is true, exercised absolute control over a large and subservient majority, but, although the legislative triumph of its measures was thus placed beyond the reach of doubt, there was no concealing the fact, that the speeches of the opposition members were producing, and were likely further to produce, a most serious impression on the public mind. This result—the great end and aim of free discussion—it became necessary for the administration to avert. It could not be prevented without a violation of the spirit of the constitution, but Narvaez was not a man to be balked by trifles of that sort. As usual, he spared circumlocution and pretence, and went directly to his point. On the 8th of January, the Minister of Finance made his appearance in the Cortes, in full uniform, and, ascending the tribune, read the draft of a brief statute, wherein her Majesty, with the approbation of the Cortes, declared, in a single clause, that the whole budget was a law, in the lump, as it stood, to the same effect as if duly considered and adopted in each and all of its parts. The Chamber was taken aback. Indignation, astonishment, and denunciation were in the countenances and on the lips of the opposition. Even the trained bands of the Ministry were staggered by the downright boldness of the blow. But there was no child's play meant. The decree was introduced to be adopted, and it was soon understood that, when that work should be done, the Cortes were to be prorogued, with a view to their speedy dissolution. The project was referred to a committee of ministerial partisans, who, after taking their own time, reported it back to the house, precisely as it had been given to them. Some of the opposition presses, which took strong ground against the outrage, had the editions of their papers which were most offensive suppressed by order of the authorities. In the meantime, when the project came again before the house, a few prominent Deputies of the opposition were allowed, for appearance' sake, to deliver speeches against it. I had the good fortune to hear the most of them, and some were singularly eloquent and powerful. The ablest speakers on the government side rejoined, and Narvaez himself concluded the debate. By the end of the month, the whole ceremony was through, and the law passed by an overwhelming majority. The "previous question" might have done the thing with a little more despatch, and after what we are in the habit of considering—but why, I know not—a more republican manner. No process, however, which is known to legislation, Eastern or Western, could have compassed its object with more perfect simplicity and success.

The Deputies, having performed their functions, were adjourned, from time to time, till the Senate could give its countersign. In that august, but dutiful body, the result could not be long in doubt; but even there the government pursued its usual course, and countenanced the forms of opposition. A few of the refractory Senators were permitted to refresh themselves by saying what they thought, and the coryphæi of the government did their best to counteract the poison so disseminated. It was in winding up on the ministerial side of the debate, that Bravo Murillo announced the views to which I have alluded.

"Senators," he said, "talked of a reduction of the army. They forgot that armies were an element of primary importance in modern governments. All government depended for its security on one of two things,—the influence of the clergy, or the military power. Clerical influence, the support of the late absolute government in Spain, had been destroyed,— whether for good or for ill there was no need that he should say; though, so far as his own opinion was concerned, he had no hesitation in saying that it was for ill. At all events, however, it existed no longer, and there was nothing left in its absence to protect society, to maintain order, to support government, but the military arm. It was useless to talk about relying on the municipalities, for they were not worthy of reliance; and as to the national militia, it was both costly and unsafe. It took men from the field, from the workshop, and from commerce,—paralyzing those vital departments of industry, and putting arms, besides, in dangerous hands. There was nothing left but standing armies,—and *cuidado!* let Senators bear in mind, that modern society, this society of progress, and learning, and civilization, and ideas, is not easily kept down. It requires a larger force than older societies needed, and if we happen to live in such a state of things, we must be content to meet the heavier obligations it imposes."

He then touched upon the subject of a reduction of taxes. "As to economy," he said, "it was ridiculous to ask it in the manner in which it was urged. He did not and would not pretend—he should be disparaging himself were he to pretend—that he could reduce the amount of contributions a single *cuarto*. There was not one maravedi too much levied. The country was quite rich enough to bear the present taxes. It ought to bear them, and ought not to complain of them. He was willing and anxious to practice all possible economy in the collection of the revenue, so as to make it produce what it was capable of, to the utmost. But even in that particular very little could be done at this day,—very little during this generation. He wished these things to be thoroughly understood, so that he might not hereafter be reproached with creating false hopes or making delusive promises."

When I looked, afterwards, at the authorized reports of this speech, I found that its broad doctrines and expressions had been so considerably modified, as to render them comparatively unobjectionable. The report, however, which I have given above, is correct, to my own knowledge; for I was so much startled at the bold avowal of such sentiments, that I took particular note of the speech on the spot. The reader will appreciate the force of those facts which refer to the revenue, when he learns that the estimates for 1849–50 were about twelve hundred millions of reals, or sixty millions of dollars! Sr. Lopez stated in the debate, without contradiction, that the cost of collecting was about twenty-one per cent.; so that, to realize what the Ministry asserted was the lowest amount of indispensable expenditure on the part of the central government, the nation required to be taxed at least seventy millions of dollars. "It was certainly consoling to the present generation to know," said Sr. Lopez, "and he thanked the Minister for his kindness in telling them, that things might possibly be better, after all who were now living had passed away from taxes and tax-gatherers." Justice to Sr. Murillo, however, makes it proper to add, that his subsequent financial measures have displayed ability and wisdom, and have given a new and vigorous impulse to public confidence and private enterprise.

XIV.

General Figueras.—Roca de Togores.—Alexandre Dumas.—Southern Oratory.—Olozaga.—Escosura.—Benavides.—Donoso Cortes.—Their Speeches.

THE other members of the Cabinet were without any particular parliamentary celebrity that I am aware of, and I seldom found any of them upon the floor, except the *ci-devant* General Figueras, Marquis of Constancia, and then Secretary at War. He was a bright-looking, combustible old gentleman, who made it a point to be chivalric and excited whenever the sanctity of his Department was invaded by rude questionings; and as the extent and expense of the military establishment were matters of daily comment in the Cortes, the silken banners of his eloquence had no occasion to feed the moth. A man in a passion, however, though perhaps more or less dangerous in a personal point of view, is not usually effective as an orator, and it consequently happened that the gallant Marquis rarely rose to speak without putting the house in a good humor, though he generally seemed to be in a very bad one himself. Yet his discourses, though fiery, were but "brief candles," and for this, at all events, his style deserves to be praised a good deal more than it is likely to be imitated.

The Minister of Marine Affairs, the Marquis of Molins, under his original and more euphonious name of Roca de Togores, had acquired considerable reputation as a poet and man of letters. He had the good fortune to be a friend of Alexandre Dumas, who called him "Rocca," and pronounced him "one of the first poets, and most *spirituel* men of Spain." Nay, more, the illustrious author of the "*Impressions*" did not hesitate to prophesy that "Rocca" would be a Minister if he lived,—just as their common friend, the Duke of Osuna, might at any time have been, had his tastes carried him that way. It may be, that, from this indorsement of his merits, the Marquis of Molins is known the better beyond the limits of his country; but as M. Dumas did not understand one word of Spanish, and the Duke of Osuna (rest his soul!) had no promptings from his genius to be any thing but a jockey, the Marquis himself could hardly have felt much complimented by his friend's appreciation of his abilities, literary or political. The prophecy nevertheless came true, and before the travels of Dumas were given to the world, "Rocca" was intrusted with the control of a Department, whose ancient glories might have fed his loftiest inspiration, as its actual exigencies taxed his utmost ingenuity. I may have occasion to speak of the impulse which the navy received under his administration. His parliamentary career was without interest, during the opportunities I had of observing it.

The reader would hardly care to know, with any particularity, the manner or merits of the various members of the Cortes, who, with more or less ability and domestic reputation, took part in the debates I witnessed. A traveller belonging to a more impassible and less demonstrative race can scarcely be considered a fair critic of Southern eloquence, until custom has familiarized him with its peculiarities. The vivacity and earnestness which an excitable nature imparts, even to ordinary conversation, are of course heightened by the intenser stimulus and more elevated subjects of public discussion, and the style and gesture of the speaker thus appear, to unfamiliar eyes and ears, sometimes extravagant, if not unnatural. We forget that the defect may be in our standard, not in the thing we judge. We forget that our nature is not all of nature,—that our enthusiasm seems as cold to an Italian or a Spaniard, as his lightest expression of emotion seems overdone to us. Friends, parted for a little while, in those more genial climates, rush, when they meet again, into each other's arms, though all the world be looking on. Among "the natives of the moral North," the rare caress is made almost a household secret; the most sincere and deep emotion seems most ashamed to show itself, sometimes even to its object. It is not necessary to determine under which manner lies, in general, the truer and intenser heart. It may be that feelings, like odors, are wasted by diffusion; or that, like colors, they fade from too constant exposure. There is no doubt, on the other hand, that the systematic restraint of emotion, or of its display, has sometimes the effect of deadening, if not destroying, it at last. Nature has probably some scheme of compensation by which she equalizes the substance without reference to the forms.

But, let the thing signified be as it may, there can be no doubt that the signs are constitutionally and naturally different. Every man feels it, every man under its influence is prompted to pronounce unnatural what comes in conflict with the habits of his nature, or the seeming nature given him by education. The reader, who, without previous experience and preparation, may have visited the Stanze of Raphael in the Vatican, can scarcely fail to remember how this feeling modified his first impressions of delight and wonder. The lofty attitude and gesture, the gorgeous coloring, heroic mien, and bold, broad drapery, seemed to him, doubtless, for a while, theatrical and overwrought. It needed reflection and habit, and some sympathy with the true soul of art, to teach him that he was measuring by the scale of his dull organs, his colder temperament, and unkindled taste, what was addressed to the sensibilities of a more voluptuous fibre, to feelings of a warmer birth, and minds of which imagination is the mould. The same process of criticism which made him halt in his admiration would take away from Oriental fancy every thing but its grotesqueness,—would make Ariosto a retailer of enchanted follies, Dante a madman, and Calderon a rhapsodist. The influences which fill the bright air of the South with birds of various and splendid plumage,—which hang the fruit of gold on the ungrafted boughs, and cover the uncultivated fields with miraculous bloom and fragrance,—give to the thoughts and fancies springing 'mid them the same luxuriance and glow. It is not in the colder zones that we can learn to sympathize with these. The hands which clipped the orange-gardens at Versailles were hardly fit to paint the prodigality of Cintra.

I would not by any means be understood, from the turn of the preceding reflections, as meaning to institute a comparison of excellence between the oratory of the Spanish legislative assemblies and that of similar bodies in other nations. I

have simply designed to suggest that they are different things,
regulated by canons widely different. I merely deprecate the
criticism which regards their natural dissimilarity as a ground
of objection to that style with which the critic is least familiar.
It may be, perhaps, from some lack of catholicity in my own
taste, that I thought the Spanish speakers often weakened the
effect, and marred in some particulars, in the delivery, the
grace of their most eloquent discourses. Their utterance, for
example, was frequently so rapid, as to convey a painful idea
of effort and haste; their gestures, almost universally, had the
frequency and quickness of excited conversation, rather than
the bold dignity of high passion. I was not, it is true,
fortunate enough to hear some whose reputations placed them
in the highest rank. Martinez de la Rosa—probably, on the
whole, the first orator of Spain, despite his age—was absent
as Ambassador at Rome. His rival, Galiano, to whom I
shall refer hereafter, did not speak in the Cortes, to my
knowledge, during my residence in Madrid. Sr. Olozaga,
one of the heads of the *Progresistas*,—deemed by many the
most accomplished speaker among the Deputies, and certainly
endowed with physical and mental gifts, such as might well
command a senate,—took little part in the debates of the
session. I lost by accident the only chance I had of hearing
him, at any length, on an occasion which elicited his powers.
It was a source of the more regret to me, from the fact
that he is a Castilian, which few of the most prominent
speakers are, and not only possesses the language in its
utmost purity of pronunciation and construction, but in his
manner illustrates the gravity and dignity of the national
style in its best type.

Of those whom I heard in the Cortes, the most attractive orator to me was Don Patricio de la Escosura,—certainly I have listened to very few, anywhere, with as much gratification. He had not long returned to Spain, under the amnesty of 1849,—having fled to France with Olozaga, under sentence of banishment to the Philippine Islands, after the suppression of the Madrid insurrection, in 1848. That abortive outbreak the government insisted on considering as the joint work of the *Progresistas* and Sir Henry Bulwer; and when Narvaez made bold to dismiss the plenipotentiary of one of the most powerful nations of Europe, for that cause, he was not in a vein to lay light hands on the leaders of his domestic opposition. That, with a knowledge of the parliamentary abilities of the two gentlemen referred to, he should have permitted them to return to their country and the public councils, speaks loudly for his confidence and courage, though perhaps not less for his sagacity under the circumstances. Nothing can be more popular than magnanimity, with a chivalrous nation,— nay, with the people at large, in any nation; and when a ruler has strength enough to practise it, he must be very unwise if he permits himself to lose the opportunity. But if Narvaez found the amnesty politic on the whole, Escosura's speeches must certainly have satisfied him that the good was not unqualified. The tribulation through which Don Patricio had passed had not bent the independence of his mind or speech. His denunciations were so glittering, his satire was so keen, his style so graceful, his manner so effective, that the ministerial benches often echoed the plaudits of the opposition. I have seen even Narvaez smile with genuine delight, at some pointed, happy hits of his, and have heard him cry out "*Bien!*" enthusiastically, at some eloquent apostrophe. Besides being one of the most graceful poets and scholars of his nation, Escosura had high personal gifts as a speaker. He was in the prime of life, with a good figure and attractive face. His voice was soft and musical, with an occasional tremor in it, which carried his pathos to the heart. His bolder tones were clear and ringing, and his articulation, even when most rapid and excited, was perfectly distinct. His humorous and histrionic powers, which were considerable, were managed with great adroitness, and enabled him to barb and point an insinuation, in a manner which I have never seen surpassed. Every speech that he made enhanced his reputation, and so attractive were the qualities of his character esteemed, that the name which he was building did not seem to cast one envious shadow.

Among the *Moderado* opposition, although there were several able men and effective speakers, the most formidable to the government was Don Antonio Benavides, a deputy from the district of Jaen. This gentleman had been in power himself, was thoroughly conversant with the ministerial ways of doing things, and possessed great familiarity with public affairs. His oratorical aspirations were by no means high, but he was a capital debater, in the business-like and best sense of the term. He carried into the parliamentary struggle a mind which was quick and versatile, at the same time that it was comprehensive and well poised. He was full of historical philosophy, but it was of the practical sort, and he had a sense of the ridiculous, which enabled him constantly to place in most amusing and resistless contrast the professions and practices of the administration. His cool dexterity and admirable temper were proof against ministerial interruptions and arrogance, as well as the embarrassments which the chair threw, as often as possible, in his way. He could always manage to have the last word, when he wanted it, and never took it without making it tell. He could throw an argument into a personal explanation, in spite of the rules of order and the President; and even ventured a gibe, when it served his turn, at the inviolable person of the Prime Minister. His pleasantry was too attractive for even the firmest of the ministerial adherents to be above its influence; and as nothing is so dangerous as laughter to pasteboard greatness, it was in this point of view, perhaps, that he was most obnoxious to the administration. "The honorable Deputy," said Sartorius of him one day, "has caused great merriment by his observations. It may be a question, however, whether a gentleman has reason to congratulate himself, because his rising to speak in the councils of his country is but the signal for a general smile."

"Blame me not, sir," was the reply, "for the hilarity which these details may have provoked in the chamber. I do not invent,—I only describe. If things are ridiculous, it is the fault of those who make them so. I crave your pardon, sir, for the presumption of my illustration, but I have never heard that Molière was responsible for human meanness and hypocrisy, because he made them palpable in Tartuffe and the Avare."

A single expression, in one of the speeches of Benavides, did more to affect the popularity of a prominent government measure than it is easy to conceive, where the appreciation and influence of humor are less universal and decided than in Spain. For some reason, not very comprehensible, a law was introduced to change the whole system of fiscal and civil administration in the provinces, by removing the Intendants and Political Chiefs, and creating a class of officers called Provincial Governors, in their stead. For some other reason, equally unintelligible, but probably much more nearly connected with personal interests and the dispensation of patronage than with the welfare of the capital or the nation, it was proposed that Madrid should be made an exception,—retaining her *Intendente* and *Jefe Politico* after the old fashion. There was a good deal of inquiry as to the cause of this anomaly,—no one appearing to understand why, if the system were vicious, as the government had taken pains to demonstrate, one part of it should be perpetuated any more than the rest. Benavides explained. "The offices in question are to be preserved," he said, "as part of the historical monuments of the capital. Posterity must learn that we have had Political Chiefs in Spain,—yea, and Intendants also! They are twin unities not known to other governments, and their memory should not be lost among men. The admiration of the future, which would have been wasted among so many, will be concentrated now on the solitary specimens that survive. Men will not speak hereafter of the *Jefe Politico* of Madrid,—the Madrid *Intendente*,—but the *Jefe Politico*,—the *Intendente!* They will be handed over to the grammatical treasury of nouns that have no plural! They will keep company with the Holy Father and the Ship Soberano,—the persons and things whereof there is but one!" The quiet but unequivocal allusion in the last expression to the fact that the administration had allowed the navy to remain with but one old damaged ship of the line, while the treasures of the nation were lavished in the maintenance of an army at Rome, struck a chord which vibrated through the House and the whole city. Sartorius endeavored to counteract its effect, by giving an acrimonious and personal turn to the debate; but Benavides rejoined in a few graceful and good-humored words, which fixed the laugh where he had left it.

The advantage, in point of parliamentary ability, being, as has been said, on the side of the opposition, Donoso Cortes, Marquis of Valdegamas, and then Minister at Berlin, was allowed leave of absence from his diplomatic post, to discharge his duties in the Cortes, as one of the Deputies from the district of Badajoz. Besides being a poet of very distinguished reputation, this gentleman had entered of late, with great success, upon the career of politics, and had become one of the most eminent of the *Moderado* orators and statesmen. He was regarded, at home and in France, as a person of very profound philosophy in things political, and of great sublimity in his views and theories generally. The post of honor, therefore, was given to him, in the debate on the *presupuestos*, and he immediately preceded Narvaez, by whom, as has been said, the discussion was concluded. Great expectations were formed of his effort, and crowds went to hear it. The newspapers glorified it exceedingly; the Puerta del Sol echoed its praises; and when I saw the orator, three nights afterwards, at a ball, he was still receiving congratulations, like a bridegroom in the first quarter of the honey moon. It was a singular discourse,—full of thought and power, rhapsody and rant,—illustrating in itself, as well as in the sensation which it produced, the reverence for French ideas, principles, and forms, in which the *Moderado* dynasty has almost merged the nationality of Spain.

Originally, with his political fortunes to seek, Donoso Cortes was a liberal, in no narrow signification of the term. Created a Marquis,—which seems to be a dignity specially coveted by the *Moderados*,—he naturally enough took to conservatism, and, being on excellent terms with those in power, he felt still more deeply—as gentlemen in such case always do—the absolute necessity of maintaining the social and established order. His school of poetry, indeed,—which is the romantic,—inclined him to invest with reverent and mystic awe the sacred rulers of mankind; and that inclination was not likely to be diminished by the fact, that the poet imagined he could see the wand of state hidden among his own laurels. Having had no practical experience in government, and but little opportunity to watch the operation of systems genuinely constitutional, he had to seek what he could find in books. The affinities of party led him towards the oracles at Paris, and his own mental constitution taught him to prefer their eloquent abstractions to the practical and plainer lessons of British and American example. Even among the disciples of the doctrines which he professed, his peculiar tendency was to romanticize and Germanize. It was his taste to vaticinate like Lamartine, and crusade with the sacerdotalism of Montalembert, rather than follow the severe analysis and unequalled generalization of De Tocqueville and Guizot. Like all abstractionists, and particularly the poetical, he frequently fell into the vice of mistaking words for ideas, and of setting up as philosophy what was simply phraseology. His speeches and writings, however, were, as I have said, considered by the mass as both profound and sublime. Philosophical forms and processes are, in themselves, of great edification and refreshment to many readers and hearers, and when they are accompanied by a certain warmth and earnestness of imagination and expression are often none the less popular from having nothing in them. The speech of Valdegamas, on the occasion referred to, was so characteristic of his own peculiarities, and furnishes so curious a clew to the political doctrines and tendencies of his party, that it deserves a paragraph or two as a pendant to the Senatorial effort of the Minister of Finance.

The question before the house was a very simple one. The Constitution required the budget to be submitted to the Cortes, for the purpose, obviously, of examination and discussion. The government, however, proposed that its whole financial policy and *projet*, thus submitted, should be indorsed and adopted at once, without further debate. It was a plain question of expediency,—not of constitutionality. It would have been folly to suppose that the constitution intended to compel inquiry, when the representatives of the people desired none; or to enforce discussion, when they found nothing to discuss. It was for the legislature, under a due sense of public duty, to determine as to the propriety of the thing; but, that determination once arrived at, there could be no rational doubt of the legislative right to act on it, or of the constitutional legitimacy and obligation of such action. It was to this view of the case that Olozaga and Escosura directed themselves, and it was in reducing and confining the controversy to this issue, after a long and discursive debate, that Narvaez displayed the clearness and directness of his acute and vigorous mind.

The Marquis of Valdegamas, on the contrary, appeared to consider the whole politics of Europe as involved in the question, which he chose to treat as a trial of strength between monarchy and socialism. After the fashion of the French conservative orators, he assumed socialism and democracy to be identical. Economical questions he then anathematized as among the most wicked and pernicious devices which the Tempter had taught the socialists; and proceeded with great gravity to prove, after his manner, that financial economy, though quite an interesting matter, was still only of third or fourth rate importance,—that it was too inflammatory a subject to be handled at that moment, and was rather difficult to dispose of satisfactorily at any time. The last of these propositions, at all events, might have been proved without any unusual exertion; but the orator had no idea of letting it pass into the ranks of things established, without something more than the ordinary treatment of plain truth.

"The nation is not firm," he said. "Since that epoch of tremendous memory (the last French Revolution) there has been nothing firm in Europe. Spain is the firmest of the nations, and you see what Spain is. This Congress is the best, and yet you see what this Congress is. Spain, wavering as you behold her, is at this moment to the Continent as an oasis in Zahara. I have talked with the wise, and have seen how worthless is wisdom. I have listened to the valiant, and have learned the insignificance of valor now. I have appealed to the prudent, and have found how weak, in the emergency, is prudence! It seems as if the statesmen of Europe had lost their gift of counsel. Human reason is in eclipse,—human institutions tremble in the wind,—nations are precipitated into sudden and mighty downfall.... At this day, over the whole continent, all paths—even the most opposite—conduct but to perdition. Here, resistance destroys; there, concession is fatal. Where weakness is death, there are weak princes. Where ambition is ruin, there are ambitious princes. Where perdition shall come of talent, there God has given ability to kings. As it is with monarchs, so it is with ideas. The most magnificent and the vilest have the same results. If you doubt it, turn your eyes towards Paris and towards Venice, and behold what has come of demagogism, and what has come of the superb idea of Italian independence! As with ideas and with monarchs, so is it with other men. Where one man could save society, that man exists not; or, if he does exist, God scatters some poison for him in the air. Where one man can overturn society, that man appears,—that man is borne aloft upon the palms of men,—that man finds every road open and level before him. Do you question it? Look from the tomb of Marshal Bugeaud to the throne of Mazzini! As it is with ideas and kings and other men, so it is with parties. . . . Where the salvation of society depends on the dissolution of old parties, and their amalgamation into new ones, there parties refuse to be dissolved, and are not dissolved. This is what happens now in France. . . . Where the salvation of society appeals to parties,—that they cling to their old banners,—that they tear not their bosoms,—that they keep themselves together, and fight together, in great and noble battles,—where all this is needful, as in Spain, that society may live,—there—here—do parties leap to dissolution! . . . Gentlemen! the true cause of the deep and awful evil with which Europe is overwhelmed is this alone,—that the idea of divine authority and of human authority has altogether disappeared. This is what scourges Europe,—what scourges society,—what afflicts the world,—and it is from this that nations have become ungovernable. It is this that explains what I have never heard explained, and what, nevertheless, is of easy explanation. . . .

"All who have travelled through France agree in saying that you cannot meet a Frenchman who is a republican. I can bear witness to the truth of this, for I have just passed through France. Why then, and how then, is it, if there be no republicans, that the republic exists? The republic exists in France—nay, it will continue to exist—*because the republican is the necessary form of government among a people who are ungovernable.* Where the people are not to be ruled, government necessarily takes the republican shape. And this is why the republic subsists and will subsist in France. Little matters it whether the republic be, as it is, resisted by the will of men, if it be upheld, as it is, by the very necessity of things!"

Having spoken of human and divine authority as equally forgotten in the world, the orator proceeded to anticipate and meet the question as to the connection that exists between politics and religion. He attributed to "civilization" two phases,—the one affirmative and catholic, the other negative and revolutionary. The former established three affirmations, religious and political. The first of these was the existence of a God and of a king; the second, the dominion of God over all things, and of the king over his realm; the third, the exercise of that dominion, by actual government, in both cases. Civilization in its revolutionary phase, presented three negations: first, that of the deist, who denied the providence of God, and that of the constitutional monarchist, who denied to the king the exercise of his dominion; second, that of the pantheist, whose political correlative was the republican; and and third that of the atheist, whose yoke-fellow was of course the socialist. The good and perfect Christian, it is needless to say, was matched with the legitimist and the absolutist. "Europe," cried the philosopher, "has entered upon the second negation, and is striding towards the third, which is the last,—the abyss,—beyond which is darkness only."

It would be tedious, though very curious, to follow the speaker through the extraordinary processes by which he showed, that, from this impending catastrophe, Catholicity and standing armies were the only asylums of refuge. Russia, he asserted, was at present powerless, because she had only wrought on Europe heretofore through the Germanic Confederation, which had now ceased to exist, or rather passed into chaos. It might be, he said, that after revolutions had dissolved society and dispersed its standing armies, and after Socialism had destroyed patriotism by destroying property, Russia might sweep, with her Sclavonic millions, in wild triumph over Europe. Only England could avert this, in any case; but England, alas! lacked Catholicity, without which there could be no victory in such a contest! "I say, Sir," he exclaimed, "that Catholicity is the only remedy against Socialism, because Catholicity involves the only doctrine which is the absolute contradiction of Socialism. What is Catholicity? It is wisdom and humility. What is Socialism? It is pride and barbarism. Like the Babylonian king, it is at once king and beast."

Then followed a demonstration of the costliness of republics, and the cheapness of despotisms. Standing armies, it was asserted, were in fact the only cheap machinery of government. This led to a parallel, touching and eloquent in some of its passages, between the soldier and the priest, but in which I am afraid the preference was rather given to the soldier,—as under the *Moderado* administration was practically the case in Spain, both as regards consideration and pay. The discourse wound up with an appeal to the Deputies, to despise economy at such a crisis and not peril a great cause by wasting the energies and distracting the unity of conservatism in fruitless and discordant debate. Legislative bodies, he warned them, might compass their own ruin by their impracticability. If they would neither govern nor let govern, but only discuss, they could not stand.

"What has become of the Frankfort Assembly?" he asked them; "of that Assembly in whose ranks were sages, nobles, and philosophers, the wisest, the most honored, the most profound? Where is it? Whither has it gone? Never did the world behold a senate more august,—an end more lamentable! One universal shout of acclamation welcomed its birth,—it died amid a hissing as universal! Germany lodged it like a goddess in a temple,—the same Germany looked on while it perished like a harlot in a ditch!"

The reader who only sees this speech, in its mere nakedness, and in the imperfect shape which I have given it,—with its melancholy pessimism, its hopeless distrust of human intelligence and virtue and the providence of God,—the solemn sophistry with which it would persuade men to surrender the hard-won liberty of thought and action, whereof the legislature in which it was delivered was the offspring, and the political existence of the speaker himself a triumph,—the reader, I say, who sees but this, will wonder that a constitu-

20

tional congress should have received the discourse with any demonstration but a hiss like that which said farewell to the Frankfort Assembly. Bursts of disapprobation did, in fact, occasionally sweep across the Chamber,—indignant denials of the principles promulged, and the deductions drawn from them. But still the speech was eminently successful. Its forms were stately, imaginative, and oratorical,—its expressions glowing with intense conviction. The orator had enthusiasm, grace, boldness, fire,—all the volatile elements which evaporate after the moment of inspiration, yet make that moment glorious. When men came to read what had excited them so much, there were many who thought, with an old Carlist general of my acquaintance, that Donoso Cortes was "a *pedante*, with his head in the clouds." But the mass did not stop to read, and the majority of those who did, though they admitted it to be "*un poco metafisico*," insisted, with great positiveness, that it was "*muy sublime*" nevertheless.

XV.

The Senate.—Alcalá Galiano.—The Cortes of 1823.—The Athenæum.—Galiano's Lectures there.

THE Palace of the Senate is on the Plaza de los Ministerios, not far from the late chamber of the Deputies, but inconveniently distant, I should think, from their present place of session. It occupies the site of a church, formerly belonging to an adjoining convent of Austin friars, and is without any architectural merit or pretension. In front of it, across the Plaza, is the palace of the Queen Mother,—a most unsightly edifice, not long erected,—which might be taken for an immense conservatory, were it not that the pile of window-glass, which constitutes the resemblance, is of various and glaring colors.

The Senate Chamber is precisely "the pleasing land of drowsy-head," in which legislators with the life-tenure usually dream through their unagitating duties. There is little that you see or hear, as you sit in the small galleries, to disturb the calm, respectable stagnation, whose spirit broods over the illustrious assemblage. Even the echoes are solemn with a monotony of their own, and the graceful oval of the hall—avoiding all obtrusiveness of angles—seems as if intended to furnish that repose to the eye, which an assured position and comfortable dignity so naturally spread over the mind. The churchmen, who nod while the Marquis of —— is speaking, are in the purple of extreme preferment. Why should they,—or the invalid generals, the broken-down or retired ministers, the gratified favorites, the pensioned placemen, the effete nobility, who are around them,—why should they, whose ambition has been successful, or exhausted or check-mated, trouble themselves with making or listening to speeches? What's Hecuba to them? Their business is to vote with the government, and to be dignified,—an easy duty and a pleasant privilege! It would be unreasonable to expect that they should mar the enjoyment of the one, by travelling beyond the requirements of the other. A stray *Progresista*—or an impracticable young *Moderado*, who has not arrived at years of political discretion, or lost the habits of the lower house, or the hope of yet ruling in Israel—may be permitted to vex the repose and crucify the spirits of the elders by his discourses and his questionings. But empty benches, dull ears, and extinguishing majorities will subdue at last even the most burning fever of eloquence and patriotism. Rare, therefore, in the main, is the tempest of discussion which ever ruffles the soft plumes of the halberdiers, whose dainty raiment gives an air of feudal pageantry to what in fact is hardly, in its spirit or its operation, an institution of the nineteenth century. Strange, that the Cortes of 1820–23 held their sessions in this same hall, and that many, whose hearts were warmest and whose voices were loudest in the eloquent conflicts of those stormy days, should be seated—conservatives among the most conservative—high on the benches which echo most faithfully the mandates of the present power! Is it the weakness or the wisdom of age which so frequently changes the radical of twenty-five into the high-tory of sixty? Weakness inconceivable or wisdom inscrutable it must surely have been, which brought Martinez de la Rosa and Alcalá Galiano to sit under the Presidency and follow the vote of the Marquis of Miraflores,—the defender of Ferdinand the Seventh and the eulogist of his despotism.

I have said that Galiano did not address the Senate, that I am aware, during my residence in Madrid. Although allied in party doctrines and association with the existing government, he seemed at that time rather lukewarm in his devotion, or at all events indisposed to make any display of it. A brother-senator of his, not ill inclined to gossip, told me that Galiano had applied to ministers, not long before, for some preferment, which they had refused. "*Y es natural se ofenda!*" my informant added;—"It is natural he should not be pleased!" No better evidence could be afforded of the strength of the *Moderados* at that day, or at least of their confident belief that they were strong, than their indifference to the support of so distinguished and able a man,—one so remarkable, especially, for those peculiar powers which are most formidable in opposition. In the Chamber of Deputies it is likely that the veteran tribune might have commanded almost anything, in reason, that he had desired. It was his misfortune, however, to be *arrinconado*—cornered, as they expressively call it—in the upper house, the deadening *vis inertiæ* of which was quite enough to paralyze all the satire, sarcasm, and denunciation he had wielded in his palmiest days. It was not, therefore, worth their while to propitiate him, when his parliamentary suffocation was so easy and economical. Alas! too, he had fallen away from the faith of his youth, and the wily politicians whom he dealt with, knew that he could no longer summon followers for his own revenge, with the trumpet he had ceased to sound when popular institutions were in danger. It was but the familiar case—so often paralleled in English history—of the irresistible leader of the people ennobled into the insignificant peer.

Galiano entered the Cortes, during the second constitutional period, as a deputy from Cadiz, his native city. In the legislature of that day were many able men, of large experience in public affairs, some of whom had successfully improved their opportunities for parliamentary distinction in the Cortes of 1812–14. Though comparatively young and inexpert in politics and public speaking, Galiano was not long in rivalling the most conspicuous of his associates, and soon established for himself a national reputation, by the boldness of his doctrines and the brilliancy of his eloquence. In 1823, when the Cortes were in session at Seville, and the approach of the Duc d'Angoulême rendered their removal necessary, the king—who, although he had committed himself to the constitution by every variety of gratuitous and supererogatory perjury, was still in active correspondence with its enemies and the chief of the invaders—refused positively to move a single step. This was an unexpected and startling blow, for Spanish loyalty absurdly forbade the violation of the royal will or person, and yet the presence of the executive was indispensable both to the constitutional action of the legislature and the maintenance of its prestige. The Cortes were in great consternation, for the peril was imminent, and the briefest delay might be fatal. To the boldest and wisest there seemed no alternative but an immediate dissolution, which involved the utter overthrow of liberal institutions. At this critical moment, Galiano startled the chamber by the introduction of a resolution, which assumed that, under the provisions of the constitution, the action of the king had vacated the throne. The proposition was a plank in their shipwreck, and was enthusiastically welcomed. Ferdinand, declared to be no longer king, was forced to conform to the will of the representatives of the nation. He was directed to prepare at once for the journey, and as he was a coward, he obeyed. In a very few hours he was under escort to Cadiz, whither the whole government, executive and legislative, hastened. So narrow was the escape of the Cortes, and so fickle the temper of the multitude, that the next day, the most important of the public archives were sacked and their contents thrown into the Guadalquivir, while the people ran loyally and madly through the streets, crying, "*Viva el rey disoluto!*"—"Long live the dissolute [absolute] king!"

Although the measure proposed by Galiano had no other effect than to save the legislature for the moment, and to prolong for yet a little while the ineffectual struggle of the liberal party with domestic treachery and foreign arms, it, as a matter of course, rendered him one of the most prominent marks of royal persecution. Upon the surrender of Cadiz, he fled to England, where, under sentence of death at home, he displayed for many years the fortitude and resignation, in poverty and exile, which are the best tests of a large mind and a great heart. He devoted himself for his support to the teaching of his native language, and lightened the heavy moments of his leisure by the cultivation of his intellectual tastes. He made himself not only familiar, but learnedly and critically so, with the literature of England; and his attainments in French and Italian scholarship are said to be equally profound and graceful. At the death of Ferdinand, he returned to his country, where his eminent services and sacrifices commended him at once to public confidence. Ten years of privation and reflection, however, with some practical experience of popular instability and the horrors of civil strife, had altogether changed his political philosophy. He attached himself, with many of the ablest of his liberal contemporaries, to the conservative cause, which he has since upheld with progressive enthusiasm, as minister, senator, and public teacher. Indeed, his views are yet more ultra in their new direction than formerly in their radical tendency; so that a humorous writer says, "He spent the earlier portion of his life in proving that the throne was a useless form, and would now, if possible, persuade the people that they ought to have two at the least." A change of opinion is, to vulgar minds, so sure an evidence of dishonesty, that nothing but Galiano's consistent poverty could have saved his reputation from the obloquy which always follows apostasy, actual or imputed. After having sacrificed an independent fortune in the maintenance of his principles, he has been a minister and has not repaid himself. Even political slander is forced to respect the motives which have been proof against temptation, necessity, and opportunity. Had he been less an orator and more a statesman or even a demagogue,—less a man of books and more a man of the world,—Galiano would probably be now, with his ability and knowledge, one of the leading spirits in the politics of Europe. As it is, he is a man of genius, and lives in humble lodgings,—all Madrid flocks to hear him at the Athenæum, yet no one wonders when a cabinet, whose members might go to school to him, refuses him a petty pension to mend his broken fortunes!

The Athenæum is an excellent institution, established in a convenient building on the Calle de la Montera. It has a capital reading-room, where you can always find the British periodicals and reviews, with the leading journals from the Continent. Its library, which is quite large, is well selected, and the collection of coins and cabinet of minerals, though small, are beginning to be esteemed. It has several professorships for the delivery of gratuitous lectures on scientific and literary subjects, and some of the chairs are filled by persons of conspicuous attainments and ability. When I was admitted to the privileges which are so liberally accorded by its rules to strangers, Galiano was in the midst of a course on modern history, and had reached the stirring times of the first French Revolution. The subject, always full of interest in itself, was of course doubly attractive in such hands; and so general was the desire to hear, that, but for the personal kindness of the speaker, I should have been unable to find a place in the overflowing hall. It is impossible for me to recall the various occasions on which I thus availed myself of his good offices to sit under his instruction, without feeling that each gave me new and enlarged ideas of the power and charm of speech.

It was said of one Romero Alpuente, a prominent Deputy of the older constitutional days, and so justly said as to become proverbial, that he was *"feamente feo,"*—" uglily ugly!" It would be scarcely fair to print the phrase in connection with the name of Galiano, were it not constantly and familiarly applied by his contemporaries to the disadvantages of feature and expression which he is able so signally to overcome. His stature is short, besides, and his gesture ungraceful. When I heard him, he had to struggle with the additional difficulty of speaking, literally *ex cathedra*, seated after the most orthodox professorial fashion, and with a table before him. Nor was there any thing in the theme which enabled the speaker to establish that personal sympathy between himself and his audience which is the mainspring of oratorical power. It was a theme for disquisition, for analysis, for generalization, for high thought, but not for passion. Only a plain, old man sat before us, to work what wonders he could, simply with his mind and tongue. Yet, if eloquence consists in the ability to sway men's understandings and lead captive their wills by speech,—to make them lose themselves and their own thoughts in the orator and his,—I have no hesitation in saying, that, in spite of all the disadvantages under which he spoke, Galiano produced on me more the effect of eloquence than any one I have ever heard. I cannot imagine any thing to surpass the magnificence of his occasional improvisations. The gorgeous language in which they were uttered may perhaps have led me away by its music; but this seemed to be their least attraction, so striking were the thoughts which they embodied, so copious the illustrations, so full the whole of fire and light and genius! There seemed something almost miraculous in the unfailing fluency, which, without the hesitation of a moment or the disarrangement of a word, went steadily through the most intricate phrases, the profoundest reflections, the freest range of imagination, never leaving the sense for an instant clouded, or the beauty of the diction sullied with one stain! The enthusiasm of the crowd must have been indeed irrepressible, to have overcome, so frequently and enthusiastically as it did, the habitual decorum and self-restraint of a Spanish audience.

XVI.

THE EX-REGENT ESPARTERO AND HIS RIVAL, NARVAEZ.—THE CARLIST WAR AND ITS CONCLUSION.—DOWNFALL OF ESPARTERO, AND ITS CAUSES.—LOVE OF TITLES AND HONORS.—ORDERS OF KNIGHTHOOD.

THE decree which recalled the Ex-Regent Espartero from banishment, in 1847, created him at the same time Senator of the realm. Since his return, however, he has had the wisdom to take but little part in the political movements of the day, and although he is still recognised as the head of the *Progresista* party, his name is rarely mentioned in connection with actual public affairs. During my whole stay in Madrid he was absent from his seat in the Senate, and was devoting himself, as I understood, to the cultivation of his estate near Logroño, and the improvement of agriculture in his neighborhood. It is not singular that a man, whose experience of popular fickleness and ingratitude has been so melancholy, should prefer the quiet occupations and pleasures of rural life to a renewal of those struggles which have already cost him so much; but it is nevertheless greatly to be lamented that the nation should be deprived of services so important as those which he has shown himself able to render. I believe that his retirement is a source of regret to the moderate and well-thinking men of all parties, for I am sure that I heard him spoken of more frequently with personal consideration and affection than any other public man in Spain.

In a former chapter, and in connection with the progress of constitutional government since the death of Ferdinand, I had occasion to speak of the downfall of Espartero as paving the way to the rapid and brilliant career of Narvaez. The characters of the two men are in strong contrast in almost all particulars except personal bravery, and the triumph of Narvaez over such an opponent is, of itself, as good a key to the spirit of Spanish politics as any that could be furnished. Down to the time of their conflict, there can be no doubt that Espartero stood far before his rival in his claims upon the gratitude of the country. Under circumstances of the most discouraging character, he had succeeded—partly by his conduct in the field, and partly by adroit negotiation—in putting an end to the cruel and desolating civil war which the adherents of Don Carlos had kept up so long. His political opponents, it is true, have sneered at the Treaty of Vergara,—by which the claims of the Pretender were extinguished in 1839, —as a bargain, corruptly purchased from the Carlist General, Maroto, and involving no high exercise of civil or military talent. Success is of course an uncertain criterion of merit, but the tale which events tell is very apt, nevertheless, to have some truth in it. For several years, the cause of the Spanish Pretender had held its own, against the best efforts of the government. The national treasury had been exhausted in vain, the best armies had been baffled, and the most distinguished generals, one after another, had returned from the inglorious field, unsuccessful at all events, if not disgraced. The trumpets of the rebels had been sounded at the very gates of Madrid, and their *guerrillas* had scoured the plains of Andalusia, La Mancha, and Castile. Until the intervention of Espartero as commander-in-chief of the national forces, there was as little prospect of a termination to the struggle, as when the banners of Don Carlos were first planted on the stubborn hills of Biscay. That the new leader, without any advantages which his predecessors had not enjoyed, should have been able to consummate what they had so signally failed in, is, of itself, some evidence that he had personal qualities superior to theirs. But that conclusion becomes irresistible, when it is considered that he did not assume the control of the government cause until after the spirit of its supporters had been broken by years of failure,—after the resources of the nation had been crippled by the long and costly maintenance of a large war establishment,—and after impunity, if not success, had given consistency and confidence to rebellion. That, after pressing the enemy so closely as to incline them from necessity to compromise, he should have chosen to finish the war by treaty rather than by bloodshed, would have been as honorable to his wisdom as to his humanity, had the contest been between strangers. But in a civil war,—a war which divided families, separated provinces, arrayed friend against friend and brother against brother, in which neither party could be victorious without carrying desolation to the hearths of its own members, as sadly as to the homes of the vanquished,—only a savage would deny that the course which Espartero chose entitled him, in a tenfold degree, to the love and gratitude of his country. Still deeper and still stronger ought that love and gratitude to be, in contemplation of the fact, that the restoration of peace, by the *Convenio de Vergara*, removed the main impediment which, till that time, had arrested the progress of Spain in freedom, civilization, and development.

Whatever may have been the weakness of the Ex-Regent's civil administration, practically considered, I have found very few who have denied to him integrity of purpose. Indeed, so far as the causes of his downfall were intrinsic in his character and conduct, they appear to have depended mainly upon principles and feelings which do him infinite honor. It is said—and probably with truth, for his friends do not generally deny it—that physical infirmity and the luxurious habits contracted during his residence in South America, rendered Espartero personally inactive and indolent, when not under the influence of any duty which stimulated his energies. But this—though an unhappy defect in any statesman, and especially in a Spanish ruler—was not by any means the chief secret of his overthrow. He was unfortunate enough to have a conscience. He was at heart, and in all his heart's sincerity, a lover of constitutional freedom. He had fought to maintain the constitutional dynasty, and had sworn to support the constitution. Under no circumstances, therefore, could he be brought to violate what he felt that he owed to the liberal institutions which had made him—the son of a Manchegan peasant—Duke of Victory and Regent of Spain. He felt the obligation of his trust, and he kept it sacred. Being a ruler with but limited prerogatives, he would not go beyond them, to advance the interests of his party or consolidate or preserve his own power. Throughout his whole administration, history will recognize a faithful effort to obey and execute the laws, in the true spirit of a liberal, an enlightened, and a conscientious patriotism.

That, even with such determinations and so much manly resolution to fulfil them, Espartero should have added another to the number of good men exiled by national ingratitude, will not surprise any one who has studied Spanish history and politics. Republican France was governed by the administrative system and ideas of the kingdom and the empire,— and constitutional Spain has not yet learned to discard the machinery and appliances of the despotism she has overturned. The court and the capital are still the fountains of power. It is there that ministers are made and unmade; there that the springs are touched which move the army and the people. The habits of centuries have not given way, and cannot soon give way, before the institutions of but a few years. To suppress the intrigues which assail government, secretly and openly, the government must use despotic measures, or be itself suppressed. Nothing less decided is understood or felt, as yet. Public opinion cannot be concentrated with sufficient rapidity, and constitutional means cannot be directed with sufficient energy and promptness, to countervail sedition. The evil is a practical one, dependent on circumstances not institutions, and has to be met practically. This, Espartero would not do. He had no talent for intrigue, and he would not usurp. That he fell was not therefore his fault, in a strict sense, although perhaps greatly so in the sense of that patriotism which impels an honest man, strong in his good motives, to violate the law in an emergency, in order that he may preserve the state.

But the Regent had other causes of defeat to struggle with. He was favorable to a reasonable modification of the tariff on imports, and this of course secured him the deadly hostility of Catalonia,—that fruitful nursery of dangerous and obstinate revolt. The apprehension of a treaty of commerce, which he was supposed to contemplate, with England, gave him the opposition of those of the commercial class, whose affinities were with France, and whose political economy was made up of French ideas. He was supposed to be, to a certain extent, under British influence, which animated the hostility of the whole *afrancesado* portion of the population. His humble birth and high position made him envied and hated, and his successful career against the Carlists had enlisted the whole legitimist feeling, almost undividedly, in opposition to him. Private jealousies, and the desire to supplant him in influence when his Regency should expire at the Queen's majority, made many of the leaders in his own party his opponents likewise. Against all these powerful elements in combination, what marvel that honesty and integrity should have proved insufficient to sustain him?

It was of circumstances like these that Narvaez had the opportunity and the tact to avail himself. Bold, active, unscrupulous, able, he was the individual, of all others, for a crisis in which a man was needed rather than a constitution. He used his elements, in combination, to break down Espartero, and then he broke down, with the other elements, each of those that separately stood in his own way. According to the principles on which he obtained power, he exercised it. Through those principles he kept it, and will most probably return to it. Where there was an evil, he sought the appropriate remedy,—in the constitution and the laws, if he could readily find it there, but wherever else he could find it, if they did not contain it. He respected constitutional forms where they did not interfere with the substance of his authority, and he was always sure to adopt them if he readily could, when he found it necessary to invade the substance of the constitution. That he often did wrong, no one can doubt; that his principles and practices all tended towards the perpetuation of his own power, is just as indisputable. But it cannot be denied, I think, that he served his country far better in the main, than if he had confined his government within the appointed limits of the constitution. The evil of usurpation was for the time a lesser one than that of anarchy. He gave strength to the central power, where it was weak, and crushed almost to extinction the spirit of petty and local faction and insubordination. He repressed rivalries and suppressed revolts, which indecision would have nursed into civil war. By making his administration thoroughly national, he commanded respect for the government at home and the nation abroad. Finally, and above all things, he kept the country at peace within and without, so that industry began to thrive, internal improvement to awaken, agriculture and commerce to start into new life. For the first time within the memory of man, the capitalists of the nation, and even of other nations, began to feel that investments were safe; that the confidence of to-day would not be turned to ruin by the revolution of to-morrow. Through his means the ground has thus been made more safe for constitutional rulers to come. He has extirpated the once prevalent idea, that constitutional government is only an organized license, and has given the people an opportunity of seeing and feeling, for themselves, that even arbitrary rule, if wise, is better than no authority at all. A gentler and weaker hand may now guide the wild horses which he has broken to the rein. The time may not perhaps have come, as yet, when the system of

Espartero will altogether suffice for Spain; but the vigor of Narvaez has brought it much nearer than it would have been, after a quarter of a century of premature republicanism. Each of the rivals, in his way, has deserved well of his country; but to human eyes it would have seemed wiser had Narvaez preceded Espartero.

It will have struck the reader, probably, in going over these brief sketches of the men who rule the destinies or hold high places in the veneration of the Spanish people, that most of them have sprung from humble origin, and won their power and reputation for themselves. This is a significant fact, and shows, beyond dispute, that the popular element is fully at work in the Peninsula, under all the shapes which political opinion may take. The court and army of Don Carlos, representing as they did the ultra-legitimist principle, would have furnished as palpable an illustration of the same fact. In speculating hereafter upon the political future of Spain, I may have occasion to recur to this, as giving some clew to her destiny. For the present, I only allude to it as in amusing contrast with the thirst for rank and title which seems to pervade all classes of political aspirants, and those, especially, whose elevation is least due to the distinctions of society. In the moment of triumph, the most radical party seems to forget its professions and the prestige which they gave. The *Progresista* progresses straightways into a countship, if he can, and the *Moderado* is moderate, if he asks no more than a marquisate. Crosses and decorations, ribbons and buttons, are sought and given without stint,—so that unlucky is the man of moderate pretensions in Madrid who has not a uniform, at least, to wear on gala-days. Knights of the royal orders are as plentiful as colonels in our Southern States. The list of Grand Crosses in the order of Charles the Third occupies eight pages of the Court Guide,—that of similar dignitaries in the order of Isabella the Catholic goes somewhat over ten. In the latter list the reader will be surprised to know that two respectable Turkish functionaries—Fuad Effendi and Seid Mohammed Emir Aali Bajá—have the pleasure of seeing their names enrolled! It would be curious if the orthodox queen, whose memory the order was designed to honor, could burst her cerements at Granada, and behold the cross she loved and worshipped resting, in her name, upon the bosom of the infidel! Almost as curious it might be to know the infidel's own thoughts, as he puts on the emblem of a worship he despises, and reflects that the poor creature whose name it bears had no pretentions to a soul! But whatever the Turk might think, the Spaniard likes the cross exceedingly. "If we were to have a democracy in Spain," said my old friend, the Carlist general, "we should call each other *Serenísimo ciudadano! Ciudadano príncipe!* (Most serene citizen! Prince citizen!) at the least."

XVII.

Loyalty.—The Queen.—Guizot and Infante.—Regicides.—Necessity of an able Prince.—The Queen's Embarazo.—Public Rejoicings and Ceremonial.—Diplomatic Congratulations and Reception.—The King.

THERE is no trait more prominent in the national character of the Spaniards, than the loyalty with which they have always borne themselves towards their kings, even when it was least deserved and most ungratefully requited. Certainly no prince, whom history records, did more than Ferdinand the Seventh, to goad and irritate a people whom it seemed the business of his life to wrong. There were men, all through the nation, whom he had maddened into hatred of his person by the most ingenious refinements of insult and persecution. There were times, when only his personal prestige —indeed his personal existence—stood between the people and their permanent liberation from a despotism which shamed the vilest annals of the Roman Empire. No one ever had a better right than he to expect the vengeance of men, in anticipation of the justice of Heaven. But although his private habits afforded the most frequent and favorable opportunities for assassination, while his public conduct was perpetually prompting and deserving national retribution, he passed through his tyrannical and vicious life without being once in peril of the dagger or the scaffold. The Spaniards are proud of this, and doubtless it does credit to their patience and forbearance; though, perhaps, it pushed these virtues almost into weakness. When Quiroga was in London, after the constitutional defeat of 1823, an eminent personage suggested to him, that, if the liberal party had dealt with Ferdinand as he deserved, they would have saved their country from oppression and themselves from death or exile. "It may be true, your ——," was the lofty answer, "but killing kings has never been a Spanish custom,—*Nunca ha sido uso en España, matar reyes.*"

But though it may have been "a large economy . . . to save the like," there was prudence as well as principle involved in it. The spilling of their monarch's blood would have precipitated on the Spaniards all the reactionary elements of Europe. The intervention, which afterwards disgraced France chiefly, would have been Cossack likewise. The darling project of the French, to make the Ebro the boundary of their dominions, would have been consummated, it may be, by the concession and the guaranty, to other powers, of beautiful and fertile Andalusia. Another dismemberment, like that of Poland, would probably have brought additional reproach upon the century, while all of Europe that pretended to be liberal would have looked on again with folded arms. It was well, therefore, for humanity and for the cause of freedom, not less than for the weal of Spain, that Ferdinand was spared. Not long ago the Spaniards had an opportunity of using, with no small effect, the advantage which their history thus gave them over their less conscientious neighbors.

In 1842, I think, but certainly while Espartero held the regency, the *Moderados* and the French their allies attempted to create the impression, that the Infantas—now the Queen and the Duchess of Montpensier—were not personally safe in the hands of the *Progresistas*. By way of giving currency and effect to the imputation, M. Guizot took occasion to say, in the Chamber of Deputies, that France would regard as a cause of intervention any attempt to do violence to the royal persons. The insult was exceedingly gratuitous, and excited general indignation in Spain. It was especially ill-brooked at Madrid, and an admirable speech in which it was retorted, by Don Facundo Infante, a constitutionalist of the old school, shook the capital with applause. "The quondam Professor of Modern History," he said, "is ignorant, perhaps, that there is no such word as 'regicide' in our vocabulary. The thing which it signifies is not known to our history, and we have had no use for the name in our language.* There are, unhappily, some nations whose annals supply the deficiency of ours. It would be well if our neighbors would tell us,—before we trust them with the guardianship of our monarchs,—how many of their own they can remember, from the days of Henri Quatre, who have not been the victims, or at all events the aim, of violence, or banishment, or murder!"

The present Queen of Spain had obviously no dream of peril from her subjects, during the period of which I write. She mingled freely with them on the Prado and in the gardens of the Retiro every evening,—generally in an open carriage, and accompanied only by her servants, and a lady and gentle-

* Since the above was written, the attempted murder of Queen Isabella by the madman Gomez has made the honest boast of the orator no longer just. The outrage, however, did but elicit a burst of abhorrence so universal, as to show that the nation could neither have sympathy with the crime, nor be corrupted by the example of the assassin.

man or two in waiting. The simplicity of her *cortége* was strikingly in contrast with the array of cavalry and cocked pistols under the protection of which the President of the French Republic went out, at the same time, to fraternize with his fellow-citizens. Upon the promenade, and as she passed along the streets, the greeting of the people to Queen Isabella was cordial and apparently sincere. Her bearing towards all was full of kindness, in accordance with the thorough amiability which is remarkable in her disposition. Her face, though not regarded as attractive generally, has an expression of sadness, at times, which is very touching, and it is impossible, I think, to see her often, without being satisfied that palace-doors have not shut sorrow from her. That her domestic relations were far from being happy seemed to be generally conceded, and if, after having been made the victim of state policy and diplomatic intrigue, she were in fact mindless of obligations which were forced on her, it would be but what has happened a thousand times, where neither the temptations nor the opportunities of royalty were added to the recklessness of youth and disappointment. From all accounts, she is entirely without ambition, and well disposed to part with any of her prerogatives as queen, which interfere with her leisure and freedom as a woman.

It would be well, indeed, for Isabella the Second, and signally a blessing to her people, if, even for the pride of governing, she could be brought to feel a graver interest in the responsibilities and duties of her station. At the present stage of Spanish affairs, the monarch should be something more than an estimable person or a respectable figure in a pageant. Not all the ability and energy of the most vigorous ministry can supply the absence of those qualities in the individual who holds the sceptre. Men, taken from the people and lifted suddenly to power, are followed necessarily by envy and resentment. They may make themselves dukes and marquises, but they cannot overcome the popular persuasion that the only sanction of their authority is the fact of their possessing it. Their measures will be scrutinized, at the best, with invidious acuteness; their motives questioned with all the distrust of rivalry. They may use the name and lean on the prerogatives of the monarch, but if the people know that it is the ministers who govern, not the king, the moral strength of the government will fall as short of what it ought to be, as the prestige of a subject falls short of a king's.

As a matter of course, this is not meant to be said of all constitutional monarchies; for where the people govern through the legislature and the cabinet, the personal qualities of the monarch, provided they be tolerable, are of no particular importance. A responsible ministry is quite as good, in such case, as a wise and vigorous king. But where, as in Spain, constitutional government has not yet grown into a habit,—where the influence of the people has not learned to make itself felt by concentration of opinion and unity of action,—the case is very different. There, the legislature has comparatively little to do with the direction of administrative affairs, and it is the executive government which actually governs. In such countries and under such circumstances royalty is a substantive thing, and has an opportunity of displaying itself in its most effective and useful phase as an institution. But, for that purpose, the individual who is invested with the royal prerogatives must be able to wield them himself. His personal and known and visible participation is indispensable, to save the state from those continual and embittered contests of private ambition, which are apt to be the bane of popular institutions in their earlier stages. Of the exercise of power by the monarch, there may be question, so far as policy is concerned, but there can be no complaint as to its legitimacy. His dignity and superiority, being beyond cavil, cannot be the cause of jealousy. Any man may intrigue to be made a Secretary, in the stead of another whom he knows to have no better right than he; but no man in his sane mind—unless he means to be a rebel—will endeavor to supplant his king. Even if the monarch steps beyond the line of his legitimate authority, his usurpation, whether for good or for evil, has at all events some pretexts and prescriptions, which make it comparatively respectable. A ministerial despotism, on the contrary, is not only bad in what it does, but in itself. It involves an insult as well as a wrong, and is hated and conspired against accordingly. In Spain, where the sense of personal equality among the people is as strong as their reverence for the throne and loyalty to him who fills it, this is particularly true; and the personal character of the monarch, and the share he takes in the government of which he is the head, are proportionally more important than in countries where those sentiments prevail less actively. Narvaez, born king of Spain, or representing the will of a prince who was known to have a will of his own, would have been able to do more in a single year for the welfare of his country, than in ten, perhaps, as prime minister in name, and dictator in fact. He would have had no palace intrigues to make him tremble for his place, no small cabals of *pretendientes* to silence or suppress, no envy or repining of other subjects at the power which he—a subject only—wielded. He would have gone on and would still be ruling,—sternly, and at all times despotically it may be, but still consistently and ably,—instead of being badgered and cross-questioned by Gonzalez Bravo and supplanted by Bravo Murillo.

But whatever may be the deficiency of Isabella the Second in the qualities which made illustrious the long-descended name she bears, and whatever may be the tone of the court gossip in regard to her conduct as a woman, she is, as I have said, certainly popular among her subjects. Identified as she is with the cause of free institutions, for which the nation has sacrificed so much, it is not strange that—other things apart—they should regard her person with something of the enthusiasm which rallied them around her rights and throne. During my visit, it was officially announced that the birth of an heir to the crown might be looked for in a few months, and the occasion developed a degree of earnest congratulation and solicitude throughout the realm, which left no doubt of the Queen's hold upon the popular affection. It may give the reader some notion of Spanish peculiarities, to describe the public manifestations which attended and followed so interesting a disclosure.

On the 14th of February, the Duke of Valencia, in full and magnificent uniform, arrested the attention of each branch of the legislature, separately, by reading a communication he had received from the proper officer of her Majesty's household, in which the state of the royal health was reported, from the certificate of the chief physician of the palace. The news could not have been very unexpected, for the subject had already been discussed in the fashionable circles and the newspapers. Indeed, for some time previous, the principal streets leading from the palace to the Prado had been sanded carefully for the comfort of her Majesty in driving, and the press had alluded to the fact, and the cause of it, without any reserve. The announcement, nevertheless, was received with great enthusiasm by the legislature. The Chamber of Deputies especially sent forth shouts of *Viva la Reina!* which might have been heard almost in the royal apartments. Immediate steps were taken upon all sides to congratulate the Queen. The Chamber of Deputies disputed for some time as to whether they should present themselves in mass, or be represented by a committee. Sr. Olozaga, who is rather a stickler for the dignity of the representative department, protested against parading the whole body, in its official capacity, through the streets. Narvaez had the tact to agree with him, and the matter was compromised by the appointment of a committee, with the understanding that all the rest of the members might go in company, if they chose. No one, of course, was impolitic enough to be absent, even if any one desired to be, which, in the general jubilee, I very much doubt. The Presidents of the two houses made fine speeches, her Majesty answered with great patriotism and amiability, and for the moment all party distinctions seemed to have been forgotten in the overflowing of loyal enthusiasm. The Cortes having set the example, there seemed, for a fortnight at least, to be a general descent, upon the palace, of all public bodies and functionaries who could lay the slightest claim to congratulatory privileges. Only the President of the United States, on his way to the Springs or to a railroad opening, was ever so overwhelmed with discourses; and although the subject was not one which afforded much scope, it was treated, nevertheless, in all the sublime varieties of what the Spanish grammarians call "figurative syntax." I was present at the demonstration made by the diplomatic corps,—having but a few days before been privately presented,—and although the grotesqueness of the idea could not but force itself upon me during the whole ceremony, I was impressed by its magnificence and the cordial spirit which seemed to animate all who took part in it.

Sir Henry Wotton says that "to make a complete staircase is a curious piece of architecture," and I was never more forcibly struck with the effect which that stately portion of an edifice may be made to produce, than when we were passing up the principal stairway of the palace, on the evening in question. The steps and balustrade, of exquisite white marble, were made more brilliant by the crimson contrast of rich carpeting, and the muskets and halberds of the guard, who saluted us at the entrance and on every platform, had a festive glitter in the flood of softened light. A few moments of easy ascent carrried us to the door of the superb ante-chamber, where the aids of the military personages in attendance and a number of officers of the household waited, in rich uniforms. In the adjoining apartment of the suite we found the principal members of the diplomatic body already assembled, and it was not long before we were ushered, with the usual ceremonial, into the presence-chamber. Upon the opposite side of the magnificent saloon to that from which we entered, stood the Queen, beside a table covered with crimson velvet. The King was on her left, and on the other side of the table stood Narvaez, with the Ministers of Finance and Grace and Justice.

At the head of the chamber was the Minister of State, with the rest of his colleagues, and at the foot the Count of Sevilla la Nueva, the Introducer of Ambassadors. Behind their Majesties were some attendants of high rank. The chiefs of the different legations, in the due order of precedence, with the Pope's Nuncio at their head, arranged themselves in line opposite the royal persons. Behind each minister stood his secretary, and the other members of his diplomatic family. When the whole pageant was in right array, it was gorgeous in the extreme; for the apartment was lofty and superbly lighted, its architecture and furniture were all that taste and luxury could devise, and the various splendor of the uniforms and court-dresses elicited the admiration of those who were most accustomed to such displays.

As soon as we had subsided into our places, the Nuncio produced a congratulatory address in Spanish, on the part of himself and his colleagues, which he read with great earnestness and deliberation, but with a provokingly Italian accent, which was almost too much for the gravity of more than one of the dignified assemblage. When he had finished, her Majesty, in a distinct tone, but very rapidly, read an expression of her thanks and "sweet hopes." She then proceeded towards the Nuncio, whom she saluted very graciously, and, after conversing with him for a few moments, passed down the line of the Ambassadors, saying a few words to each in his turn. The King followed her, but seemed to be in no great haste to finish his part of the performance,—so that her Majesty was compelled to wait some time for him, with the Introducer of Ambassadors, at the foot of the saloon. She obviously did not bear the delay very patiently,—as was quite natural,

—and when the King finally joined her, she made her exit with him at once, by a door opposite to us. The curious in such matters may be edified by the information, that their Majesties retired facing the diplomatic body,—making three several bows as they moved across the apartment, and another at the door, as they were in the act of passing through it.

It was the first time that I had been near the King, for a sufficiently long time to observe him particularly. He is of short stature, exceedingly juvenile and effeminate in his appearance, with a "shrill treble" in his voice, and a downy, incipient moustache. Whether he deserves one half the unamiable and disparaging things which are said of him may well be doubted by any one who knows the reckless license of court scandal; but there is no risk, I am sure, in saying that neither Lavater nor Spurzheim would hasten to select him, from outward signs, as the model of a ruler among men.

XVIII.

SOCIAL CUSTOMS IN MADRID.—ENTERTAINMENTS.—SOCIETY AND ITS SPIRIT.—IMITATION OF THE FRENCH.—THE ACADEMY AND THE PRESS.—SOCIALISM.—ETIQUETTE.—SOCIAL FRANKNESS AND CORDIALITY.

IN all the capitals of Europe, the general tone of society among the higher classes is, of course, given by the court; but Madrid is so emphatically "*la Corte*,"—the Court and nothing else,—that every movement at the Palace vibrates through the whole circumference of the social circle. The Queen, who is as generous as she is gay, had been in the habit of throwing open the royal saloons to her lieges without stint, and I found that traditions of her splendid balls and routs, during the preceding winters, were quite rife among the gossips of fashion. Indeed, I met with a party of young noblemen who had come from Belgium, all the way, in the praiseworthy expectation of realizing sundry wonderful accounts which had been given them by some of their luckier friends, who were in Madrid the year before. Unhappily, however, the events to which I have alluded disappointed the hopes and calculations of the dancing world, during the season of my visit, and confined the entertainments at the palace to a few operatic performances. As a consequence, scarcely any one seemed disposed to open or carry on the usual festive campaign, and several of my acquaintance, who had promised me marvels when the season opened, were careful to tell me, when it was over, that they had never seen Madrid so little like itself. The few general entertainments which were given were probably a fair type of the many which would have kept them company under more favorable auspices; but as it is no part of my plan to chronicle a stranger's experience of private hospitality, I must leave the reader to imagine, that wealth and social cultivation have the same results in Madrid as all the world over.

In telling the story of my former rambles in Spain, I took occasion to say something about the rarity of invitations to dinner, which some travellers complain of so bitterly. It is not the custom of the country to feed the hungry after that fashion,—and whether it be a fault or a virtue, Madrid, in that particular, is like the rest of the kingdom. Any one who makes up his mind to be a dweller in the capital must resign himself to the inevitable necessity, for the most part, of casting his own bread upon the waters, and finding it for himself when he can. With but few exceptions, the foreigners resident at Madrid are the only Amphitryons, and there are those of them, no doubt, who are consequently remembered in the same spirit which taught the weary pilgrims to

"drink, and pray
For the kind soul of Sybil Grey."

The prodigal abundance—which loads the tables and supports the medical faculty, regular and irregular, wherever Anglo-Saxondom, or its remotest offshoot, stretches—forms no part of Spanish social economy. The *tertulias*, or evening receptions—which are so natural, so pleasant, and so free, that no one can enjoy them long, without regarding them as one of the most charming fashions of social intercourse—are altogether without gastronomic embellishments. A little *orchata*, lemonade and cake, with perhaps a cup of tea where foreign tastes have been acquired, are all that a large company will desire, to help them, with music and conversation, through a long and agreeable evening. If cards are introduced, as they frequently are, it is not often that the game gets the better of prudence. In the more aristocratic saloons, where *écarté* is popular, the stakes are generally made up by the bystanders,— and the loser invariably resigns his seat to his neighbor, as soon as fate determines against him. The amusement of one is thus made the amusement of all, and there is a natural and constant diffusion of that social electricity, which we are too apt, in this country, to suppose can only be disseminated by the ponderous machinery of a supper.

Some ill-natured commentators upon Spanish customs have been disposed to attribute the fast-day character of these entertainments to the poverty of the people, or their economy, rather than their moderation. I have no idea that there is any foundation whatever for that impression. People would be called together less frequently, no doubt, if it were necessary to tempt them by costly preparations; and it is more than probable, that the Spaniards, like all the rest of the children of men, would say Ha! ha! among the banquets, if there were any, as the war-horses are wont to, among the trumpets. Yet this last would only happen from the common weakness of all flesh and the superiority of temptation to human powers of resistance. I am quite persuaded, in spite of it, that the present system is the result of both taste and principle. The Spaniards are notoriously an abstemious people, in the very bosom of abundance; hence, to be moderate is to them natural. In the midst, too, of all their distinctions of rank and class,—their stars and crosses and uniforms,—they are, as I have frequently repeated, more practically observant of personal equality than any people I have seen. A social habit, therefore, which puts rich and poor upon a level, so far as they may instrinsically deserve to be, is entirely in accordance with their instincts. Fond, too, as they are of pleasant intercourse, it is but reasonable that they should adhere, with some pertinacity, to observances which remove the ban so often put by adverse fortune, elsewhere, on social talents or accomplishments. Halleck's "Fanny" could never have been a poem of Spanish life. The "dwelling of the proud and poor" would not have closed its doors or lost its visitors, because there was no longer a chandelier in the drawing-room. If the inmates had been worth cultivating, the world would have sought and found them, as usual, on the next pleasant evening after the notary had called to protest the bill. Not that, in Spain, adversity is altogether without the shadows which make its pathway cold and gloomy everywhere; but that social pleasure is made to depend more upon the men and women who enjoy and give it, than on the adventitious circumstances which surround them, and these may consequently take to themselves wings, without carrying every thing along with them.

Madrid, however, is no very accurate or favorable type of the national character and customs, in the particulars of which I have been speaking. Socially, indeed,—it is strange, but it is true,—the capital is the most un-Spanish city in the kingdom. There is less of the national freedom and frankness there, more ostentation, more pretension, more servility in the imitation of foreign tastes and habits, than in all the rest of Spain put together. I have heard some of the Madrileños rebel sturdily against this conclusion; but it is just, nevertheless, and I, for one, certainly adopt it in no unfriendly spirit. The persons to whom I refer insisted that foreigners visit Spain merely to enjoy its peculiarities,—the points in which it differs from the more modernized countries of Europe. Looking at the people merely in the picturesque point of view, travellers, they said, are disappointed at finding that the French bonnet and hat have superseded the *mantilla* and *calañes* on the Prado,—that *boleros* and the *ole* are not danced in polite society,—and that well-bred men and women in Madrid are dressed and bear themselves like well-bred people in the other capitals of Europe. Hence it is, they said, that strangers pronounce Madrid un-Spanish. Going to the Peninsula as to a *bal de costume*, they are disappointed at not finding the maskers and mummers as fantastic as they had expected.

There would be a good deal of force in this, if it told the whole truth. No people are under an obligation to be stationary for the amusement of picturesque tourists. Intercourse with other nations would be of but little service, were we not at liberty to learn and willing to be taught any improvement on our national usages. Though, therefore, I consider it very barbarous taste to supplant the *mantilla* by any French or English contrivance whatever, I see no reason why those who think differently should not be allowed to indulge their notions accordingly. With far greater readiness,

I admit both the wisdom and civilization of introducing the French system of cookery, to the fullest extent. Any one who prefers the *puchero* of his fathers ought of course to be tolerated in adhering to it himself, provided he gives to others the choice between it and something better. But, on the other hand, it is entirely in accordance with the most orthodox *Españolismo*, for a man to prefer what the culinary genius of the Palais Royal has done for humanity, to all the combinations of *garbanzos* and *tocino* that have come down from the days of King Roderick. Neither patriotism, nor prescription, nor "reverence," has any thing to do with so vital a matter.

But the customs of Madrid go very far beyond these reasonable limits. The dynasty and its associations have infused the French mind, as far as possible, into the national body, and the French raiment in which they have clothed the latter is consequently worth noticing as a type of the inward transformation. French habits have been introduced,—French tastes domesticated,—French ideas, and doctrines, and even prejudices, incorporated into the national stock,— not because they are better than the old, but because they are French. What foreigners admire most in the Spanish character and manners is that which is most characteristic. The Madrid theory seems to be, that to adhere to what is characteristic and national is to linger behind the age. In the most elevated circles—in the very palace itself—the French language is spoken, not merely as a matter of diplomatic necessity or convenience, but of choice; and Spanish is hardly tolerated there, even between Spaniards. The personal example of the Queen, who is especially fond of her native language, has failed to check this corruption of the public taste. It has gone so far, that not only the ephemeral productions of the press, but even the best-conducted journals, and the works of some of the most popular writers, are filled with glaring Gallicisms. The Dictionary of the Academy itself—the standard and test of purity in the Castilian—is naturalizing these interpolations so steadily and progressively, that a witty censor, not long back, insisted on having the last edition translated into Spanish! The discourse of a prominent Senator of the *Moderado* party, delivered while I was in Madrid on the occasion of his admission to the Academy, was amusingly and justly criticized in detail, by a writer in the *Clamor Público*, for its palpable introduction of unauthorized French words and idioms. The thing was made too plain to be above even a foreigner's appreciation.

As has been heretofore observed, in speaking of the Madrid press, the newspapers have not only adopted the French form and arrangement, but are mostly printed, as nearly all the best books are, from French type. The French political philosophy which may be current at the time furnishes, in like manner, to the journalists on both sides, the greater part of their maxims and logic. Sometimes the effect of this is very amusing. For example, if there be any thing on earth of which a Spaniard is, from his moral and physical constitution, incapable, that thing, it may be safely said, is socialism. Your genuine Iberian may do many things both strange and wild, in a political way, but his peculiarities must always have a practical turn. He will "pronounce," with his shouldered musket, in the *plaza*,—he will shoot a *Jefe Politico*,—hunt a broken-down minister to the very frontier,—turn *guerrillero*, and go through five years of countermarching and starvation, to break down an existing dynasty or give the king of his choice " his own again,"—but socialist, Fourierist, communist, or transcendentalist of any species, he cannot be. He has not the stuff in him of which these sorts of people are made. His romance, his human instalment of insanity, does not run in that direction. He has excellent common sense, in the first place, besides a keen perception of the ridiculous, and a contempt for metaphysics generally. " You are metaphysical," says Babieca, the horse of the Cid, to Rozinante, in one of the sonnets prefixed to the first edition of Don Quixote. "'T is that I eat not!" is the Manchegan charger's reply. The Spaniard, everywhere, is of Rozinante's opinion, that too nice speculation is a windy business, furnishing small entertainment for man or horse.

In spite of this,—which is as indisputably a trait of the Spanish character as loyalty or constancy, or any of its virtues or vices,—there was not a conservative paper in all Madrid, that did not daily and principally enlarge upon the horrors of the socialist doctrines, and invoke the energies of the country and the powers of the government to check the progress of liberal politics, as involving socialism and its consequences, of necessity. M. Proudhon was the great bugbear. French democracy had run riot, and declared all property to be robbery; therefore there was no safety for any thing, in Spain, that savored of concession to the people. The reasoning was not very conclusive, but still it was generally adopted, and the perservation of " *el orden* "—" order"—seemed, by general consent, to be regarded by the whole conservative party as the only purpose for which government was instituted. The party of progress, on the other hand, did not fail, I must admit, to give some color to the pretensions of the enemy. The magnificent generalities of the French republican orators were too high-sounding in Castilian for journalist nature to resist, and phrases, which might perhaps, have been potent, and consequently dangerous, at the Hôtel de Ville, were now and then let loose from the columns of a liberal newspaper. It needed great folly to suppose that such abstractions could be any thing more than simply ridiculous in Spain. Yet it was mortifying to see how frequently the political discussions, both in print and in the Cortes, were made to turn, almost exclusively, upon them. It will be worth while to observe the course which things of the sort will take, now that France has adopted the *coup d'état*, which is emphatically a Spanish (or Turkish) invention.

The etiquette of Madrid was, in most particulars, very rational. Strangers, on arriving in the city, were expected to leave cards for those persons on whose civility they had any claim. The promptness or delay with which the courtesy was acknowledged, furnished a pretty fair test of the cordiality with which a more particular acquaintance was likely to be encouraged. On New-Year's day, or from that to Twelfth-day, every one sent cards to all his acquaintance, and a neglect of that attention was construed, in the absence of explanation, to indicate a wish for the suspension of visiting intercourse. It was an easy civility, however, and few disregarded it. You had only to make out a list, and your servant did the rest. Persons about to enter upon the holy estate of matrimony, announced the fact to all with whom they desired to continue their social relations, by sending round a card, in their joint names, giving the direction of their intended residence and an invitation to visit them. Formal visits were generally made between two and five in the afternoon, yet few persons received formally, and it was generally polite to send a card, always so to leave one in person, without asking to be admitted. Most families of any social position had stated evenings —once in a week or a fortnight—on which they expected visitors, as a matter of course, and it was regarded as unsocial, if not uncivil, for even an ordinary acquaintance to neglect presenting himself, occasionally, at these unpretending reunions.

In the more fashionable houses, the evening receptions did not begin before nine o'clock. They generally lasted until near midnight, about which hour, if there was a ball elsewhere, the company would separate to meet again. Such hours, of course, were not likely to encourage early rising, and I have heard it said of some fair ladies, that, on their way home from the dance of Saturday night, they would now and then point the moral of earthly vanity, by hearing mass in their faded flowers! The gay and passionate, who had the vigor of youth as well as its hopes and promptings, no doubt found enjoyment in this,—at any rate for a while; but there were others on whom it must have imposed a melancholy servitude. Power was to be sought, as well as pleasure, even in the saloons of Madrid, and many an intrigue to overturn a ministry or circumvent an opposition was planned and thwarted amid festal light and music. Politicians, diplomatists, and the higher order of *pretendientes*, were usually watchers, therefore, on such occasions. Many a weary and sad Major Pendennis went through a nightly tribulation, which all the honors and profits of the Court would have but ill repaid. I could not help thinking, sometimes, how natural it was that affairs should occasionally go wrong, when the brains on which their conduct depended were so often throbbing, at the dawn, with the fever of sleepless revelry. It was on account of such habits, most probably, that the ministerial bureaus were so rarely accessible, for any purposes of business, before the afternoon. No one who knows, from experience, how little of the working day is left when the morning is gone, can be surprised, after knowing this fact, at the delays and postponements in which the public offices of Spain so proverbially abound.

It was not, of course, among the polkas and mazurkas—which are danced, all the world over, to the same music, well or ill played—that the characteristics of Spanish society were to be particularly sought, even so far as they were to be found, at all, in Madrid. The quiet *tertulia*, among quiet people, was more interesting to a stranger, on that account, than the rout which followed it. The one he could see almost anywhere, with perhaps some little variety in its accidents; the other he could, on the whole, find nowhere else. With respectable introductions, he could have access, on almost every night of the week, to *tertulias*, literary, political, or merely social, according to his taste. A fair acquaintance with the Spanish language would be necessary to his complete enjoyment and appreciation of them; for although he would seldom be without some one to speak with him in his own tongue, or, at all events, in French, yet the conversation—except, as I have said, in the more courtly circles—was, for the most part, carried on in Spanish, and its spirit and style were mainly national. The unreserve with which he would hear persons and things discussed, according to the predominating opinion of the company, would surprise him a little, at first; but he would soon find himself regarded as having undergone a sort of matriculation, which involved confidence as well as cordiality. Whatever he might find to be the degree of sensibility manifested by the Spaniards, as a people, to any impeachment of their national intelligence or dignity, he would soon learn, that, as individuals, they were as open as any to respectful and kindly interrogation or suggestion. If he should fail to understand them fully and appreciate them fairly, it would be his own fault; for, lack what they might in other things, they would show him no want of frankness. If, in the midst of the very kindness which made him at home upon the briefest acquaintance, he should perceive an attentive politeness, approaching so near to formality as now and then to embarrass him, he would soon be brought to understand and admire it as the expression of habitual consideration for the feelings of others. He would value it the more, when he learned, from its universality, that what was elsewhere chiefly a thing of manners and education, was there a genial instinct developed into a social charity.

XIX.

THEATRES AND DRAMATIC LITERATURE.—ACTORS AND THEIR STYLE.—ROMEA AND MATILDE DIAZ.—BRETON DE LOS HERREROS AND HIS PLAYS.—RUBÍ.—ISABEL LA CATÓLICA.—HISTORICAL DRAMAS.—THEATRICAL POLICE.—LITERARY REWARDS.—COPYRIGHT.—COUNT OF SAN LUIS.

THE Teatro de Oriente, when I was in Madrid, being still as Ferdinand left it, there was no theatre or opera-house on a scale worthy of a capital. Indeed, with the exception of the private operas at the palace, it was admitted, on all hands, that the season was without musical attractions. The drama fared much better,—and although the minor theatres, with ballet and vaudeville, were more generally attended, the Teatro Español (known for nearly half a century as the Teatro del Príncipe,—the Prince's Theatre) was constantly presenting plays of the best character, in quite a high style of art. This theatre is the property of the *Ayuntamiento* of Madrid, at whose risk and for whose account it was conducted; but the worshipful fathers of the city, with a discretion not usually belonging to their class, had placed its management in the hands of Don Julian Romea, a capital actor,—who was, besides, no mean poet, and said to be one of the best dramatic critics in Spain. Under his auspices and the very liberal encouragement of the Count of San Luis, then Minister of the Interior, the best poetical talent of the country was called into requisition, and the Español had become an excellent school of taste for both actors and authors. Its audience was generally made up of the most cultivated people, and evinced a discrimination in applause and censure, that bespoke the habit of hearing and seeing good models. The theatre itself—then the best in the city, though not the largest—was very comfortably arranged for the spectators, although so narrowly provided with accommodations behind the scenes, as to require the removal of the more cumbrous decorations to a distance, whenever the production of a novelty increased the usual supply. The machinery and the *mise en scène* were, nevertheless, quite modern and artistic, on the whole, so that little was left to be desired, in those particulars, by such as were content to enjoy the " legitimate" department.

What has been said in regard to the oratory of the Spaniards, applies with equal force to the elocution of their stage. There is, among the best of their tragic artists, what strikes as exaggeration one who is accustomed to our standards. It is not the depth of their passion, nor indeed its violence, but rather its vivacity, that produces this impression. They have a quickness and restlessness of manner which seems at war with dignity. There is too much gesticulation,—too little repose,—an incessant twinkle, which takes the place of both blaze and heat. As the kings at some of our theatres insist upon wearing their crowns and robes of state in the street and on the battle-field as well as in their bed-chambers, lest they be mistaken for common people,—so the Spanish tragedians seem to think that a hero or heroine must say and do every thing after a peculiar fashion,—if not a heroic one. Instead of holding the mirror up to nature, they are constantly and majestically watching their own looking-glasses. This criticism, I am aware, may possibly be open to the reply which I have admitted may be made to my observations on the kindred subject. Yet I do not think it is fairly so. I am the better satisfied that it is not the result of prejudice, or of my habituation to a different style, from the fact that I do not think it possible for a Spaniard to have enjoyed, with a keener relish than I did, the excellent comic acting, and the admirable representations of daily life, which were so frequent upon the Madrid stage.

Romea, who generally filled the best tragic parts, is less obnoxious to the remarks just made, than any actor of his nation that I have seen. If, on the contrary, he has a leading defect, it is that he is too cold,—that he has chastened his style into tameness. The features of the tragic mask will not bear too much rounding, and from forgetting this he has made them sometimes inexpressive, when seen from a spectator's distance. It is a fault, however, which springs, in him, from the tastes and scruples of a scholar, and is in a great degree relieved by a thorough comprehension of his parts, and a nice and graceful observance of all the proprieties and probabilities of his art. He has a good voice and great command of it, an admirable articulation, and exceeding skill in the appropriate adornment of a striking person.

The wife of Romea, better known as Matilde Diaz, is regarded as the best tragic actress in the kingdom, and has unbounded popularity in Madrid. An unfortunate tendency to *embonpoint* has made her figure emphatically what Byron hated, and has of course greatly impaired the spirituality which first gave reputation to her acting. She redeems this misfortune, however, by a sweet, expressive face, a melodious voice, and a great deal of tragic feeling and poetical appreciation. Her recitation of her noble native language is, at times, the perfection of spoken music, and her tender passages would indeed be perfect, altogether, were it not that, with Rosalind, she sometimes "will weep for nothing, like Diana in the fountain." Whether Matilde has made this excess of sweet sorrow the fashion, I do not know; but it is the fashion,—and her rival, Lamadrid, who likewise has a good deal of tragic power, carries it to the extreme of the pocket-handkerchief style, which makes the griefs of Mrs. Haller so affecting.

Breton de los Herreros is the most popular dramatic author of the day in Spain,—perhaps the only writer in the annals of the drama, anywhere, who has ever received the enthusiastic compliment of having a whole play encored. Though his fertility is quite equal to his skill, there was nothing new from him during my visit. His latest comedy then, called *Quien es Ella?* "Who is she?"—had appeared in 1849, and was occasionally performed, though without producing any great sensation. It was an attempt to introduce upon the stage the celebrated writer, Don Francisco de Quevedo y Villegas, one of the first names in Spanish literature. To make an effective character, in a work of fiction, out of a literary man, is for obvious reasons no very easy task under any circumstances; and although Quevedo's connection with public affairs gives some interest of a dramatic nature to his history, it is as a wit, an epigrammatist, a satirist, a poet of a bold and lofty genius, that he dwells chiefly in the remembrance of his countrymen. With the exception of Cervantes, there is probably no writer whose sayings are as frequently upon the lips of the people, and not even Cervantes has ascribed to him one tithe of the unwritten sayings which are handed down by tradition as Quevedo's. Like Swift, whom he resembles in some particulars,—and those not always the most creditable to either,—he is as thoroughly individualized by these sayings as man can be. While, therefore, it was easy enough for so facile a poet and clever an artist as Breton to catch the salient points of so striking a character and mind and manner, it was not so easy to fill the public idea of so renowned a man,—to make that out of him which every one knew him to have been, and desired to see reproduced. With a great deal of merit, therefore, *Quien es Ella?* fell short of its purpose, and took but little hold of the public mind as a play,—though it very deservedly added to its author's reputation as a poet and scholar. If Breton had taken the same view of his own capacity which the critics seem to have adopted, he would probably not have undertaken a work of the sort. His plays are considered attractive, more from the grace and sprightliness of the dialogue, and their abounding wit, than from their delineation of character or interest of plot. Indeed, his pieces in one act are, I believe, the most popular; and that he is called the Scribe of Spain is some proof of the general opinion, that the loftier walks of the drama are not those which he treads most successfully. That he has published some sixty plays, entitles him, however, to a little consideration for the faults

"Quas aut incuria fudit,
Aut humana parum cavit natura."

The triumph of the season was the drama of *Isabel la Católica*, whose author, Don Tomas Rodriguez Rubí, a young poet from Malaga, had already won for himself a brilliant reputation. It was received with enthusiasm, night after night, by crowded houses, although the length of the performance, which lasted nearly five hours, might well have excused a more temperate display of admiration. The author was called out, as is the Spanish custom, to receive wreaths and bravos, and even the Queen did him the honor to make one of his audience. The play, as its title indicates, is founded on the eventful history of the Catholic Sovereigns,—a theme which the learning and genius of Prescott give us a right to be proud of, as in some degree our own. It seems to have been the object of Rubí to present a succession of striking historical pictures, rather than to construct a regular drama. The plot—if indeed there be a definite, pervading thread to the story—is at the best a rambling one, and the incidents are, certainly, quite treasonable to historic truth. Ferdinand, bad and morose, is thrown entirely into the shade, as king if not as husband, and Isabella is made the magnanimous victim of a tender and reciprocated, though innocent, passion for the Great Captain, Gonzalo de Córdova. Gonzalo is painted as a showy and sentimental hero of romance, and Columbus, who of course appears, is made to say and do many things, philosophical and geographical as well as personal, which would have astonished him quite as much as his predictions mystified the doctors of theology.

There is, of course, no particular reason why a dramatist should be held to strict account for the accuracy of all the situations in which it may please him to depict historical personages; nor do I conceive that he is under any obligation, as a matter of conscience, to cling to the authentic chronicles, as

Mr. Bisset has stuck to the Annual Register. There are certain limits, however, beyond which a popular writer cannot go, without doing some harm,—certain landmarks which ought, by all means, to be left standing. It might be proved, at this day, beyond the peradventure of Archbishop Whately's most impregnable logic, that Richard the Third of England was as erect in stature as the herald Mercury, and as good a king as Hamlet's father. Yet all the historical societies in Christendom could not make him otherwise than crook-back and tyrant, as long as Shakespeare should continue to be read and listened to. Many good people, I am sure, have died, entertaining impressions, as matters of faith, which they supposed they had derived from the Scriptures, and so would have fought for, but which had no better (and happily no worse) origin than Milton's Paradise Lost. Where a play, or any work of fiction, is sufficiently meritorious to become a permanent part of the national literature, and is founded on an interesting and important passage of the national life, it is the better rule, certainly, to take as few liberties as may be with the main historical fabric, and at all events not to turn the whole matter upside down. The history of which posterity has the luck to get possession is, at the best, but a skeleton, and a poet has quite scope enough for his fancy and imagination, in clothing it with flesh and raiment and giving it the speech and motion of a living creature. There are so many things of which the story has been left untold, and may, therefore, be told as one pleases, that it is hardly worth while to pervert the few which have been faithfully handed down. If a man wishes to make his characters pure fictions, there is no need of his giving them historical names. If, on the other hand, he professes to write a historical drama, he ought to have something of history in it, besides the names and the pictures. It was a very classical thing in Canova, no doubt, to model a statue of Napoleon, naked, with a globe and Victory in his right hand,—for Napoleon was a man and a conqueror, and the Romans commemorated such after that fashion. But it was a poor invention indeed, and a scanty genius, (with deference be it said,) which could make nothing newer or better than a disrobed Roman Emperor out of Bonaparte and the epics of which he was the hero! Why call the marble by the Corsican's name, when, but for the face, it might have answered as well for Titus or Augustus? The angels in periwigs, at the *Caridad* of Seville, may be in worse taste, but are not a whit less characteristic or significant.

But whatever may be the critical objections to *Isabel la Católica*, as a specimen of dramatic art, it certainly has very high merit as a poem, and is full of fine and striking situations. Its effect was, of course, greatly assisted by the scenic accompaniments and the gorgeous pageantry for which the subject gave such scope. But this was by no means all. The versification is stately and heroic; the poetry, excellent throughout, is, in many passages, of a high order; and the tone and spirit of the whole work are lofty and thoughtful. The author, as I have said, was praised and garlanded. It will hardly be believed that this must have been done by the special permission of the *Jefe Político*, who, but a day or two before, had published a long edict, of which the following was an article:—

"*Sixth.* It shall likewise be necessary to obtain, beforehand, permission to throw verses, crowns, or flowers upon the stage in honor of an artist; it being absolutely forbidden to throw any other thing expressive of satisfaction or censure, and likewise for the audience to address words or signs to the actors, as well as for the actors to direct such to the audience."

The name of the liberal and enlightened functionary who waged such war upon the consecrated prerogatives of the pit was Don José Zaragoza!

But the good fortune of Rubí was not confined to the relaxation, in his favor, of the *Jefe Político's* theatrical discipline. He received a substantial remuneration for his labors, which spoke as well for the public taste as for the liberality of the law regarding literary property. The existing statutes on this latter point prohibit the performance of any play without the author's consent, and give the copyright to him during his life, with remainder to his heirs or assigns for twenty-five years. During all this time he and they have the right to exact from the managers of all theatres where the play may be performed a certain percentage on the receipts, and to occupy or have the control of a certain number of places. Ten per cent. is the rate allowed, where the play has three acts or more, and three per cent., where there are but one or two acts; but these rates are doubled on the first three nights of performance. From this source, a free benefit, and the printing of the work, Rubí had realized, after the first fourteen nights, the sum of thirty-six thousand reals, or eighteen hundred dollars. As the author of the best work performed during the dramatic year, he received, according to law, the premium of five hundred dollars. In addition to this and to the emoluments which were likely to follow from future performances, there was settled on him, by the Commissary of the Crusade, a yearly pension of four hundred dollars. The fund on which the pension was fixed proceeds from the sale of dispensations, which relieve the purchasers from the necessity of complying with some of the minor requisitions of church discipline. The Commissary-General was of opinion that the play had contributed, by the elevation of its tone, to the advancement of the cause of religion, and determined to reward it accordingly. May the race of such Commissaries never become extinct!

I give these facts, as they appeared in the newspapers at the time, supposing that they will be of interest to the reader, as showing the public feeling towards literature and the respectable inducements which are held out for its cultivation, at least in one department. So far as such happy results are due to the laws, the Count of San Luis is entitled to the credit of having produced them. They do honor to his intelligence and taste. If he had been as familiar with Hamlet as he is with the dramatic poetry of his own country, he could not have more certainly provided against that "ill report" of the players, in his lifetime, than which even "a bad epitaph" is better.

XX.

Literature.—Books, Booksellers, and Book-Stalls.—Book-Hunting in Madrid.—Publishers.—Standard Works.—Historical and Geographical Dictionary of Madoz.—Cheap Publications.—Mr. Ticknor's History of Spanish Literature.—Its Character and Translation.—Gayangos.—Vedia.

WERE I called upon to choose between two cant words, I should say, that, so far as Madrid afforded a criterion and a stranger could judge, there was more "movement" than "progress" in literature, at the time of my visit to Spain. A good many works, original and translated, were issuing from the press, and there seemed to be a fair demand for them and a general disposition to read them; but there was not one really good bookstore in the whole city, and scarcely a publishing house of any enterprise or liberality. Besides this, and notwithstanding the generally creditable style of the newspapers, and their obvious disposition to cater for a certain degree of literary taste among their readers, there was not in Madrid a review, or magazine, or any literary periodical worthy of notice.

It is not easy to imagine any thing much drearier than a book-hunt in the Spanish capital. The established bookstores are, in general, mere shops, very few of which are supplied with catalogues; the most of them being unprovided, likewise, in the absence of the master, with any one who has even a speculative idea as to what the shelves contain. You present yourself at the counter, in the rear of which lie the treasures. The proprietor is not at home. "*Ha ido á la calle,*"—"He has gone into the street." His representative looks around after you have made your inquiry, shakes his head slowly, and answers, "*Creo que no!*"—"I believe not!" It is not worth while to appeal from his judgment. Your doubts will convert his belief into a certainty, and you thus take your leave with the most abiding conviction, that the gentleman who has given you your answer has made it take the negative form, for no earthly reason but to save himself the trouble of a search. This is the style in the principal bookstores on the main streets. It, however, fell within the range of my duties to procure, if possible, certain works which were somewhat rare, and I was compelled, in pursuit of them, to make a pilgrimage to most of the depositories of old and second-hand works. As a general rule, the proprietors of these establishments have not the remotest idea of the character or value of the books which belong to them. They buy them, often, by the *arroba*, like old iron, or rags, or paper, and arrive, as well as they can, at the prices that should be asked for them, by a series of ingenious experiments upon those who desire to purchase. If they happen, once in their lives, to have had a casual high bid, which they have refused in hope of a higher, neither time nor tide will ever induce them to sell the book in question for any thing less,—though it rot in waiting for a customer. The theory of moderate profits and speedy sales forms no part of their political economy. If a stranger presents himself, the standard rises. He is presumed not to inquire for any thing but what he wants, and to be able and willing to pay for what suits him. Should he be so unfortunate as to look twice at the same book, he must give up all hope of obtaining it, except on the owner's terms. The matter is resolved into a question of endurance in the bookseller's mind, and he regards it as settled that he will secure his price, if he can keep his patience. Being a Spaniard, he is quite equal to that.

A foreigner is not only troubled thus, himself, but becomes a cause of trouble to others. The unhappy book-fancier who follows in his wake is sure to find the market with an "upward tendency," and to learn, by way of justification, that a *caballero ingles* was there the day before, and was willing to give greatly more than the price demanded. Having myself, on several occasions, not far apart, discovered at one of these establishments certain works, which I had been long looking for and was anxious to obtain,—and having very cheerfully paid for them what the seller regarded as a high price, though, in view of my objects, it was very little,—I was amused at hearing, from a friend who frequented the same stall, that books on the subject to which mine related had of late become very valuable, as there was a young Englishman in town, who would buy them at any price.

By far the greater part of the book-stalls, where curious books are to be found, are in the open air. Sometimes they are arranged on shelves around a court, or on one side of a *plaza*, or against a church, or in some entry or open passage. Now and then they occupy the ground-floor of a house in some by-street,—the apartments which contain them being only lighted through the doors, which are of course left always open. In the latter case, you will find the proprietor, in the winter season, with cloak and hat on, sitting over his *brasero,* half torpid with cold. He will give you good day when you enter, and perhaps go through the form of removing the ashes from his coals; but he will rarely afford any other evidence that he is aware of your existence, unless you ask him a question. You will soon find, in most cases, that the best way of ascertaining what you desire to know is to examine for yourself, and you will accordingly prosecute your inspection, until your blood and curiosity fall below the freezing point. You will then bid him "Remain with God!" and he will tell you, in reply, to "Go with God!" so that you and your errand will be to him, when you depart, the mystery you were when you entered.

When the stall is entirely open to the weather, the owner sometimes has a sort of small sentry-box, to hold himself and his *brasero* with the most valuable of his properties,—sometimes he keeps watch and ward from the window of his lodgings, near the roof of an opposite tenement,—sometimes he walks up and down, *muy embozado,* in his cloak. It is a rare thing for him to manifest any more interest in your proceedings, than a sentinel at the door of a picture-gallery. If you keep the peace, and neither damage nor steal any thing, he does not appear to think that he has any concern with you. I confess that, on the whole, I was not displeased at being thus left entirely to myself. The modern system of salesmanship has become so much like persecution reduced to a science, that it is quite a luxury to be allowed the use of your own discretion, without being dragooned, by a shopkeeper's deputy, into looking at what you do not care to see, or buying what you would not have. A man in his sane mind, with the usual organs of speech, has a right to be treated as if he knows what he wants and is able to ask for it. At the same time, I am willing to admit, that, when he does make a demand for information, he is entitled to receive it in a somewhat more explicit and reliable shape than the mass of a Madrid *librero's* explanations.

It is not very likely that a mode of bookselling, so far behind the locomotive style of traffic which the century has brought forth, will long continue, even in the lonely by-places and chilly courts of Madrid. An intelligent Catalan, at the time of my visit, had already established a shop on the Calle de Alcalá, near the Prado, where he purchased second-hand books of all sorts, to sell, not to keep. He advertised, every morning, his principal acquisitions of the day before, with the prices, usually moderate, at which he was prepared to dispose of them. The result was, that it was necessary to be early on the ground, if you desired to secure your bargains. Books of rarity and value were constantly passing through his hands, and I am sure that he sold, in a month, more than a year's trade of all his cloak-wearing competitors put together. His advantage consisted in knowing something about his books and his business, and in being willing to put up with a small advance, for the sake of turning over his capital. Time was, when even Spaniards themselves were compelled to send to London in search of Spanish books which were really scarce. The agents of the London trade were always on the alert in the Spanish cities, and if any thing worth having found its way to the stalls,—as, in the changes of those days, was constantly happening,—they had every chance to capture it, before ordinary purchasers could know any thing about it. The Catalan of the Alcalá will put a stop to this, if he has not done so already. His constant demand must afford him the control of the market, and the publication of his lists will give the race to the swiftest. The example he has set, of intelligence and enterprise, cannot fail, by its success, to open the eyes of the booksellers proper, and perhaps stir them from their ancient stagnation. Before I left the city, it had begun to teach them lessons in the philosophy of advertising, and there was an almost daily increase in the number and extent of the notices of book-sales which headed the columns of the *Diario de Avisos*.

It is not to be inferred from the unpromising picture thus drawn, that the press of Madrid was altogether idle, or the hunter of books entirely without resources. The best French works, standard and ephemeral, together with Baudry's republications from the English, and a fair collection of Spanish books, could be found at Monier's on the Carrera de San Gerónimo. It may be interesting to the reader to know that the oily old man, with a pen in his mouth, who does the chief honors of that place, is the proprietor of the night-capped head and the "torso adorned with a shirt," which were thrust out a window to welcome M. Dumas to Madrid, on the morning when the illustrious Alexandre found himself in a strange court, where two women and five cats were sitting round a *brasero!* There were two or three shops, besides, on the Calle de Carretas, not far from the Puerta del Sol, where the best Spanish standard works, and occasionally some new publications, were sold, with great dignity and severity, at the most inflexibly high prices. It was next to impossible, however, so far as modern books were concerned, to find a copy of any publication for sale, except at the shop of the publisher. Getting out a work, of any size or character, was considered as forming quite an epoch in the history of the house, and for the pride of the thing,—as well perhaps as for the sake of realizing all the profits of a limited market,—every man seemed disposed to monopolize the control of his own handiwork.

The publishing establishment of "*La Publicidad,*" on the Calle de Correos, was probably the most extensive in Madrid. It certainly gave greater evidences of vitality than any other, in the number and style of its issues, as well as their literary caste. Two series, which were well advanced in 1850, were sufficient to give character to the concern. These were a republication of the best standard writers, from the formation of the language to the present day,—and another, of the *Codigos Españoles,*—the main body of Spanish written law. Of the first-named series, nineteen or twenty octavo volumes, out of the forty-five in preparation, have already appeared, and the first edition of several of the works had been absorbed so speedily, that a second was about to be issued while I was in Spain. The reprint of the *Codigos* was far advanced, and the volumes which had been printed were edited with learning and care, under the direction of the most distinguished jurists and legal antiquaries of Madrid. The Count of San Luis, with his usual solicitude for the advancement of letters,—when they did not interfere with "order," or meddle with ministers, or their doings or places,—gave the *Codigos* the full encouragement and support of his Department. He issued an order, directing all the municipalities representing two hundred householders or more to subscribe to the work, and credit themselves for the subscription on their tax accounts. All the *employés,* " active and passive," of the government, pensioners as well as office-holders, were authorized, by royal order, to have their subscriptions paid, if they should choose to make them, out of the arrears of their pensions and salaries. After reading the sad though humorous and graceful descriptions of the *" cesantes "* and the *" clases pasivas "* by Gil y Zárate, one hardly knows whether to smile or sigh over the fate of the poor people to whom the royal order was so gracious. After living or starving on promises and hope, they must have found great consolation, in the absence of food and fire, from being permitted to refresh themselves, out of their unpaid pittances, with quarto copies of the laws of the Visigoths! The learned jurisconsults of the Middle Ages should certainly not be offended at finding themselves gathered together in the pawn-brokers' shops, like Bible-Society bibles on the gin-counters in London!

The same sort of encouragement had been lent by the government to the eminent *Progresista* Deputy, Don Pascual Madoz, in aid of his publication which I have already mentioned,—the "Geographical, Statistical, and Historical Dictionary of Spain and her Dependencies." This is not the place for notices of books, but the work of Madoz well deserves to be referred to, as indicating both the existence and encouragement, in Spain, of a high degree of literary energy and spirit. In a country where every facility existed,—where statistical details were regularly collected and made accessible, —where there was constant intercourse between the various districts, and where universal education and an active and intelligent press had been long at work,—even there, it would have been no easy matter to do justice to the promises made on Don Pascual's title page. With scarcely any of those circumstances to aid him, he has nevertheless kept himself fully up to the level of his task. Fifteen large octavo volumes, the fruit of fifteen active and toilsome years, had already appeared, when I left Spain, and but one more was wanting, to complete the publication. As far as it had gone, it was, with great propriety, styled, by the Madrid journals, "a monumental work." There was not a village or a parish in the kingdom omitted. In regard to all, the details were as copious as could be desired. The historical notices were written with impartiality and fulness,—the political, artistic, and antiquarian dissertations, with liberality, taste, and learning. Statistical information of the most varied character—collected by the author himself, whose parliamentary career is notable for his accuracy in such matters—was for the first time given to the world. Commercial, agricultural, scientific, and professional knowledge, of a high grade, made the Dictionary valuable as an authority, no less than as a compendium for common reference. The literary merit of the whole was as considerable as its other recommendations, and it may, indeed, be doubted whether any other country possesses at this day a more worthy and complete epitome of itself. It is the more remarkable, too, from the fact, that in the midst of duties so multifarious as its preparation must have imposed, and principally on himself in person, the author has been active as a politician, and prominent and useful as a legislator and statesman. Few orators in the Chamber of Deputies carried more weight than he. None had more readiness, more energy, or a larger stock of the manageable information which tells in debate. He was one of the leaders of the liberal party, and had, as he deserved, its confidence; although, as he did not make a trade of politics, and was not afraid to say and do what he thought right, he was occasionally regarded as "impracticable,"—an epithet applied in Spain, as out of it, to the political riders who will not jockey to win. In fine, he was one of the best illustrations extant of the Catalan character,—

"Impiger, iracundus, inexorabilis, acer,"—

morally, intellectually, and in action.

In the "Glimpses of Spain" I had occasion to remark that the system of cheap publications, in numbers, had extended itself to Spain, and had been the means, as with us, of flooding the country with all manner of worthless and prurient trash. In Madrid this was particularly conspicuous. The appetite for all things French which prevailed there caused the novels from Paris to be chief in demand; and an activity of the press, which might have produced an indefinite diffusion of useful and elevating knowledge and have given a permanent impulse to the national literature, was wasted on translations of the very worst and most pernicious of the *feuilletons*. During the discussions in the Cortes upon the subject of reducing the postage on printed matter, one of the most respectable journals took occasion to insist, that it was the policy of the government to discourage, rather than to favor, the diffusion of the publications which the measure would most affect. It was but a scheme, the writer said, "to give scanty alms to hungry translators,—to put a premium on rendering bad French into worse Spanish." There was, I think, a general concurrence of opinion among the best-informed men, to the same effect. It seemed to be the impression, that as long as the booksellers could find a ready market for foreign extravagances which cost them nothing, they would continue to hold back from the literary labor of their own country the encouragement for which it was suffering so much. The activity which was displayed in the circulation of the bane, seemed to have stimulated an equal zeal in the preparation of the antidote. A literary friend informed me that the "Key to Paradise" was perhaps the only book which divided the suffrages of the trade with the "Mysteries of Paris."

When I left Madrid, the admirable "History of Spanish Literature," by our countryman, Mr. George Ticknor, was in the hands of Don Pascual de Gayangos, the celebrated Arabic scholar and antiquarian, and his friend Don Enrique Vedia, a gentleman of fine taste and accomplishments, for translation. Although it was impossible for any work to have received more unqualified commendation, from the whole body of Spanish literati, than Mr. Ticknor's history, and although the translators were men of the highest merit and reputation, there was great difficulty, nevertheless, in finding a publisher with sufficient spirit to take any liberal share in the enterprise. I have since seen a copy of the first volume, very elegantly printed, and bearing date at Madrid, but whether the publishing houses were entitled to any of the credit of its production I have not learned. Their unwillingness to engage in the adventure was a conspicuous illustration of their want of liberality and taste,—as well, perhaps, as of a similar defect in the book-buying public. There is, in the Spanish language, no thorough history of the national literature. The only native work that I am acquainted with, which professes to give a comprehensive view of the subject, at any length, is the *Resumen Histórico*, forming part of the *Manual de Literatura*, published in 1844 by Gil y Zárate, for the instruction of youth. It was not, of course, at all within the scope of such a work to meet the requisitions of an accurate scholarship. Sismondi's brilliant though superficial treatise has been translated, and was published at Seville, some ten years ago, but is not, I believe, to be readily obtained. Of the translation of Bouterwek's more learned and profound, though still imperfect work, only a single volume has seen the light. This was published, with many valuable annotations, in 1829; an epoch at which there was, unhappily, but little encouragement in Spain for labors of the sort. The length of time which elapsed, since its cold and discouraging reception, of course precludes all hope of the work's being completed. Amador de los Rios, one of its editors and the author of a book of some reputation, on the History of the Jews in Spain, was said to be engaged in 1850, on a work of his own, upon the same subject. It was generally believed, however, that he was not altogether suited to the task.

Mr. Ticknor's History is every thing that could be desired, to supply what is thus felt, in Spain, to be a pressing literary want. It is a history of books, as well as of literature. The variety, completeness, and accuracy of its details were—as I had occasion to know—a source of gratified surprise to the most learned of the Spanish literary archæologists. The acuteness and profundity of its criticisms, and its perfect comprehension and appreciation of the Spanish mind and taste and spirit, were regarded by the most eminent of the native writers and thinkers as all that a Spaniard could have been able to attain, and next to miraculous in a foreigner. A distinguished man of letters—whose opinion would be regarded

as oracular in Spain, and whose familiar acquaintance with
French and English literature rendered the basis of his judgment as broad as that of almost any one—told me that he
regarded Mr. Ticknor's work as "the best history of a literature" that he had ever seen. With the prestige of all this in
its favor,—and the security, besides, that any accidental error
or omission would be certainly remedied or supplied by the
translators,—so that the book could, at once, pass from their
hands into a standard authority,—its publication was hindered,
nevertheless, by the difficulties to which I have referred. That
it should have appeared, at last, in spite of them, is certainly
creditable to the zeal and energy of the editors, and bespeaks
a confidence in the literary discernment of the community,
which augurs something better for the future.

XXI.

QUINTANA.—THE JUNTA CENTRAL.—QUINTANA'S POLITICAL AND LITERARY LIFE AND WORKS.—NICASIO GALLEGO.—HIS POLITICAL CAREER AND POEMS.—DEBATES ON THE INQUISITION.—CLERICAL LIBERALITY.—DOS DE MAYO.—MARTINEZ DE LA ROSA.—HIS POLITICAL AND LITERARY LIFE AND WORKS.—ESTATUTO REAL.

OF the eminent literary persons whose career began before the revolutions of the present century, and whose works are numbered among the classics of the language, there survive now, in Madrid, but two, Don Manuel Josef Quintana and Don Juan Nicasio Gallego. The one a civilian, the other a priest,—both of them poets and both prominent in political service,—they have the further bond of a common devotion to the cause of rational liberty, and of common suffering for their efforts to establish and maintain it.

Quintana was born in 1772, and educated at Salamanca, under the direction of Melendez Valdez. He did not devote himself long or actively to the profession of the law, though it continued to be his nominal pursuit, but soon became one of the little band of men of letters whose leader—and in some sort patron—was the wise and accomplished Jovellanos. Of his first productions, which were dramatic, the tragedy of "Don Pelayo" gave him earliest distinction. A volume of lyric poetry, published about the same time, full of noble inspiration and a burning, lofty patriotism, commended him still further to the love and admiration of his countrymen. These works were followed by a volume of lives of celebrated Spaniards, to which, of later years, he has added several biographies, remarkable for their learning, grace, and historic impartiality. In 1808 he gave to the press several volumes of selections from Spanish poetry, commencing at the days of Juan de Mena and embracing the choicest productions of the best masters, with historical and critical annotations. The convulsions which followed the invasion of Napoleon drove Quintana at once into the arena of active and troubled life. The position of Secretary to the *Junta Central*, which he was called to fill, was perhaps the most important civil station, at that time, in the public gift, and to the ability with which Quintana discharged its duties, and the eloquence and power of the state papers which came from his hands, was attributable mainly the hold of the *Junta* upon public confidence. "It was a happy selection for that body," says the Count of Toreno, in his History. "The public opinion of the *Junta*, and of its plans and ideas, was formed from the masterly expositions of the Secretary." Certainly no writer of his day was capable of addressing to the people appeals so stirring as those with which, in poetry and prose, he kindled and sustained the national enthusiasm.

With the downfall of the constitution in 1814, fell the Cortes of which Quintana was a conspicuous member, and the day of tribulation began for him, as for all the ablest and worthiest of his countrymen. He was thrown into a cell in the fortress of Pamplona,—cut off from books and friends, and even denied the use of writing materials,—until the constitutional reaction of 1820. Upon that revival of free institutions, he was at once elevated to the Directorship of Public Instruction,—an office created by the constitution, and, in the hands of a statesman so enlightened and liberal as Quintana, one of the mightiest engines of national regeneration. The public acts of those days attest the wisdom and comprehensiveness of his ideas and administration, and there can be no doubt that there were seeds of knowledge and sound doctrine sown among the people, during the short reign of his system, which have sprung up to the best fruit in more recent times. The reëstablishment of despotism, in 1823, of course put an end to Quintana's public labors. He was fortunate in being allowed to cultivate his literary tastes in a quiet and distant province, where he remained until 1833, when the death of Ferdinand the Seventh recalled him to his old duties, and threw on him new honors. Created a member of the House of *Proceres* (or Peers) under the *Estatuto Real*, he prepared, in 1836, in conjunction with Gallego and others, a plan of public instruction, which was adopted by the government. In his legislative capacity he was the author of many able reports upon important political and economical questions, and when the present constitutional system was finally adopted, he was made a Senator. During the minority of Queen Isabella, he was intrusted with the direction of her education, and he is now President of the Council of Public Instruction. Of the distinguished positions to which he has, from time to time, been called, several have been the gift of administrations and parties to which he was opposed,— an honorable tribute to his ability and patriotism, and to the consistent integrity with which he has clung to the political principles of his early manhood. The persecutions and privations of a troubled life, and the insensible but steady change which is wrought in most men by the experience of years and of human affairs, have done little towards extinguishing the enthusiasm of the veteran *Progresista*. While others—and many of them among the most conspicuous of the original constitutionalists—have been tempted by the love of place or repose, or driven by their disgust for popular fickleness and ingratitude, almost into the arms of the system which they once abhorred, he has remained as he began. Too able and too clear-sighted to have overlooked the follies of his party, he has had the wisdom to foresee and the patience to await the ultimate triumph of the permanent over the transient.

If the bulk of Quintana's literary productions is less than might have been expected from his long and industrious life, it is because, during the greater part of it, he has sacrificed the leisure and tastes of a scholar to the sterner duties of a patriot. In the preface to an edition of his poems, in 1821, he speaks of several works which he had already nearly completed, when the war of the Peninsula broke out. "Since then," he says, "the duty of devoting myself to labors of a far different kind, the necessity of moving constantly from place to place, and the whirlwind of misfortune, persecution, and imprisonment, which has raged around me, have scattered my manuscripts, consumed the best years of my life, and set my literary plans at naught. The present circumstances of the country render it impossible for me to renew these last. Other writers will fall upon calmer times, and doubtless will be blessed with better fortune." In the edition of Quintana's works which has recently been published as a part of the series of standard authors referred to in the last chapter, there appear, for the first time, a number of letters addressed by him to Lord Holland, in 1823 and 1824, and containing a history of the curious and important political events of that day. Additional value is given to them by a striking analysis of the political history of Spain, from the reign of Charles the Third down to the period at which the letters were written. Upon this subject, and more especially in reference to the incidents which passed under the author's personal observation, the letters are a valuable contribution to the history of the century. The epoch is one of which little is truly known out of Spain, and in regard to which but little that is worth reading has been written there. The work of the Marquis of Miraflores, which is the principal source of information, is executed in the most partial and illiberal spirit, as if its author had but one idea in producing it,—that of recanting and atoning for all his previous enthusiasm in behalf of liberal and rational ideas.

In passing to and from my apartments in the House of Cordero, on the Calle de Pontejos, I had often given place upon the stairs to a venerable gentleman, apparently in robust health, of fine stature, and full of energy and vigor. The habit—soon acquired abroad, if it be not natural—of meddling but little with other people and their affairs, had prevented my making any inquiries in regard to him, and I had been more than a month in the same house with Sr. Quintana, and hearing his footsteps at night in the apartments above me, without knowing that he was my neighbor. The happy accident through which I made the discovery was the means, also, of giving me the honor of his acquaintance, under favorable auspices. It was a gratification which I should ill repay, were

I to say more than that he is surrounded in his old age by all the appliances which can make the enjoyment of a man of taste, education, and moderate desires,—the centre of a circle of quiet and cultivated friends, whose regard is dearer to him than the public homage, and from whom his learning, accomplishments, and virtues win reverence as profound as their affection. Few poets have lived to realize such pleasant disappointment as he,—in comparing the actual decline of his life with the melancholy anticipations expressed in his "Farewell to Youth." Few public men have lived through so many storms, to see the shadows fall so peacefully on so serene an evening.

Though but five years the junior of Quintana, Nicasio Gallego belongs, in a literary point of view, to a later epoch. Scarcely any of his most admired poems were given to the public until after Quintana's reputation had become national. During the French invasion, he was too busily occupied with public affairs to

"meditate the thankless Muse."

In the upheaving of all things old, and the confusion of things new and old as well, which made that period remarkable in Spain, the *Junta Central,* which had the reins of the provisional government, was overwhelmed with projects of legal and constitutional reform. All the political theorists in the land had set their heads and hands industriously to work, and all the subordinate *juntas* and pragmatical corporations sent in their recipes for the preparation of Utopias, warranted to last. To give to these multiform schemes the consideration to which they were entitled, on the score of merit or policy, and to cull from among them such as might be worthy to be ingrafted on the permanent legislation of the country, was of course impossible for an administrative body, in the throbs and throes of a revolution. A board was accordingly constituted for that purpose, and Nicasio Gallego was one of its most prominent and useful members. To the Cortes of 1810 he was an active and able Deputy, and distinguished himself especially by his zeal in advocating and perfecting the laws which secured the freedom of the press. His reported speech against the proposition to establish a censorship is full of large ideas and a manly and liberal philosophy. It is the more deserving of note, as the production of an ecclesiastic, controverting the narrower views which were urged, in the name of religion, by others of his class. Justice, however, requires it to be said, in this connection, that there was no measure before the Cortes of those days, involving the popular freedom and its guaranties, which did not find among the clergy who were Deputies some of its most able and strenuous supporters. Of this fact the discussion in regard to the Inquisition furnishes a curious and instructive illustration, well worthy the attention of those who think and write as if the odor of a roasted heretic were the only sweet-smelling savor in the Spanish clerical nostrils.

Services so eminent and patriotic as those of Gallego could not escape the vengeance of Ferdinand; and upon the return of his Majesty, Don Nicasio was made the victim of a state prosecution which lasted eighteen months, and ended in his imprisonment, for four years, in the Carthusian Convent of Jerez, without even the decent formality of a judicial sentence. From Jerez he was transferred to the Convent of Loreto, in the midst of a wilderness not many leagues from Seville. His Muse, always sluggish, was not greatly quickened by these vicissitudes; but the few poems which saw the light during his confinement are among the best of his productions.

On the return of the liberal party to power, in 1820, Gallego received a distinguished ecclesiastical preferment, of which Ferdinand took the earliest occasion to deprive him, when the wheel again went round. A life of trial and humiliation was the lot of the poet for the next ten years, during which he had an opportunity of tasting the bitterness of that exile shared by so many of his countrymen, and by himself so touchingly described :—

> "Otros, gimiendo por su patria amada,
> El agua beben de estranjeros rios,
> Mil veces con sus lagrimas mezclada."

To the desire for repose, so natural after so much weary and sad turmoil, is perhaps attributable, in some degree, the pertinacity with which he has resisted all attempts to bring him again before the world, by the publication of his works.

When Ferdinand died, the road of advancement lay open to Gallego, but he declined to accept various offers of the most honorable character. He consented, nevertheless, to act with Quintana, Lacanal, and Liñan in the preparation of a scheme of public instruction, and was, besides, for some time, a member of the Directory which had that matter in charge. Of later years, he has received the appointment of Senator, and now fills the distinguished station, likewise, of Perpetual Secretary to the Spanish Academy. The exquisite idiomatic purity of his compositions, and the almost oracular reverence in which his critical opinion is held, render the appropriateness of his selection for the last-mentioned post a matter of universal and gratified recognition.

The published poems of Gallego are so few, that only the highest order of excellence could give him the reputation he enjoys. They are chiefly lyrical and elegiac, and remarkable, according to their class, for nobleness and elevation of style and thought, or for refined and plaintive tenderness. His celebrated verses in commemoration of the Dos de Mayo,—the consecrated 2d of May, 1808,—the day on which the patriotism and self-sacrifice of Daoiz and Velarde and the enthusiasm and despair of the people of Madrid raised the bloody and at last triumphant standard of resistance to the aggression of the French,—have become as much a portion of the literature which dwells in the popular heart, as the Marseillaise in France or the "Mariners of England." The poem is published throughout the kingdom, as often as the years bring round the proud and mournful anniversary, and so admirable are both its spirit and its execution, that it challenges, at every repetition, not less the admiration of the scholar and the man of taste than the enthusiasm of those who have no canons of criticism but their feelings. Indeed, without entering into any critical analysis, I know no better idea of Gallego's style and merit, in the class of works of which I have spoken, than that which is given by likening him to Campbell. The same loftiness and correctness,—the same purity of taste and grace of expression,—the same trumpet-like capacity to warm the blood,—are conspicuous in both of them. Unfortunately, the reproach for "soul-animating strains,—alas, too few!" is equally applicable. Gallego has, it is believed, a large number of poems, which are fated to do him only posthumous honor. A friend, writing of his vigorous old age, says that "the request to publish is the only thing to which he is deaf." He is content, no doubt, with the regard and admiration of his contemporaries already won, and is not unwilling to conciliate posterity by a legacy.

It would be hardly fair to leave unnoticed, in this little sketch of two of the veterans of Spanish literature, one who, though somewhat their junior, still belongs, both in age and eminence, to the class which they represent. I refer to Don Francisco Martinez de la Rosa, admitted, I believe, on all hands, to be the most accomplished belles-lettres scholar in the kingdom, and, if not the most prominent in any particular department of literature, remarkable, certainly, for his ability and success in almost all. The vicissitudes of his political life and opinions have divided the public sentiment in regard to his talents as a statesman, and as this division has been accompanied with considerable feeling, such as political breaches always involve, it has produced a similar diversity of sentiment in respect to the degree of his excellence as a writer. Neither passion nor party spirit, however, has been able to extinguish, even in his enemies, that respect for his untiring industry and great attainments, which is conceded equally to his personal integrity.

The first public appearance of Martinez de la Rosa was in the Cortes elected in 1813, under the new constitution. He was sent by his native city of Granada, was an active supporter of the new system, and, though only twenty-five years of age, soon ranked among the most distinguished orators of the Congress. The vindictiveness of Ferdinand was always proportioned to the worth and ability of the rebel. Martinez was accordingly prosecuted with great rigor, but although an opportunity was offered him to adjure his opinions and be free, he preferred incurring the severe penalty of confinement, for ten years, in the state-prison of the *Peñon* in Africa. With the liberal reaction of 1820, his release came, and he went back to Granada, to be welcomed with triumphal arches and returned again to the legislature of the kingdom. Time, however, had begun to produce that change in his opinions, which in the first fervor of his youth and enthusiasm the hope of royal clemency could not precipitate. The constitution of 1812 had ceased to seem to him the perfection of government, for which he had once taken it. This change soon disclosed itself in his parliamentary course, and, in the contests between the executive and the legislature, he was generally to be found on the side of ministers. On a memorable occasion in the legislative annals of that epoch, he announced it as his principle, that "*defendiendo al gobierno se defiende tambien la libertad,*"—the defence of government is the defence of liberty also! This, which has been the maxim of his whole subsequent political career, gave at the time great provocation to the liberal party, which he was regarded as deserting, and has fixed him permanently in the public mind as the adherent and advocate of power. He was elevated to the Premiership in 1822, but was compelled, by the pressure of circumstances and of legislative opposition, to resign a post for which he had not practical qualifications or administrative tact. His parliamentary defences, however, of his principles and measures at that time, are among the most masterly and eloquent recorded efforts of the Spanish tribune; and it may be fairly inferred that his reputation, both national and Continental, was of some mark, when Chateaubriand congratulated himself on being Prime-Minister of France, at the same moment that the same high place was filled by Canning in England and Martinez de la Rosa in Spain.

The return of Ferdinand to absolute power drove Martinez into exile. He remained for the most part in Paris, where he formed many distinguished political and literary associations, the former of which contributed no doubt to confirm and fix his maturer and more conservative ideas of government. During his residence abroad, which continued until 1830, he published many poetical, dramatic, and critical works, some of them of a high order of merit, and none without the marks of scholarship and taste. One of his dramas, written in French, was in the course of representation with great success in Paris, when the revolution of the "three days" broke out. His Art of Poetry,—after the fashion of Horace and Boileau,—though in itself fuller of art than poetry, like its illustrious prototypes, was accompanied by a large body of copious and admirable annotations, amounting almost to a critical history of Spanish poetical literature, and displaying, not only a profound and intimate acquaintance with the subject, but all a poet's appreciation of its spirit.

After the death of Ferdinand, the known moderation of Martinez de la Rosa in his political sentiments commended him to the Queen Regent. The *Estatuto Real* (Royal Statute), the first compromise of despotism with the new order of things, was promulgated by an administration over which he presided, and is admitted to have been his individual work. Allusion has already been made to this hybridous constitution, and it is not worth while to analyse its character here. It created a legislature composed of two branches,—the one chosen for life and eminently aristocratic in its nature and functions,—the other a chamber of *procuradores*, to be selected from time to time, and mainly by the *ayuntamientos* or corporations of the cities and towns. As these latter functionaries for the most part were the creatures of the crown, or could at any time be made so, it was felt by the mass of the constitutional party, that the Cortes of the *Estatuto* were little better than a mockery of popular representation. When the decree for the organization of the system was read, the indignation of the liberals against its authors knew no bounds. Arguëlles, the coryphæus of the old constitutional *régime*, cried out " Apostasy!" lifting his hands to his head in despair; and even in the first legislature which the ministry convoked under the Statute, there were elements of the most vigorous and determined resistance to it. Martinez had all the oratorical ability and tact which baffle or break down an opposition in debate, but he wanted the strategy and energy to divert or overcome the pressure from without. He was, besides, too scrupulous for a statesman in his country and generation. He expressed opinions because he entertained them, and adopted lines of policy for no better reason than that he believed them to be right. The chances of such a game as politics have become, in all countries, were therefore necessarily against him, and when the defects of his system and the traits of his personal character were added to what a contemporary calls his " excessive rectitude," it is no marvel that his administration was troubled and disastrous. It lasted, however, nearly eighteen months. The equally bad success of those who followed him, under the same system, might, in other circumstances, have relieved him from the charge of being less wise than his fellows; but, unfortunately, he was the author of the system itself, so that, in one shape or the other, he must bear the responsibility of his own reverses and, it may be, of theirs.

Since the repeal of the *Estatuto*, and under the constitutions which have succeeded it, Martinez de la Rosa has been a member of the Cortes from time to time, and has maintained the parliamentary reputation of his more vigorous years, under all the disadvantages of age and the loss of political prestige. He was a Deputy when I was in Madrid, but was absent, as I have stated, as Ambassador at Rome. A warm and active sympathy with the Head of the Church, in his misfortunes, was certainly both natural and proper in a country so thoroughly and devotedly Catholic as Spain. The virtues of Pius the Ninth entitled him, besides, to veneration and affectionate regard, independent altogether of the homage which was rendered to his ecclesiastical supremacy. He was undoubtedly the pioneer in the liberal movement which has shaken Europe during the last few years, and there can be but little question, that, if he had been left to himself, to conduct with prudence and moderation what he had begun with wisdom and good faith, there would not now be seen the spectacle of a French army keeping watch and ward in the Eternal City. The presence of so distinguished a personage as Martinez de la Rosa, invested with the highest powers and dignities known to diplomatic custom, and following the exiled Pontiff through all the stages of his pilgrimage, was therefore, in every sense, appropriate and worthy of a reverent and generous people. It was nevertheless a striking instance of that perpetual change in men and nations, whereof all history is but the record, that

Spain herself, so frequently the victim of foreign intervention, should have sent an army to intervene in the domestic affairs of Rome; and that an individual who had so often denounced the hateful principle, and had himself so suffered from its operation, should have been the bearer of his country's mandate, to do unto others what she would not that others should do unto her. "For my part," says Montaigne, "I am with much more difficulty induced to believe in a man's consistency than in any other virtue in him; while there is nothing I so readily believe as his inconsistency; and whoso will meditate upon the matter, closely and abstractedly, will agree with me." As to the consistency of nations, not even that universal moraliser thought it worth while to moralise.

Besides the works to which reference has already been made, Martinez de la Rosa has subsequently found leisure for the production of many, both in poetry and prose, and some of them at least are likely to become a permanent portion of the national literature. His most elaborate work in prose-fiction —the historical novel called Isabel de Solis—has not been received with general approbation, the better opinion being that it lacks both spirit and invention. The historical biography of Hernan Perez del Pulgar is, however, an admirable specimen of its class, and would, in the judgment of many, be sufficient to make a reputation. Critical opinion, nevertheless, is divided even upon that point, and some have been found to denounce the whole production as a waste of time and labor on a worthless subject,—an attempt to write a chronicle of knightly days, in the obsolete language that belonged to them. Some time back, one of the prominent journals of Madrid was polite and amiable enough to announce, that, in the judgment of its editors, Martinez de la Rosa was little better than a *tonto*,—in plain language, a fool! I myself was surprised to hear a distinguished political rival say, that he was a flat poet and a dull novelist, with nothing striking about him, but large acquirements and larger vanity! In the mean time, by general consent, at home, he stands among the first of the men of letters of his day, and a recent sketch of his life announces his elevation, abroad, to the high dignity of President of the Institute of France. The balance would seem, under such circumstances, to incline somewhat in his favor, but the amusing diversity of opinion in regard to his literary merits may well serve to illustrate the uncertainty of contemporary fame, and to justify, in a new point of view, the wisdom of the philosopher of old, who said that the fortune of the happiest man alive was like the luck of a wrestler who was still in the ring.

XXII.

Standing Armies.—The Spanish Army, its Condition and Political Influence.—Immense Number of Generals.—The Scientific Corps.—Their Organization and Merits.—The Navy, its Improvement and Personnel.—Its Organization.—The Cuban Expeditions.—Discriminating Duties under our Act of 1834.—Development of Agriculture and Internal Improvements in Spain, in Consequence.—Santander.—Railroads.—The Canal of Castile.—Competition.

THE organization of standing armies has always been regarded as a step forward in the civilization of Europe. Not that there is any thing particularly humanising in horse, foot, and dragoons, of themselves or as an institution, but that, as men, since the days of Cain, have had a proneness to slay their brethren, it was a wise and happy thought to intrust the indulgence of that human weakness to a representative class, educated, equipped, and paid for the purpose, and to leave the rest of society leisure and opportunity for more profitable labor and gentler entertainment. No one needs be told how military establishments, like all other establishments clothed with public power for public purposes, have habitually, and on principle, used that power for their own. When kings grow into tyrants and priests into stipendiaries,—when republican Representatives resolve the whole task of legislation into making themselves Presidents, or profiting by the President-making of others,—it can be no matter of surprise that the drum and trumpet should have taught no better lesson of conscience and duty.

In Spain the weight of the army in political affairs has been a crying evil, since the very commencement of the liberal system. Its *pronunciamientos* have been always influential, and often omnipotent. Its leaders have found military service —or the rank which they have reached without it—a passport to the highest places of the state. The legislature is full of them,—the ministerial bench is rarely free from them. They are the boldest intriguers, the most open and avowed self-seekers. Where a civilian finds a pretext necessary, a brigadier-general affects none. If the government displeases him, he is indignant and confesses it. He represents an estate of the realm, and he has no hesitation in proclaiming that he will make himself feared, if the rulers will not love him.

Unfortunately, the evil of these things, though very obvious, is of very difficult cure. A nation like Spain, which has been for half a century in constant war, must of necessity have incurred heavy obligations to her soldiery. She has debts of gratitude to be paid in honors, and debts of a more substantial sort to be more substantially satisfied. As a portion of her wars have been dynastic,—and as in many of her political contentions the bayonet has done the duty of the ballot-box,— the victorious dynasty and the triumphant party have necessarily involved themselves in pledges to their troops, which must for a while not only forbid any serious reduction of the military scale, so far as the officers are concerned, but render it dangerous to resist the demands of popular chieftains.

There are external causes, too, at the present moment, which make it almost impossible for Spain to contract her army and its influence within the proper scope of a constitutional system. Of these, the troubled and uncertain state of Europe is obviously, an important one, but the chief obstacle is to be found in the proximity of France and the extent and efficacy of French influence. There seems to be a sort of spiritual or phreno-magnetic *rapport* proclaimed, if not existing, between Spain and her extraordinary neighbor. It has become almost a concession, that, if there is a revolution in France, there must be one in Spain, with or without cause. If there is a reaction at Paris, Madrid straightway becomes reactionary, whether there be or be not any thing to react from. A "crisis" at the one place is almost sure to produce a "crisis" at the other, without the remotest regard to the existence or non-existence of any thing critical. The patient smacks his lips, simply because the mesmerist has a disposition to drink. I have already alluded to the extent of this influence, but chiefly in reference to the absurdities in which it results. Its more serious consequences are quite as numerous. There was a popular outbreak in Madrid after the overthrow of Louis Philippe, merely because Louis Philippe had been overthrown. The government strengthened itself for its own preservation immediately after that outbreak, as was natural enough; but the increase of its powers was made a fixed political principle, as soon as it was perceived that in France it had become fashionable to shoot "fraternity." Since the accession of Louis Napoleon to the Prince-Presidency and the Empire, there is no knowing what might happen, were there any body in Madrid who was nephew to an uncle. Indeed, it would not be strange, if, before these reflections should see the light, there were a temporary interruption of the constitutional progress of Spain and the happiness and improvement of her people, by some Gallic harlequinade or other, on the model of the *coup d'état.*

Excluding the troops in the colonies, the Spanish army, in actual service in the Peninsula and the adjacent islands, was stated by Sr. Moron, in the Chamber of Deputies, to consist of one hundred and four thousand men. On the first of January, 1849, and throwing out of the calculation all subsequent additions, which were numerous, there were neither more nor less than six hundred and sixty-two general officers, the most of them comparatively recent promotions, distributed through that army! By the Blue Book of 1850, seventy-nine of these appear to have been lieutenant-generals. The French army, of about five times the number of soldiers, had about one third the number of generals, and the proportion was still smaller in Prussia. In Austria, with more than four times as many men, there were scarcely more than half as many commanders. It is true that the military system of Spain provides for the enrolment and reduction into service, on occasion, of what is called the *reserva*, or reserved division of the levies, so that the enormous disproportion which the statistics show between the rank and file and their superior officers, ought to be considered with a trifling qualification, on that account. But taking all things into the calculation,—not forgetting the troops in the colonies, or overlooking the necessity of supernumerary promotions, during the progress and at the close of a civil war of protracted duration,—it must be admitted that there is little to redeem the military establishment of Spain from mere absurdity in the particular referred to. Even if the *reserva* were called by circumstances into activity, there is not much in the history of the past to induce the belief, that the opportunity would be taken to make the officers deserve their honors by the laborious discharge of duty. On the contrary, it is more than likely that the occasion would be greedily seized to enlarge the list of *generales*, &c., yet more extensively, and to decorate with new ribbons and crosses, if such could be found, those who had already reached the summit of actual rank.

In his guide-book, published about the middle of 1849, and containing a great deal of useful compendious information, Mellado states that the *empleados* connected with the War Department amounted to about eleven thousand, exclusive of soldiers. It will not thus be deemed at all remarkable that the *presupuesto*, or budget of 1850, should have appropriated nearly sixteen millions of dollars to that branch of the public service. When it is considered that the ordinary provision for the Naval Department, in the same year, reached about three millions and a half, and that a very large increase in the navy has since been rendered necessary, by the piratical plans which have been agitated in the United States, it will be seen that Spain would have abundant reasons for being represented in the Peace-Congresses.

With whatever truth the contrary may have been said twenty years ago, there can be no question that the Spanish army, at the period of my visit, was in a high state of discipline, and thoroughly instructed in the best improvements of modern military science. The regiments which went to Rome attracted great admiration, although the duty assigned to them afforded but little opportunity for the display of their more substantial qualifications. I saw some of them after their return, and heard ample testimony borne by competent judges, without national bias, to the excellence of their equipment and drill. The garrison of Madrid was composed of a very fine body of men,—both infantry and cavalry,—lithe, active, and strikingly martial in their bearing. I could not help frequently observing, however, among the company officers of the line, a manifest inferiority to the rank and file in soldierlike appearance. It was mainly attributable, I thought, to the comparative youth and immaturity of the captains and lieutenants, some of whom seemed hardly fit to encounter the rudeness of war's alarms. It is still but fair to say, that the worst enemies of the army, as a political engine, were constrained to acknowledge the personal bravery of its officers. It would indeed be hard to find a more gallant band of gentlemen, and it was on that account the more to be regretted that so many of them should be tempted, by a corrupting political system, to hang upon the favor of a court.

Captain Widdrington[1]—whose professional pursuits, as well as his long residence and opportunities of observation in Spain, entitle his judgment to great respect—speaks very favorably of the education and attainments of the officers attached to the scientific departments. The period to which he refers was about that of Ferdinand's death, and the improvement which

[1] In a review of the "Glimpses of Spain," the London *Athenæum*—referring to the favorable notice I had taken of this gentleman's admirable books on Peninsular affairs—was liberal enough to suggest, as the source of my commendation, that no doubt the captain wrote "U. S." after his name! I should be glad if it were true, but as it is not, I must be content with having introduced to the *Athenæum* an officer of whom the Royal Navy ought to be proud, and an author of whose name it was scarcely reputable in a literary journal to be ignorant.

has taken place, since that time, in the preparatory system, would no doubt render his commendation more generally applicable now. Although, however, it is true, as he observes, that the artillery and engineer corps have always been remarkable for the liberality of their political sentiments, and have almost universally encountered the greatest sacrifices in the maintenance of such opinions, it is equally true, that they have habitually refrained, more than any other branches of the army, from intermeddling with the ordinary politics of the country. No doubt the direction of their intellectual occupations has had a good deal to do with this, and there is even more, perhaps, in the fact, that they have intellectual occupation of some sort, without any particular reference to its nature. The mathematics do not fit a man peculiarly for playing *pretendiente*, if the inclination occurs to him; yet it is not likely to occur to him, if he has the mathematics, or any thing else, in his head, by which he earns an honorable livelihood, with mental improvement and a respectable position. But that the engineers and artillery officers are not politicians generally, is probably owing to the particular organization of those corps, more than to any other cause. Promotion, with them, follows the rigid rule of seniority; whereas, in the other divisions, he who has friends, male or female, in the palace or about it, rises soonest and most infallibly. The visible good effect of the stricter system ought certainly to suggest to the law-makers the propriety of extending it to the whole military establishment. Promotion, given as the extraordinary reward of extraordinary merit, in the legitimate field of a soldier's duties, is of course an incentive to honorable and just ambition, and elevates the character of the army, while it prejudices no other interest of the state. But where advancement is the prize of ante-chamber servility, political subserviency, or small intrigue, it can have no beneficial public result, military or civil. Numerous instances of its ridiculous and prejudicial consequences were very familiar, when I was in Madrid, to all who knew any thing of public men and political affairs. With us, the habit of looking to military chiefs as political leaders, merely because they have fought battles, is bad enough, no doubt,—and none the less so, because now and then the education and habits of the camp may have developed eminent executive qualities in particular individuals. That must, in spite of exceptions, be in the main a vicious rule, which regards any thing aside from fitness, in the choice of agents for any purpose. But with us, the soldier, wise or unwise, takes off his spurs when he becomes a political leader. His military career may secure his elevation, but it ends when that begins. General Narvaez, as Prime-Minister, might wear on state occasions, if it pleased him, the uniform of a Captain-General. It would be odd, with us, to see a President inaugurated in epaulettes. As long as the Spanish system lasts, irregularity and uncertainty must be looked for, and constitutional government cannot be said to exist in its purity. Our system will probably give us many bad rulers; but they will be simply inferior Presidents, not dangerous generals.

In the Spanish navy, promotion is likewise dependent upon fixed rules, and the result is identical with that which has already been adverted to, in connection with the scientific corps of the land-service. It is a very rare thing for naval officers to be heard of in association with political intrigues, or, indeed, anything political; although they are remarkable as a class for their ability, and for the extent of their general, as well as professional attainments. This fact illustrates the political wisdom of their organization, even more decidedly than the same result following the same cause in those divisions of the army to which it is applicable. Until lately, the Spanish navy had been for many years in a state of sad inactivity; and the opportunity for any practical exercise of the scientific acquirements which the routine of the service prescribes, was extremely insignificant. Sailors and naval commanders cannot be made or occupied without ships, and the disasters of the preceding and the present century had not only destroyed the proud armaments of Spain and exhausted the means of their restoration, but in a great degree broken the spirit which might have repaired her fortunes on the sea. All the temptations which leisure creates were therefore thrown in the way of the officers of the navy. Ambitious, and at the same time capable and well-educated, they had every inducement to seek, in the palace or the halls of legislation, the command which they had no quarter-decks to supply. The influence which countervailed so natural a tendency must have been strong, especially when they beheld field-marshals and generals changing into senators and secretaries all around them, and when there was scarcely a scale of power into which some one did not fling, before their eyes, a sword no heavier than theirs.

I have said, that the necessity of defending her colonies from the aggressive expeditions of our buccaneers has produced a decided augmentation of the Spanish navy within a few years past. In addition to the regular budget for 1850, a million and a half of dollars were appropriated, by special decree, in March of the same year, principally to the construction of steam-ships. Considerable activity had previously been given to the workshops at Ferrol and La Carraca, and the then Secretary, the Marquis of Molins, had devoted himself with considerable energy and enthusiasm to the renovation of his Department and the increase of its efficiency. The same policy has been pursued with constant vigor down to the present time. Liberal and wise appropriations have been successively granted in furtherance of it. Large purchases for the Spanish arsenals have been made in our own timber-markets. The naval schools have been reorganized; the modern improvements in naval architecture have been studiously consulted; the quiet acquisitions in nautical science, which men like Navarrete had for years been hiving, have found scope for their display and application. The national pride has become enlisted, and the opposition but rivals the government in encouraging and following its suggestions.

Independently, indeed, of the principal cause of all this, which has been mentioned, the increase of the navy was absolutely required by the improving commercial activity and prospects of the kingdom. Not that trade has been doubled, as the navy has been,—but that the military marine was so utterly unequal to the discharge of its proper duties, as to need a complete reorganization, in order to meet the most moderate advance in commerce. Public measures or events are rarely to be regarded in the exclusive light of cause or effect. They are generally both. An increase of naval strength, suggested by an increase of commerce calling for protection, must, in its turn and by the very protection which it affords, give an impulse to commercial development. A commercial marine, upon the other hand, developed by any cause whatever, must not only create and enforce a necessity for the increase of naval power, but must furnish the means of naval growth, in a body of experienced and hardy seamen and in the awakened interest and sympathy of the nation. It may thus turn out, that the attempts of a portion of our floating and licentious population to enrich themselves at the expense of Spain and her colonies, and of our national good name, may be one means of burnishing once more the rusted trident of the Peninsula, and restoring the goodly trade which once flourished under its guardianship.

There is a portion of our national legislation, in reference to Spain, which shows how important results may sometimes follow from causes apparently wide of them. It perhaps illustrates quite as well the remark just now made, as to the double light in which public measures ought commonly to be regarded. I refer to the matter of "discriminating duties," levied on Spanish vessels from the West Indies, under the act of 1834. The reader may perhaps remember an able and statesmanlike communication on the subject, made by Mr. Secretary Corwin, to Congress, during its last unprofitable session. The act was passed as a measure of retaliation, and would, perhaps, have been sufficiently just, if it had not been unwise. It very soon resulted in excluding Spanish vessels from our ports, and to the extent of throwing the carrying-trade between the United States and the Islands into the hands of our ship-owners, it answered its purpose speedily and bravely. But our legislators seemed to forget that a carrying-trade implies commodities to be carried, as well as vessels to carry them. They lost sight of the fact, that the articles of merchandise which we contributed to the consumption of the Islands could nearly all be purchased elsewhere, and that the advantage which our ports enjoyed, from their proximity, could readily be counterbalanced by custom-house facilities and exemptions, extended to importations in Spanish bottoms. These facilities and exemptions were in fact afforded. Other nations, wiser than we, were willing to produce and sell, and let the Spaniards themselves carry. The consequence followed, that a large portion of the demand from the Spanish West Indies was diverted to other markets, so that our trade with them is now confined in a great degree to our own products, and to certain ponderous articles of no very great value, which our locality enables us to monopolize in spite of our legislation. The large mass of foreign commodities which we formerly sold them are now purchased by them, directly, from the same sources which furnish our own supplies. Even in the articles which we continue to furnish, the sum of our trade bears no proportion whatever to the immense increase of the West India demand. The benefit, therefore, which our shipping interests may seem to have reaped in some particulars from the measure in question, has been most dearly paid for by sacrifices which are now too obvious to escape the attention of any political economists, except members of Congress on the eve or in the reaction of a Presidential campaign.

But the result, as it affects the United States, is not the point to which the purposes of this work would make me direct the reader's attention. Driven from our ports, by the onerous duties imposed on them and the vexations with which the imposition was often accompanied, the Spanish ship-owners naturally enough sought their home-markets, whenever the articles required by the colonial trade could be found there. The new demand and opportunity of shipment, in their turn, quickened production and supply. Large quantities of rice, which till then had almost rotted on the Mediterranean coasts of Spain, began to fill the warehouses of Cuba, in the stead of our rice which was excluded. Bread-stuffs, which had found no outlet from the boundless and inexhaustible grain-growing regions of Castile, began to pour through the gates of Santander. A new and extraordinary impulse was given to the trade of that city. Numerous mills were erected in its vicinity; new quays were built; all commercial facilities were, as far as possible, augmented. Internal improvements were begun, and with vigor, for their usefulness and profit were certain. A new source of wealth was in fact created,—a new development given at the same moment to agriculture and commerce, and all the collateral departments of both. By the last information from the province, it appears that, under the direction of an English company, a railway from Santander to Alar was about to be commenced at both ends of the line, and that a continuation of the same work from Alar to Burgos and Valladolid was already partially under contract. The Canal de Castilla, originally projected by the wise foresight of the Marquis of Ensanada, about the middle of the last century, was to have had one of its *termini* at Santander, and there has been of late an active movement towards its completion. Indeed, the rivalry which at present exists between those who are interested in the canal, and the company having in charge the Valladolid branch of the railway alluded to, furnishes the best evidence of the importance of the interests involved and the spirit which they have awakened.

The consumption of Castilian bread-stuffs in the West Indies has now become so general, and the improvements which have been made in their preparation and packing have rendered them so desirable, that it is much to be doubted whether any change in our policy, thus late, can open the way to profitable rivalry. The works of internal improvement to which I have alluded, and the other enterprises connected with them, are in a great degree sustained by the colossal capital of the Cuban merchants and bankers, so that there is but little probability of their failure from lack of liberal support. The experiment on our part is nevertheless worth trying, for as political economy is the science of selfishness, we had as well be scientific, like the rest. If the Spaniards be wise, they will take care of themselves, on the same principle, and not commit the folly of starting in the race of unrestricted competition, until they have trained themselves for it, like their competitors, by a course of rational self-protection.

XXIII.

Ecclesiastical System and Reforms.—Abolition of the Inquisition.—Its Character.—Llorente.—Campomanes.—Floridablanca and Jovellanos.—The Monastic Orders.—Their Suppression.—Confiscation of Church Property.—Reforms of the Church System.—Pay of the Clergy.—Character of the Secular Clergy.—Clerical Influence.—Toleration in Spain.—Protestant Travellers and Prejudices.—Exaggerations, &c.

NO entirely correct idea can be given of the state of Spain, under her present institutions, without some reference to her ecclesiastical system. The subject, nevertheless, is one which it is not easy to touch without giving offence; for all experience shows that the utmost candor and the best intentions afford no security, in such matters, against the harsh judgment of those whose opinions or prejudices are invaded by an effort to be faithful to the truth.

Spain has long been considered and treated, by ultra-Protestant writers, as the reduction of the Roman Catholic Church to an absurdity. All the errors and follies and abominations of the many despots who have reigned over her,—all the evils that have been entailed on her by foreign invasion and domestic broil,—all the obstacles by which nature and circumstances have interrupted the march of her civilization,—have, in their turn, been set down to the influence of her clergy, and the pernicious doctrines they have taught. When public, or literary, or religious opinion has once begun to run in a particular channel, observation generally takes the same direction. The foregone conclusion is a sort of mould for the facts which come after it. Men explain the phenomena by the theory, instead of correcting the theory by the phenomena. The religious view to which I have adverted has thus shaped the observation of nine-tenths of the travellers who have visited Spain from Protestant countries. Almost every one of them has contributed his statement of illustrative facts to the common stock,—many of them in the best faith,—some of them because such things make up a lively and picturesque book,—others because they have discovered that nothing sells so well as a little piquant uncharitableness. Of this last the trade is perfectly aware, and can calculate you the probabilities of the market accordingly.

While the anti-Catholic feeling thus induces a disposition to resent, as too partial, the most moderately favorable view of Spanish ecclesiastical matters, the Catholic sentiment, on its part, is somewhat prone to censure the concessions which impartiality demands. This is natural enough, certainly. By systematic denunciation of any cause, you may readily provoke its advocates into admiration, or at all events into the sturdiest defence, of its very errors and vices. Every one remembers what a hero persecution made out of Wilkes. But although the effort to write down Catholicity, by writing down Spain, may account very satisfactorily for the adverse feeling and effort of the Catholic press, it furnishes no reason for blindness or concealment on the part of those who desire to look at the field of controversy without favor or animosity. Even with the profoundest respect for the faith which is professed by Spain as a nation, and for the sincere convictions of those who maintain it, a man cannot read Spanish history, or know the Spanish nation, and ignore the fact, that the institutions with which the national religion has, until lately, been surrounded, have had much to do with the decay of public prosperity. To this many of the most eminent of the Peninsular divines and statesmen have borne ample testimony, on solemn public occasions, and among intelligent men in Spain there is, at the present day, no difference of opinion in regard to it. It is a question entirely outside that of faith, and is wisely and properly so regarded. As to the right and prudence of the particular ecclesiastical reforms which have taken place since the inauguration of the liberal system, there has been and continues to be much dispute; but, that reform of some sort was needed, seems to be the concession of all parties whose opinions are worth recording.

On the other hand, again, I am quite as well satisfied, that the extreme Protestant opinion, so popular in England and this country, with regard to Spain, is very much exaggerated, and has grossly magnified the abuses of the Spanish Church, as well as unjustly disparaged its clergy. When the various ecclesiastical changes of the century were under consideration, the subject was approached with all the care which its importance suggested. Not a step was taken without full and often hostile investigation; and the members of the liberal party, clerical as well as lay, brought to light, without forbearance or reserve, all the details which went to show the necessity of the reforms in contemplation. In a country where there is no established religion,—where every denomination is under the severe and constant scrutiny of those who entertain antagonistical opinions,—it may not always be easy to arrive, by confession, at the whole truth, when its exposure would be unpleasant. Men will conceal from the criticism of opponents what they have no disposition to uphold themselves. But in Spain there was no anti-Catholic organization to scrutinize or censure. If there was no reason for exaggerating, there was no temptation to soften down the truth. To use their own expressive phrase,—*todo se quedó en casa*,—it all remained within doors,—a family secret. Besides this, whatever may be their habit when the national pride is involved in controversy with strangers, the Spaniards in their domestic discussions are not generally self-flatterers. They laugh at what is ridiculous among themselves with as keen a relish, and denounce what is worthy of denunciation with as healthy an earnestness, as if they had no part or lot in the absurdity or the sin. Not even John Bull can grumble more sturdily than they, though their pride is perhaps less visible than his, through the holes they pick in their mantles. I allude to these things for the purpose of showing the reliance justly to be placed upon the estimates made by the Spaniards themselves of their ecclesiastical abuses. I cannot but consider them far better guides than the opinions formed by strangers, upon observation necessarily limited, and not always had from an intelligent or impartial point of view. There is a perverseness, sometimes, in sectarian animosity, which would find apples of discord in the very garden of Eden.

The principal changes which the revolutions of this century have wrought in the Spanish ecclesiastical establishment are three,—the suppression of the Inquisition, the abolition of the monastic orders, and the assertion of a more direct and absolute control by the government over the revenues and administrative polity of the Church. The decree levelled by Napoleon at the Inquisition, soon after his invasion, was of comparatively small practical importance,—the invasion itself having very summarily put an end, for the time, to the power and oppressiveness of the institution. The action, moreover, of a foreign and intrusive government, was perhaps more likely to rally the resistance than to conciliate the respect of the people, or to concentrate their moral force upon any reform, no matter how salutary in itself. The movement in question was nevertheless a useful precursor to the action of the national Cortes, which, by solemn decree, in 1813, pronounced the existence of the Inquisition incompatible with the constitution. I have already alluded to the discussions which preceded the adoption of this measure. They were reported, at the time, in a separate volume, unconnected with the ordinary debates of the Cortes, and had an extensive circulation and, I have no doubt, an excellent effect. I know no work, the perusal of which would do more towards the removal of religious and political prejudice from a candid mind. I have never turned to it without an increased respect for the intelligence and liberality of the Spanish clergy, as well as the political sagacity, boldness, and, at the same time, moderation, of the much abused Cortes of that day.

With Ferdinand the Seventh, the Holy Office resumed its sway, in 1814, but having been again suppressed by the constitutionalists, in 1820, it has never since been revived. It had in fact long ceased to perform the bloodier functions which made it most odious. An unhappy woman, who in 1781 was burned at Seville as a witch, was the last who suffered its awful ministrations. Her execution was particularly extraordinary, when we consider the character of the reigning monarch, and the great liberality which distinguished the measures of his government. It excited so much abhorrence, as to prevent the possibility of a repetition.

The Inquisition has been the subject of such merited execration from the whole civilized world, that any attempt to qualify the general estimate of its enormities is not likely to receive even fair consideration. It is nevertheless proper to observe, that, among the most enlightened and liberal of the Spaniards, the work of Llorente, on which so much historical judgment is predicated, holds no very high place as a trustworthy narrative. The author, his compatriots say, had all the spirit of a renegade, and, after having derived from the Inquisition, in its day, all the honors and profits of its secretaryship, was not unwilling to reap the credit of candor and repentance, by exaggerating the sins to which he had given countenance. Many of the most important records, on which his statements profess to be founded, were destroyed by him, under the direction of Joseph Bonaparte. There may have been good reason for this, but the result of it is, that the personal veracity of Llorente is the only existing guaranty for the truth of much that has passed into history. Unfortunately, however, for the tribunal, there is quite enough known from other sources, to make its abolition a cause of just delight to all who sympathize with freedom, or have an interest in the progress of our race. That it was in fact a political engine, quite as much as a religious institution,—at all events of later years,—there is now, I believe, no doubt; and much of the odium which it has thrown on the Church will, one of these days, I am sure, be transferred to the State, which deserves it. But no change of historical opinion upon that point can weaken men's detestation of its principles, or palliate the iniquity of its practices.

The measures of the Cortes of 1813, in regard to the Holy Office, were accompanied by corresponding legislation with respect to monastic institutions. In this, as in the other case, the initiative had been taken by Napoleon and the government of Joseph, whose military resources, being entirely independent of the popular prejudices, and unaffected by the influence of the monks over the more ignorant portions of the people, enabled them to take boldly, and at once, a step which would have required infinite caution and delay on the part of the revolutionary authorities. Even after the movement made by the French, the Cortes found it necessary to deal tenderly with the matter, and the provisions of their legislation in regard to it looked only to the most prudent and gradual reform. Such as they were, however, they were not saved by their wisdom from the destruction with which the whole of the liberal system was overwhelmed, on the return of Ferdinand. In 1820, the reform, thus interrupted, was renewed and prosecuted in a bolder spirit, and, by way of securing its permanency, the possessions of the different orders were sold to private purchasers, under the direction and with the guaranty of the government.

It is not proposed to enter here into the vexed question as to the right of the civil ruler, for the benefit of the whole of the governed, to appropriate to the public treasury, or throw into the operative hands of individuals, the property lying "dead" (as the law has it) in the possession of ecclesiastical communities. In the absence of any particular constitutional justification of such measures, their propriety depends, perhaps, upon the simple and fundamental inquiry, whether nations, like individuals, possess the right of self-preservation. So far as the laws of Spain are concerned, the whole subject underwent the most learned and scrupulous examination during the reign of Charles the Third. The works of Campomanes and Moñino (afterwards Count of Floridablanca) demonstrate, in the fullest and most satisfactory manner, that the accumulation of property in mortmain was in palpable violation of the letter and spirit of the fundamental institutions of the realm. The celebrated work of Jovellanos, on the *Ley Agraria*, published in the succeeding reign, was equally demonstrative of its ruinous influence upon agriculture, and the general national prosperity. Whether these eminent jurists and statesmen were at fault or not in their conclusions, the legislation of subsequent times has, at all events, been predicated on the assumption of their correctness.

Upon the second overthrow of the constitutional party, in 1823, the monastic institutions were reëstablished, and the whole of the property which had belonged to them was wrested from the purchasers and their aliences, to be devoted to its original purposes, without any return of purchase-money or allowance for improvements. Indeed, the parties in possession were compelled, where the monks required it, to restore the whole, at their own expense, to the condition in which they had purchased it. Whatever may have been the rights of the ecclesiastics, the iniquity of this proceeding, so far as the government was concerned, is beyond apology. Many families were ruined by it, and large numbers of innocent and industrious persons exposed to great pecuniary loss. The deep and general resentment which it provoked was, however, directed chiefly against the monks, and was aggravated in time, and by additional causes of dissatisfaction, into decided and uncompromising hostility. The final overthrow of the monastic system, and the stringency of the measures which were adopted with a view to it, may be in a great degree attributed to the existence of this feeling and its primary cause. The first of the *Moderado* cabinets were disposed to temporise with the subject, and attempted to legitimate their limited interference with it, by some of the articles of the Council of Trent. But the monks, in the mean time, took such active and open part in the Carlist rebellion, as to leave the government no pretext for casuistry, and no safety in forbearance. Self-preservation and the popular pressure from without soon put an end to delay and scruples. The final blow was stricken, by royal decree, in the spring of 1836, under the administration of Mendizabal, and the Cortes, in the summer of 1837, gave to the action of the Executive the deliberate and authoritative sanction of the national will. All convents, colleges, and communities of monks were at once suppressed, (with a few temporary and special exceptions,) and the nunneries were reduced to the smallest number capable of containing those of their inmates who were unwilling to reënter the world. The prohibition of religious vows, from that time forth, insured the gradual diminution and ultimate extinction of the whole monastic body.

The monks thus ejected from their cloisters (*exclaustrados*, as they are called) passed, many of them usefully, into the service of religion as parish priests. Others remained, here and there, in charge of the churches belonging to their orders, which were preserved as works of art, or were regarded as essential to the religious necessities of their neighborhoods. The great majority dedicated themselves to such secular employment as they could procure, and many of them grew into useful and excellent citizens; while others, incapacitated by the habits of long years, soon surrendered industrious pursuits for idleness and mendicancy. The decree of suppression provided for the support of the *exclaustrados,* out of the fund to be raised by the sale of conventual property. It was, however, but a miserable pittance at best,—not intended, for obvious reasons, to be altogether relied on,—and it has always been paid with sad irregularity. In many cases, therefore, where private charity has not interfered, the lot of the aged and infirm monks and nuns has been cruelly destitute. A few instances within my own observation satisfied me that, like every sudden and sweeping change of public policy,—no matter how just and wise in itself,—the reformation of conventual abuses has been purchased at the expense of grievous individual wrong and suffering. But general rules, unhappily, can hardly be framed so as to avoid particular results which make their application painful; and the philanthropy of statesmen is not much to be complained of, if the aggregate of good is, on the whole, upon its side.

The traveller, who looks at Spain from the picturesque point of view, has certainly small cause to thank the political necessity which has removed the cord and cowl from the dim cloisters where their shadows fell. Decay has commenced its work, already, upon many of the magnificent temples which the care of the friars kept perfect. Stately buildings, once wealthily endowed, where architecture and the kindred arts accumulated all their pomp, seem naked now, and are lonely and desolate, without them. Gardens and groves which they tended—plantations and vineyards which might have been the heritage of princes—have been parcelled out among small proprietors, until subdivision seems to have made them insignificant. Green patches of forest, rare in Spain, which their intelligence and taste had induced them to preserve untouched, through all their tribulations, have disappeared, in some places, before the axe of the lay proprietor. Ruined walls, dismantled towers and belfries, meet the eye of the wayfarer sadly, as he crosses the deserted plains or the wild mountains,—making the solitude and gloom of the landscape yet more impressive and severe. On the streets, and in the public walks and places, the bright colors of the national costume are relieved no longer, for the artist's joy, by the dark groups in sombre drapery, that used to be the theme of every pencil. A striking characteristic of Spanish scenery and life has passed altogether away.

But men live, now-a-days, for something more than pictures. The monks had lost public respect, and with it their usefulness. The distribution, which has destroyed the beauty of the convent lands, has no doubt doubled the productiveness of their soil. The alms which supported the monastery, and kept its architecture and its ornaments from decay, have remained in the peasant's hands, for the comfort of his family or the improvement of the little spot he cultivates. The spiritual instruction of the young and ignorant has become the care of the secular clergy, whose education and higher gifts, intellectual and moral, make the change a national blessing. The impoverished industry and neglected agriculture of the land have received an accession of vigorous labor, no longer tempted into sloth by the seductions of a privileged and sensual life. In the cities and larger towns, the convent buildings have been displaced, to make room for private dwellings of more or less convenience and elegance, or have been appropriated as public offices or repositories of works of art. The extensive grounds, which were monopolized by some of the orders, in the crowded midst of populous quarters, have been converted into walks or squares, dedicated to the public health and recreation. In a word, what was intended, in the beginning, as the object of monastic endowments, has been to some extent realized. What was meant for the good of all, though intrusted to a few, has been taken from the few who used it as their own, and distributed, rudely it may be, but yet effectually, among the many who were entitled to and needed it.

The number of the inmates of the monastic institutions in Spain has been ridiculously exaggerated. Widdrington speaks of an extraordinary statement in the Edinburgh Review, setting them down at four hundred thousand, some twenty years ago; and the reader will probably remember estimates, almost as remarkable, in the books of statistics to which he may have referred. According to the Count of Toreno, there were, in 1808, at the time of the French invasion, 92,727 religious in Spain including monks, nuns, lay brethren and sisters, servants, and dependents. When the measures of suppression were adopted, there were, by the estimate of Mellado, about twenty-six hundred convents in all, being at least five hundred less than at the epoch of which Toreno speaks. Their inmates, according to the best accessible information, did not much exceed forty thousand in number, in 1836, and of these about thirteen thousand were nuns. In his notes to the translation of the statistical work of Moreau de Jonnés, published in 1835, Don Pascual Madoz carries the number of religious beyond ninety thousand; but his estimate is founded on the census of 1797, which it would seem strange that he should have adopted, were it not that the extensive data which it furnished gave additional strength to the *Progresista* side of the then excited Church controversy. So true it is that figures, which according to the common proverb "cannot lie," are invariably found, in political dispute, to arrive as nearly at the reputed impossibility, as the purposes of the disputants may require.

That, according to the most moderate and probable view of the facts, there should, in a population of not more than twelve millions, have been forty thousand persons withdrawn from those practical and substantial duties which, in the order of Providence, are a part of the destiny and obligation of every human creature, and from which no state can safely or consistently discharge its citizens,—is quite justification enough for the legislative action which put an end to such a drain on the public industry, and such a check on production, population, and wealth. The "*descansada vida*" of Fray Luis de Leon—a life of mystic reverie and contemplation—may not be inconsistent with the social uses of humanity, in the few whose genius or temperament, like his, suggests it. In them it may be but the nurse of lofty and poetic thought, the prompter of religious musings, which may delight and teach mankind. But for the most of men, the "*mundanal ruido,*" —the worldly noise,—the echo of the thoughts and feelings, the labors, hopes, and sufferings of other men,—is needful to prevent their hearkening only to the eternal whispering of self. Contemplation, pursued as a calling in life, is apt to degenerate into a trade. Its sphere in a Carthusian's cell cannot be a very wide one, nor its objects many or healthful. It would be but poor astronomy to have one's observatory in the bottom of a well,—poor philosophy to suppose truth was only to be found there! When I visited the Escorial, a tottering sacristan, who showed us the Pantheon of the kings, said, in a melancholy, humble tone,—which vividly recalled Sterne's old Franciscan,—that he had been thrice *exclaustrado*, and yet trusted in the mercy of God! A friend informed me, almost in the same connection, that he had seen the Padre ——, a distinguished and irreproachable brother of the same monastery, dance the polka after his secularization, with all imaginable glee. Here were the two extremes,—the man of the tombs and the man of the world. I could not help thinking that the mercy of God was as likely to be with him who trod the earth cheerfully, as with him whose thoughts, like his occupation, were in the mansions of decay beneath it.

In the series of legislative measures which the ecclesiastical reformation of Spain required, the estates which had been accumulated by the Church proper were of too great importance to be overlooked. Indeed, the movements which began during the reign of Charles the Third were rather in regard to the property held by the secular clergy, than that belonging to the monastic establishments. The views of Campomanes and Moñino took this direction chiefly; and although Jovellanos afterwards carried out his opinions to the extent of their legitimate application, it will be observed that he touched the question of convent property with a somewhat lighter hand than that which he laid on the domains of the Church. The truth is, that the monastic orders, being in fact the soldiers of the Holy Office, were most especially under its protection; and it was not prudent, if safe, even under the enlightened government of Charles, to provoke so formidable an enemy. Moderate and guarded as they were, it required all the favor of the throne to protect Campomanes and Floridablanca from the storm which the honesty and conclusiveness of their expositions had raised. Indeed, the latter of these distinguished men—after the death of the monarch to the glory of whose reign and the good of whose people he had contributed so much—was made to taste the bitterness of persecution, imprisonment, and want. That the same fate attended Jovellanos might be inferred from the customary history of his nation's benefactors, even if the details of his sufferings and wrongs were not a well-known portion of the annals of those days.

A royal decree, promulgated in 1798, upon the suggestion of Jovellanos in the Report of which I have spoken, had laid the foundation of a permanent change in the administration of Church property. It directed the sale of the real estate belonging to hospitals, brotherhoods, &c., and the investment of the proceeds in the public funds for the benefit of those establishments. It likewise invited the higher clergy, as a matter of policy and patriotism, to dispose of the property attached to the various Church foundations under their control, and to pursue the same course of investment with the moneys to be realized therefrom. This decree was approved by the Court of Rome, and carried into effect for a while with considerable energy; but the consummation of its benefits was arrested by the invasion of 1808, and the policy which had dictated it was not revived until the meeting of the constitutional Cortes, in 1820. By a decree of the last-named body, reënacted in 1836, the future acquisition of estates in mortmain, under any pretext, was finally forbidden. In connection with this, and with the anti-monastic legislation already referred to, the property of the churches, chapters, brotherhoods, and other bodies of the secular clergy, passed, in due course, into the possession of the state. As a part of the same system, tithes, first-fruits, and all ecclesiastical dues whatever were absolutely abolished, so that the clergy were cut off from any immediate reliance on the people, and from all right to enforce contributions. The state thus became the fountain of Church patronage, assuming the support of the altar, and taxes for *culto y clero* (worship and clergy) were added from that time forth to the list of imposts for the ordinary purposes of government. In the budget of 1850, nearly seven millions of dollars were appropriated to this head, besides about a million dedicated to the support of the nuns who still remained in their convents. When I was in Spain, there was a mixed commission, appointed by the Pope and the government, whose labors have resulted in the *concordat* of March, 1851. By that instrument, all titles acquired under previous sales of Church property are confirmed, but the portions remaining unsold are restored, with a provision, however, for their future alienation and the investment of the proceeds in stock. The right of the Church proper to acquire real estate is, in some sort, revived, and certain orders of nuns are reëstablished. The suppression of the monks is finally acquiesced in,—although the return of the Jesuits has since been allowed. The settlement has not been satisfactory to either of the political parties, but it has compromised, at least for the present, many long-vexed questions.

When the state assumed to provide for the support of the clergy, their incomes were of course reduced. There was great room for such reduction,—the receipts of the archbishops, bishops, and other prelates of high rank, being then generally large, and in some cases enormous, with reference to the condition of the country. The present scale is sufficiently high for their proper and decorous support, although the irregularity with which the salaries were paid, particularly to the lower clergy, was any thing but creditable, and tended to throw upon the ecclesiastical policy of the liberal party a certain amount of that unpopularity which is the proper and inevitable result of injustice. If the interests of the public demand that the state should control the finances of the Church, the simplest good faith of course requires that they should be honestly administered. Above all, there should be fair dealing with a dependent class, who have now no remedy but patience and resignation. There is no point of view in which it can be either proper or expedient that the ministers of the altar should be hindered, by want, in the performance of their sacred functions, or be exposed, by the faithlessness of the civil power, to personal humiliation and distress.

Although the number of the secular clergy, like that of the monks, has been immensely exaggerated, out of Spain, there is yet no doubt that it has generally been, and still is, larger than the religious necessities of the people can justify. This is, in some degree, the result of a church establishment, consecrated by the universal opinion of the nation, and upheld by the power and *prestige* of the government. It owes something, likewise, to the devotional tendency of the Spaniards, and their disposition to surround the depository of their faith with all the dignity and influence of a numerous clergy. As a democratic institution, too,—in the midst of a monarchy,—with its honors and wealth and power accessible to all, the Church has necessarily attracted that extensive class whose aspirations have been checked in other quarters by the lack of family and fortune. But, quite as much as to these causes, the overgrown service of the Church may be traced to those general circumstances which have depressed the industry and crippled the agriculture and commerce of the nation,—thereby diminishing the sources of respectable occupation, and throwing so many of the educated youth into the few remaining channels of advancement. In this connection it may properly be observed, that the suppression of the monastic orders, so beneficial in so many regards, has not been altogether without consequences which are temporarily hurtful. It put an end to a respectable mode of subsistence for many thousands, at a time when the tardy development of the national resources created no sufficient demand for their labor in any other department. I speak not merely of those who had already assumed the monastic habit, but of the large number of young men whose families looked forward to the convents as a creditable mode of providing for their future maintenance. In time, and as the resources of the nation shall be developed, legitimate methods of support—involving labor and not idleness, contributing to the national wealth, instead of consuming it—will fill the void thus created. But for the present the reform has greatly swollen the innumerable caravan of *pretendientes*, who beset the capital and every source of public patronage. It has increased the virulence of party to an unwonted extent, by rendering the bread of so many dependent upon their access to favor. It has diminished the chances of a regular and uninterrupted system of government, by making it the interest of so many to pull down whatever stands between them and the treasury, and to exercise power, while they hold it, for purposes exclusively personal to themselves and their friends. Many a young gentleman in yellow gloves, who holds them and his cigar by the tenure of two hours' dawdling in a public office, and four hours' lounging on the Calle de la Montera, —and many another, who among the humbler crowds in the Puerta del Sol, with his threadbare cloak hiding much poverty and hunger, catches the tidings of a ministerial crisis, as a maiden hears love-music at midnight,—would have been *Padre Gregorio*, or *Padre Benito*, in former times, blessed in basket and scrip. There may be some doubt whether he is not quite as undesirable a functionary in his present shape, as he would have been in his cowl; but, at all events, there is nothing about him too sacred to be meddled with, if need be, and there is some chance of his being useful, should the future give him an opportunity.

Whatever may have been said, and with truth, of the intellectual and moral estimate properly to be formed of the monks, there has been, it must be admitted, but little cause to complain of the secular clergy. With those exceptions which the temptations and privileges of an establishment necessarily produce and encourage in all countries, the Spanish Church—abstracted from the monastic orders—has faithfully and ably discharged its duty to religion and society. The most independent and decided advocates of the reforms which have corrected its abuses have borne this tribute to its merits; and, even among the most radical *Progresistas* I have met, I have never heard its justice disputed. Of the distinguished literary men whom the nation has produced, — poets, historians, scholars,—some of the first have sprung from the bosom of the Church. In contests where freedom has been involved, there have always been champions for the right among the leaders of the clergy. In the Councils of the Catholic Church, and among its theologians, the Spanish priesthood have always occupied the first rank. How much was due to them, in the infancy of European civilization, the enthusiastic commentary of M. Guizot on the Councils of Toledo will illustrate. Almost all the monuments of real and lasting charity to be found in the Peninsula, attest the sincerity and constancy of their devotion to the practical spirit of Christianity. Lord Clarendon, for so many years Ambassador at Madrid, declared in the House of Lords, in 1839, that during his residence at that capital he had heard in the Cortes, "from the lips of Catholic prelates in that assembly, sentiments of Christian charity as pure, and dictated by as entire a spirit of toleration, as he had ever heard in their Lordships' House." An English historian of reputation [1] does not hesitate to admit that the Spanish secular clergy will sustain, honorably, a comparison with the priesthood of the Church of England. The testimony of Widdrington, after long years of patient and impartial observation in all parts of the Peninsula, is hearty and comprehensive, as to the individual worth and usefulness of the clergy proper, and the marked distinction between them and the religious orders, in character, ability, and public estimation. It is but proper for me to make these statements, so that what I have said may create no unjust impression, and

---

[1] *History of Spain*, Cabinet Cyclopædia, Vol. V, p. 258.

that the distinction may be fairly drawn between the external and accidental institutions which have surrounded the religion of Spain, and the influence which its tenets and teachers have had, in their legitimate province, upon the national mind and heart.

The history of former times must speak for itself; but I think there is very small foundation, now, for the common impression, that Spain is what we are accustomed to call "priest-ridden." Whatever may be the cause,—whether it be the fault of the clergy, or of circumstances, or of a relapse from the ancient fervor of the national enthusiasm in such matters,—certain it is, that the Church has not at this moment any decided control over the popular mind. In the rural districts, among the more ignorant and uneducated of the people, the priesthood, no doubt, exercise that sort of influence with which superior intelligence and the nature of their calling must of necessity clothe them,—an influence certainly legitimate, and desirable unless abused. But there is nothing in the history of the times to show that it passes, even there, beyond the limits which properly belong to it. So far as the educated classes are concerned,—those who control the opinion of the nation and regulate its political progression,—there is as much independence of clerical domination as could be desired. Indeed, I am not altogether sure that there is not a jealousy of it, which sometimes leads to injustice and folly. I am satisfied, that in the United States, where freedom of judgment on such questions is unlimited, the influence of the clergy upon public opinion and the press, gives them a dominion over public action, which the Church of Spain, with all its prescriptions and organizations, cannot at this day pretend to rival. This conclusion is drawn as to Spain, not merely from my own limited observation, but from what was told me by those who had the amplest opportunities of knowing, and from the tone and style in which ecclesiastical matters were handled by the various journals of Madrid. Of course, in speaking of the influence of the clergy in this country, I do not refer to any supposed ability of theirs to govern the public mind for sectarian purposes; but simply of their power, as a class, over public sentiment and those who move its tides. In this, I repeat that I have no doubt of their advantage over the Peninsular clergy. If clerical opinion had been potent, the Carlist war would have had a far different conclusion, and the legislative measures which have formed the principal subject of this chapter would never have approached their consummation. That the rebellion ended as it did, and that the Church is now a stipendiary of the state, ought to satisfy the most sceptical that ecclesiastical despotism is not a present evil. The same facts may indeed suggest a serious doubt, whether the Church, independently of the state and unsupported by its power, had ever the sway which has been ascribed to it, or deserves the whole of the responsibilities which are commonly attached to it.

Much is said, by travellers, of religious intolerance in Spain, and the matter deserves a cursory notice in this connection. Toleration by law certainly does not exist there. The Catholic is, by the constitution and the concordat, the religion of the state, and no other form of worship is allowed. That this is narrow, behind the age, and unbecoming any government which wears the semblance of liberality, it is unnecessary to say. But at the same time it is fair to observe, that upon the

Spaniards, such a provision works no hardship. The nation is Catholic, sincerely, devotedly, and thoroughly, and a constitution predicated upon any other idea would be regarded as an imputation and an anomaly. The prohibition affects no one prejudicially, except the strangers who are called to the Peninsula by business or pleasure, and their number has been heretofore so small, that it is not singular they should have been left out of the account. When the commerce of the nation increases, and the influx of foreigners becomes greater,—as from year to year it necessarily must be,—we must hope that the ban will be removed, which, merely nominal as it now practically is, can only be regarded as a vicious relic of bad times and principles.

But though the constitution does not tolerate, the people certainly do, in the most important sense of the word. A stranger might pass a year in any part of Spain that I have visited, without hearing a single inquiry as to his religious opinions, or being troubled by one impertinent interference with the entire freedom of his religious action. If a man assists at any religious service or ceremonial, he is required to take no more than that respectful and decorous part, which good breeding, of itself, would suggest to every gentleman. Whether he will assist or not, is a matter entirely within his discretion. No one will notice his absence,—certainly no one will remind him of it. Now and then he may meet a clergyman upon the street, with the *viaticum*, and he will be expected to kneel, or at all events uncover, as it passes. If his piety or his convictions forbid him to do this, he can get himself into a doorway or a by-street, where he will find some very good Catholics, doing the same thing, on account of their knees, which he is doing for his conscience. If this is not satisfactory, he ought to proceed homeward at once; but it is to be hoped that in such case he will say nothing about toleration. I am sorry to record it,—but my observation of Protestant travellers, generally, in Catholic countries has been, that many of them claim the privilege of showing on all occasions their contempt for the religion of those about them. I have seen it attempted, and indeed carried out, over and over again,—by persons who had every obligation to know better,—in Catholic cathedrals, and during the most solemn acts of public devotion. Being no Catholic myself, I claim to say this without prejudice. In Spain, such things will not be permitted. The people themselves generally participate in the services of their Church with all solemnity, and they insist that those who desire to witness their celebration should at least abstain from the manifestation of irreverence.

During two visits to Spain,—not very long, it is true, but quite long enough to give me some opportunities of observation,—I do not remember to have heard a single remark made, which ought to have wounded the sensibility of any sincere but rational Protestant. No one ever attempted to engage me in controversy upon religious matters, or to annoy me by the remotest suggestion of heresy or schism. Every one seemed willing to take his own chance, and to allow me the same privilege. By some, this would be set down to indifference; but it certainly was not bigotry, and I was well satisfied to take it for enlightened toleration. Some of the more zealous Spaniards themselves would sometimes say that the religious feeling of the nation had diminished,—that lukewarmness had of late grown general among the people. I was inclined to think that the remark was just; but I was still quite willing to reciprocate the non-intervention with which I was favored, and allow them to take their devotion at any temperature they preferred.

XXIV.

Education.—Statistics.—System of Instruction.—Schools.—Universities.—Census of 1803.—University of Madrid—of Alcalá.—Complutensian Polyglot.—Manuscripts.—Prescott's Ferdinand and Isabella.—Sabau's Translation of it.

IF a traveller is enterprising and industrious, there are few countries in which he will find it difficult to visit universities and schools, look over collegiate courses, and collect educational statistics. Spain, however, is not a statistical land. There is no organized or thorough system there for the ascertainment of numerical facts, so that even the ostensible illustration which those deceptive materials afford must, in a great degree, be wanting to any record of Peninsular observation. Statistics, nevertheless, at the best, are but a poor apology for real information as to the state of national instruction. The diffusion and the degree of knowledge are things so widely different, that the one, which figures may readily express, furnishes but little clew to the other, which they cannot,—though it is so much better worth the knowing. The line between the man who can neither read nor write and his neighbor who can barely do either, is certainly as near as need be to a mathematical line, in the matter of breadth; and yet a statistical table will make its widest distinction between these, while it will draw none between the profoundest scholar and the emptiest sciolist in rudiments. It is as if, to describe the condition of the arts in any nation, the annalist were to divide the people into two classes,—those who could paint and those who could not. The favored class might be all Raphaels or Murillos, and they might be all sign-painters, quite as well.

Nor does the visitation of seminaries of learning, or an examination of the routine which they profess to follow, afford results that are much more valuable. Education is like war. A good plan of a campaign is an excellent thing, but victories, generally, are won by good fighting. A limited course, well taught, makes better scholars than the amplest, not half carried out. It is not in what they profess to teach, that the schools of the present day are apt to be defective. If there be any fault in that particular, it is that they promise too much; and indeed attempt too much, likewise. It is the execution, therefore,—not the plan,—which must be observed, if the observation is to be worth anything; and only he who makes the experiment can fairly know how long and constant that observation must be, to entitle it to real confidence. The imperfect data which follow are consequently given to the reader, with the fullest persuasion of their insufficiency as a basis for any accurate appreciation of the state of mental culture in Spain.

It has already been said, that, by the constitution of 1812, the education of the people was made obligatory on the government. Title X. provided that primary schools should be opened in all the towns of the realm, and that universities and other institutions for instruction in literature, science, and the arts, should be established wherever it might be found expedient. The Cortes were charged with the duty of forming a proper system, subject only to the restrictions that the plan of instruction should be uniform throughout the country, and that the constitution should be taught and expounded in every establishment opened for public education. A Directory, to be composed of suitable persons, was created to superintend and regulate the working of the whole. It was of course impossible that a system could mature sufficiently for beneficial results of any extent, during the several brief reigns of the constitution of 1812. Nevertheless, the work was undertaken and prosecuted, in good faith, by the ablest men of the country; the Directory was organized; plans of study were prescribed, and the machinery was set in motion, as well as might be, under the innumerable disadvantages which surrounded the movement.

The system which now exists went into operation in 1847, when the "Department of Commerce, Instruction, and Public Works" was created by royal decree. The appropriations called for by the budget of 1850 dedicated nearly seven hundred and fifty thousand dollars to the branch of "Instruction" alone. Exclusive of private establishments of all classes, there are ten universities and forty-nine institutes under the direction of the government. The primary and other schools through the whole kingdom reach the number of about sixteen thousand. Besides the institutions thus devoted to general and ordinary education, there are many in the cities, where only particular branches are taught,—such as Commerce, Drawing, Architecture, Chemistry, Mathematics, &c. Of these, some are provided for by the government, and others are under the direction and supported by the patronage of the

Boards of Trade, and the various literary and economical societies. Independently of the funds supplied by the state, a moderate contribution is exacted from those pupils whose circumstances render it proper to call on them; but education is strictly gratuitous, in all its departments, where the parties are really destitute.

No impediment is thrown by law in the way of private teachers,—except that they are required to produce certain certificates of good character and conduct, and of having gone through a prescribed course, which is more or less extensive, in proportion to the rank of the institution they may desire to open. It will not be easy to invent any system, by which Béranger's

"Vieux maître d'école,
Fier d'enseigner ce qu'il ne savait pas,"

can be altogether got rid of. The effort to diminish the chances of his appearance is nevertheless a praiseworthy one; and while priests and pilots, physicians, lawyers, and lieutenants, are, for the most part, required to undergo an examination, before they are permitted to take the destinies of the public into their keeping, it is difficult to understand upon what principle the school-house, which is the nursery of all arts, should be flung open to all comers.

By the best statistical estimates, it appears that, in 1850, the number of pupils in the public schools alone (exclusive of the universities and institutes) was in the proportion of one to seventeen of the whole population. About 1,100,000 was set down as the number of persons then in Spain who could read, —the whole population being about 12,135,000, and the ratio therefore as one to eleven. Limited as this scale may appear, it nevertheless takes quite another aspect when compared with the estimates of Moreau de Jonnés, based on the census of 1803, and not very materially varied in 1835, if we may judge from the notes of Madoz, appended to his translation of M. de Jonnés's work. Out of a population of 10,250,000, in 1803, the number of students in all the educational establishments of the kingdom did not exceed 30,000, or about one to every 340 inhabitants. This extraordinary change—for it is extraordinary, statistical merely though its evidences be—has been mainly wrought within the last twenty years, by a small minority of thinking, educated men, struggling against a mass comparatively ignorant and open to all the influences for which ignorance paves the way. It has been wrought, under institutions only partially liberal, in the midst of civil strife, dynastic controversy, foreign interference, and the most serious fiscal derangements. It has, happily, been the result, not of a violent impulse or a moment's patriotism and enthusiasm, but of a deliberate and progressive system, gaining strength and comprehensiveness as it has advanced. There is therefore no exaggeration in saying, that it furnishes demonstrative evidence, in its way, of solid national development already, and that definite calculations for the future may, with much confidence, be based upon it.

The primary or elementary schools are simply what their name indicates. The studies which follow, and are called *estudios de segunda enseñanza*, require five years, and it is only at the end of that period, and after having undergone the prescribed examinations, that the degree of Bachelor in Philosophy can be attained. The Latin is the only ancient language which this course comprehends. To become a Licentiate or

Doctor, in any of the five Faculties,—Philosophy, Theology, Jurisprudence, Medicine, and Pharmacy,—requires an extended course in a university, varying, as to its length and the studies involved, according to the degree and the Faculty. So far as one may judge from the programme laid down and the list of works which form part of it, the system of education is certainly ample and thorough. How faithfully teachers and scholars discharge their duties I do not pretend to have had any means of knowing, upon which it would be candid to build a judgment. It may, however, with propriety be observed, that the good sense and liberal attainments of the eminent persons who had the formation of the present system, suggested to them the propriety of rendering it far less scholastic and artificial than that which it superseded. As a consequence, it will be found that the young men now leaving college, or engaged in the higher departments of university education, bring with them, or are prepared and trained to bring with them, into the world, those larger ideas, which are as necessary to their distinction or success, in the educated society of the day, as they would have been considered dangerous to the individual and the state under the regimen happily extinct.

The University of Madrid, probably the most flourishing now in the kingdom, is the successor of the venerable University of Alcalá de Henares, founded by Cardinal Ximenes de Cisneros, in the days of the Catholic sovereigns. Its transfer to the capital was begun in 1836, but it was not until about 1845 that the institution and its dependencies took their present shape. It is now complete in its departments, —its professorships filled with men of high attainments in their respective branches, and its popularity permanently established. The name of Don Pascual de Gayangos, an Arabic scholar perhaps unsurpassed in Europe, and of the most accurate and extensive learning in the various departments of modern literature, is one of those which the Spaniards are proud to refer to, as showing the grade of men who have of late years taken the chairs of their universities. In 1849, the students matriculated in the University of Madrid, and the institutions connected with it, were more than 4,500 in number; so that the good seed does not seem likely to want places in which it may be sown.

The mention of the University of Alcalá will probably recall to the reader's recollection the celebrated edition of the Bible, issued from that ancient seat of learning, under the direction of its founder, and commonly known as the Complutensian Polyglot. In regard to the antiquity and authenticity of the manuscripts resorted to in its preparation, and consequently the authority of its text, as derived from them, there has been a good deal of discussion in these later days of sceptical and analytic criticism. Mr. Prescott[1] states, upon the authority of a German Professor who visited Alcalá in 1784, that the disputed question can never be settled satisfactorily, inasmuch as the librarian of that time sold the manuscripts to a rocket-maker, as waste paper, and they duly passed off, in squibs, like baser matter. The fact, if truly reported, would certainly have been a very disgraceful one to Spain, and a sad one for the cause of accurate knowledge on a most absorbing subject. It however turns out happily, that Professor Moldenhauer was mistaken, having no doubt been misled by the

---

[1] *Ferdinand and Isabella*, Vol. III, p. 325, and note 45.

worthy librarian, who would perhaps have been willing to see the Professor himself go up on a rocket, rather than furnish *braseros* and patient attendance for his lucubrations over Hebrew manuscripts.

Don Pedro Sabau y Larroya, Professor of Jurisprudence in the University of Madrid, and Secretary to the Academy of History when I had the honor of assisting at its sessions, has translated Mr. Prescott's work, and, in a note to the passage referred to, treats the whole Moldenhauer story as a "pure calumny." The manuscripts of the Polyglot, he says, were carried from Alcalá, in 1837, to the University of Madrid, where they are now deposited. They were examined there by himself, in the presence of the Professor of Hebrew and the librarians of the establishment. As the original inventories (if any ever existed) are not now to be found, it remains yet an open question, whether some of the manuscripts may not have been mislaid or removed, and whether, indeed, some of those which remain may not have suffered injury, during the long years, and troubles, and many changes, which have rolled over and through the Peninsula, since the Cardinal went to his rest. From the description given by Sr. Sabau, which is much too long for this place, it appears that the manuscripts now open to inspection in Madrid are, in any event, of extreme and curious value. It will be strange if some enterprising Biblical scholar should not undertake the revision of them, which the German Professor sought so unsuccessfully to make. On my way home, I gave to our intelligent countryman, Mr. Henry Stevens, whom I had the pleasure to know in London, a short memorandum of the manuscripts which Sr. Sabau enumerates. He requested it for publication in that very curious and useful periodical, *Notes and Queries*. Whether it ever appeared, or the attention of those learned in such matters (which I do not pretend to be) was ever called to it, my hasty departure prevented me from knowing.

The reader, whose curiosity may induce him to turn to Sabau's Prescott, in relation to this matter, will find a good deal of unnecessary indignation displayed against the memory of the German Professor. I say the indignation is unnecessary, because, although the accusation which he makes is one of very grievous Vandalism, it can hardly be supposed that a man would travel from Germany to Spain,—and especially in those days before railroads,—for the pleasure of inventing and retailing a ridiculous story. The truth is, that Mr. Sabau, though a person of considerable ability and reputation, is not remarkable for the breadth of his views, as the notes to his translation will show. Jurisprudence has obviously not been a "gladsome light," though it may have been a bright one, to him, for the tone of his writings, generally, is neither cheerful nor charitable. He qualifies the wish expressed by Mr. Prescott, in his Preface, for the "civil and religious liberty" of Spain, by a note, in which he distinguishes between freedom from such physical compulsion and persecution as the Inquisition enforced, and freedom in a general sense. The former he is willing to accept for his country, the latter he protests against. His comments upon other passages are in the same mediæval tone, and in some places, indeed, he has softened down the manly language of his author, until it no longer represents, in any way, his just and vigorous sentiments. It is true, that Sr. Sabau has not done this without notifying the reader, and assigning his reasons; but the liberty is unpardonable, nevertheless. A translator may controvert the text, as freely and as positively as he pleases, but to alter it is not one of his privileges. If the original is challenged, it should at least be permitted to speak for itself. Even in ordinary controversy, it would be held no small advantage to have the stating of your adversary's argument, as well as of your own reply to it. A translator has his original sufficiently in his power, at the best; for it is rarely a profitable business to one man's thoughts, that they should pass through the sieve of another man's mind. There is no propriety, therefore, in adding to a necessary evil.

XXV.

Taxes and Modes of Collecting them.—Reforms in Taxation.—The Provincial Deputations and Ayuntamientos.—Grievances and Abuses.—The Customs.—Low Salaries.—Gate-Money.—Tax on Consumption.—National Debt.

IT is impossible to form even a proximate idea of the total amount which the Spanish people contribute to the support of government. The yearly estimates which the constitution requires to be presented to the Cortes contain, it is true, a detailed statement of the sources from which revenue is to be derived, and the objects of its application. But they are necessarily confined to the income and expenditures of the government, for national purposes,—leaving altogether out of consideration the large sums which are collected on provincial and municipal account. The comparative want of publicity in the levying and disbursement of these latter imposts, of course leaves room for many abuses; so that, doubtless, the proportion which the minor, unreported taxes bear to the whole contributions of the nation, is much larger than the ordinary course of such things would lead one to suppose.

Within a few years past, the system of taxation has been very much simplified. A number of special and onerous burdens—which had been imposed in particular emergencies of the state, or by occasional usurpations of the monarch, and had been made permanent, though the occasions or pretexts which produced them had been almost forgotten—have been swept away by the representatives of the people. Applying, as these did, to peculiar classes and property, they were necessarily even more odious than they were oppressive; and being, moreover, founded on mere prescription, in many of their details, they were frequently attended by extortion and injustice, for which there was no remedy. The present plan has, at all events, the merit of being, in the main, comprehensive and general, notwithstanding it gives cause for much complaint, in other particulars which will be noted.

The sources of revenue at this time are not numerous. They are principally regulated by the tax-laws of 1845 and 1847. The most important is the impost on real property, agriculture and live stock ("*Inmuebles, cultivo, y ganaderia*"), which in 1850 was so levied as to give a net product of $15,000,000. At the beginning of every year a ratable proportion of the money called for by the budget which the Cortes may adopt, is assessed to each province. The duty of dividing the whole among the several municipalities, devolves upon the *Diputacion Provincial*, which is composed, in every province, of the *Jefe Politico* and *Intendente* (or the officers who, under more recent legislation, may discharge their functions), and a certain number of Deputies, elected by a majority of those qualified to vote for members of the Cortes. The *Diputacion* is likewise clothed with the power of regulating the provincial taxes and assessments, —directing the internal affairs of the provinces,—managing their public works and property, with subjection to existing laws,—and proposing to the government, for its consideration, such matters of provincial interest and policy as the public good may from time to time suggest. The proper amount of taxes having been assessed to each municipality, the appointment among the individual contributors is made by the several *ayuntamientos*, and an equal number of the principal taxpayers themselves. The assessments are yearly. Real estate, when leased, is taxed according to its annual value to the proprietor. If unproductive, it contributes nothing. Farms, with their cattle and utensils, in the hands of the owner himself, are estimated by as close an approximation as possible to their actual, clear profits. The valuation is never arbitrary, when there are facts upon which it may be based; and indeed, so far as legislation may avail to such ends, the law provides, wisely and prudently, for the doing of justice in the assessments to both the state and the citizen. Complaints, nevertheless, as to the operation of the system, were frequent and serious, when I was in Spain, and they were repeated so often in the Cortes, by Deputies of character and moderation, as to be obviously founded on something more than the proverbial unpopularity of tax-laws throughout the world.

From the best information I could obtain, Sr. Bravo Murillo was certainly right, in saying that the amount of sixty millions of dollars was by no means larger than Spain could readily pay to the central government. The grievances, so often made the subject of remonstrance, arose from the distribution and collection of the taxes, and not from their amount. In spite of all statutory precautions, the assessments, I was informed, were very unequally and unfairly made in some of the provinces, and there existed no sufficient accessible remedy, even in cases of great hardship. But it was in the time and mode of their collection, that the public burdens were made to weigh most heavily. It was the interest of the officials to collect, if possible, by execution; the perquisites resulting to them in such case being proportionally very large. The result was, that, in seasons when the failure of any particular crop—perhaps the chief dependence of the agricultural year—would embarrass the farmers in particular districts, those districts would as certainly be the mark of the tax-gatherer's utmost extortion. The time within which execution might be levied, in case of non-payment, was entirely too short; the proceedings were arbitrary and summary in high degree, and there was no provision for the redemption of the property sold, within a definite period, no matter how great might be the sacrifice in its sale. In a country like Spain, where—although there is comparatively little destitution—there is a very large portion of the rural population whose daily labor can produce but daily bread, it will be readily seen that the severe and stringent application of coercive measures must result often in absolute ruin. This effect is the more likely to be general, when it is produced at all, from the fact that, in many of the agricultural districts, the nature of the soil, the degree of its improvement, the staples and the modes and means of their cultivation and production, are so entirely identical, that one general cause—a drought, for example—will put it out of the power of all the small farmers, alike, to contribute any thing, for the time, to the expenses of the state.

Next to the tax of which I have spoken, the customs furnish the largest item of revenue. The anticipated receipts from that source, for 1850, were eight millions of dollars, an insignificant sum enough, in view of what might be obtained by a rational—one might almost say a sane—adjustment of the tariff on imports. Notwithstanding its insignificance, however, it was a considerable improvement on the past,—the result of the improved ideas of political economy which had for some time been prevailing at Madrid. It is certainly difficult to understand how men could be blind so long to the evils and errors of the prohibitory system, whose worst absurdities they were illustrating and developing daily. It is almost as singular, that a favorable change, when once begun, should advance so tardily. Nevertheless, it is satisfactory to know that the current has set at last in the right direction, and that the tendency of Spanish legislation is now as strong towards the removal of commercial restrictions, as the proper protection of the national interests will justify. I do not say that such is the present temper of the whole nation, or that the destruction of long-established monopolies and prejudices can be accomplished at once, and without resistance; but that the thinking men of all parties, at Madrid, seem to unite in pressing such modifications of the tariff, as will finally raise it to the most productive scale for the revenue, while they at the same time foster most effectively the great interests of commerce and manufactures. That such a result is not easily attained, the experience of the United States is most ample to show. It is to be hoped that the Spaniards will profit by it and by their own, so as to avoid, on the one hand, the building up or the maintenance of a system which has no support but legislation, and the disregard, on the other, of those suggestions, by which nature and the instincts and tendencies of a people point out to its government the policy and limits of protection.

It would be tedious and unnecessary to dwell upon all the other methods of obtaining revenue which prevail in Spain. They are such as the experience of most civilized nations has devised, and perhaps, on the whole, are as fair and productive in themselves as any general scheme can be made. Of the very large percentage which is paid for their collection, I have already had occasion to speak; but although there is no evil connected with the revenue which it is more important to cure, there is perhaps none in Spain whose correction will be more difficult. It is not easy to persuade the public, anywhere, that any system can be economical, which involves the increase of salaries. Every one can perceive the difference between a small and a larger sum of money; it is not every one who will appreciate the infinitely larger difference between the services of an efficient and honest officer, and those of one who is willing to work at any price, for the sake of bread and of profiting by contingencies. There are always so many persons ready to serve the state cheaply, who have never been under an inquisition as idiots or sent to the penitentiary for crime, and who therefore, in intendment of law, are sensible and honest, that it is quite useless to assert that good men will not accept office at low rates of compensation. Demagogues will always be found to say that these excellent people can be had at minimum prices, and to prove, by addition or subtraction, the detriment which the commonwealth will suffer by rejecting their bids. By such and similar devices, the public are seduced from their propriety so far as to forget, in affairs of government, the principle so universal in private experience, —that a good thing is only to be had by paying for it. In Spain, the inferior officers of the revenue are wretchedly paid.

To live by their salaries is out of the question,—they must of course live from their offices. They must accept bribes, to permit the violation of the laws,—they must oppress where they dare, and can make it profitable,—they must take their own share of what passes through their hands. The public can never know the extent to which this is done. If the revenue falls short, other reasons can be given for it, and the fallacy of those reasons cannot be demonstrated. While, therefore, the popularity-hunters in the Cortes can show in a moment the difference to the public between a salary of one *peseta* daily and a salary of two, the advocates of the more liberal system can only rely upon probabilities and inferences, which, strong as they may be, are yet not arithmetic. Thus it is, that, although every man in Spain knows the existence of corruption in the fiscal department and throughout many of its minor details, it will be long before there will be moral courage enough in the legislature, with the cry of retrenchment ringing in its ears, to commence an economical reform, by a system of liberal compensation.

Perhaps the most odious of the Spanish taxes—certainly the most justly odious—is that called the *derecho de puertas*,—an *octroi*, or gate-duty, imitated from the French, and levied upon articles which are carried into the cities and certain authorized towns. Not the least among its evils are the large number of custom-house officers it requires, the frequent opportunities it affords for oppression and peculation, and the sort of *espionage* under which it places all travellers and carriers. But its principal vice is the restraint it puts upon the freedom of trade and intercourse between different parts of the country. No one can appreciate, without frequently observing, the infinite and petty delays and vexations to which it exposes the country people and small dealers, to whom time is of the utmost value, and upon whom it operates, perhaps, more severely in this regard, than in the mere amount of contribution which is exacted from them. It is really sad to see a line of industrious, poor fellows—who have travelled, from early dawn, to sell, perhaps, a donkey-load of charcoal—detained at the gates, as they often are, till the best hours of the morning have passed away; while the gentlemen of the customs—too few to discharge their duties promptly, or too idle to discharge them at all, except for a compensation—are quietly smoking their *cigarritos*, in shade or sunshine, according to the season. The patience, however, is remarkable, with which the sufferers will endure all this,—too happy if they are not required to empty their panniers to the very bottom, so that the official eye may see, where the official hand has failed to discover, any contraband bottle of wine or *aguardiente*.

Connected with the gate-tax in its unpopularity is the *derecho de consumo*, or tax on consumption, which is levied upon all articles consumed in the cities and towns. It is the more objectionable, since it is regarded but as a duplicate of the *derecho de puertas*,—a doing over of what is justly considered bad enough when done once. The worst of both these impositions is, that they may be applied to the same articles of trade or consumption a dozen times, if the owner thinks proper, or finds it necessary, to give them so wide a circulation. An acquaintance from Malaga, who was sojourning in Madrid, told me one day that he had directed some fruits to be sent up from home, for his own use and to be presented to his friends in the capital. They had been produced on his own farm, upon which, and on its stock, he had paid direct taxes proportionate to its crops. They had been carried into Malaga, to be stored, and he had there paid the gate-tax and the tax on consumption. "I learned yesterday," he added, "that they had arrived here, and when I had paid the charge of the *galera* for bringing them,—which was no trifle,—I was called on for the *derecho de puertas* and the *derecho de consumo* for Madrid. I have not made up my mind whether I shall not beg the *Señor carabinero* who has them in charge to favor me by eating them. *Y que le hagan buen provecho!* May they do him much good!"

In 1848 there was a royal decree, authorizing the Secretary of the Treasury to exempt from the *derecho de puertas* the raw materials used in the various manufactures of the country, and this without regard to their being of foreign or domestic origin. The measure was, no doubt, an extremely wise one, and has contributed its share towards the improvement which the manufacturing industry of Spain has, of late years, obviously undergone. By the law of *presupuestos*, in 1850, the authority was extended to such other articles as might seem to require a similar exemption,—provided always that the revenue from gate-money should not be, thereby, too seriously impaired. The latter clause was quite unnecessary, as it is not in the nature of finance ministers anywhere, and least of all in Spain, to cut down any available means of revenue, where they are allowed to exercise a discretion. Sr. Bravo Murillo, in April, 1850, published a list of about one hundred and seventy additional articles to which the freedom of the gates was given. They were principally drugs, medicinal plants, and vegetable and mineral substances employed in the various mechanic arts. Their exemption seemed but a trifle, until I reflected upon the incalculable annoyance and injustice which the levying of taxes on them must previously have wrought. There were several commodities, among them, which struck me as somewhat singular: such, for example, as live vipers, dried do., sand for scouring, human hair, do. manufactured, cantharides, canary birds, leeches, &c., &c. Even if the snakes, the birds, or the flies had not been permitted to enter the cities scot-free, without legislation, a fellow-feeling ought to have sufficed, of itself, to save the leeches, at all events, from the rude hands of the tax-gatherer.

A chapter on the finances of Spain would hardly seem complete, without some allusion to the national debt; but as this, unfortunately, is somewhat over nine hundred millions, and is not much nearer being paid than it was when contracted, it has no very practical connection with the financial interests of the day. If such things be national blessings, as is sometimes contended, the cup of the national beatitude ought certainly to be full. Every now and then some "agent of the bondholders" is said to visit Madrid, with a view to an arrangement for the punctual payment of interest. But this announcement has been made so often, and the "arrangement" is still so far from its consummation, that the "agent" is now generally regarded as a newspaper fiction, and the debt answers but little purpose, save as a shuttlecock for the players at the Stock Exchange. Rumor occasionally alludes to large fortunes, supposed to have been made from speculations in it, by persons high in authority, who are able to foretell, if not to cause, the fluctuations of its market value. There is, no doubt, truth in these reports; for Lord Bacon has wisely said, that " want supplieth itself of what is next, and many times the next way." It may be private uncharitableness to believe ill of our neighbors, but it sometimes is public wisdom not to be incredulous in regard to the sins of our rulers. The reader who is disposed to be amiable may see some prospect of the debt's being extinguished in the fact that $160,602 were applied in July, 1852, to the redemption of preferred securities!

XXVI.

INTERNAL IMPROVEMENTS.—AGRICULTURAL AND MINERAL WEALTH.—NATURAL OBSTACLES.—PRESENT FACILITIES FOR TRAVEL AND TRANSPORTATION.—SAFETY OF THE ROADS.—POLICE.—NEW ROADS AND CANALS.—ADMINISTRATION OF ROADS AND CANALS.—RAILROADS PROJECTED AND COMPLETED.—RAILROAD COMMITTEE OF THE CORTES.—ROYAL DECREE AND PARTICIPATION OF THE GOVERNMENT IN THE MANAGEMENT OF RAILROADS.—INFLUX OF CAPITAL, AND ITS RESULTS.

IF there be any one subject of greater interest, at this moment, to Spain, than all others, it is a comprehensive and thorough system of internal improvements. It is a matter vital to her prosperity in all points of view,—not merely with reference to the development of her material resources, but to the diffusion of liberal and enlightened opinions, and the spread of civilization among her people. During the Carlist war, it was notorious that the Pretender had no strength—almost no party—in the cities and large towns, and wherever intelligence was diffused. His strongholds were in the fastnesses of the hills, the almost inaccessible valleys, and wherever the isolation of the people from the rest of the world was most complete. I do not, of course, speak, in this connection, of the footing which Don Carlos maintained in the Basque Provinces. His popularity there was altogether independent of any attachment to his person, or to the despotic and retrograde principles of which he was the representative. He was identified by the intelligent and sturdy inhabitants with their *fueros*, or prescriptive privileges, and it was for these, and not for him or his cause, as is commonly supposed, that their unyielding struggle was kept up. But, elsewhere, the devotion of the rural districts to the Pretender was universally proportioned, in its intensity and its extent, to the degree of their remoteness from the sources of information, and the difficulty of their intercourse with the other portions of the kingdom. And so it must always be. New ideas cannot enter rapidly, or be accepted with intelligent welcome, where the people who are to carry or receive them have only access to each other, and to the living stream of human thought and movement, by mule-paths over rugged mountains. It is not to be expected that men can get rid of their swaddling-clothes, while they are compelled to lie in the cradles in which they were rocked. I think it is Sidney Smith who says that "the wisdom of our ancestors is the usual topic, whenever the folly of their descendants is to be defended"; but how are men to get beyond the follies of their progenitors, if they have no opportunity to acquire wisdom of their own? When the oracle foretold to Philip that he might cleave the wall with his wedge of gold, it presupposed some crevice, through which the work might be begun.

To see what might be done for the material wealth of Spain, by a judicious system of internal improvements, it is only necessary to look for a moment at her geographical position and resources. Though not abounding in ports of the first class, she has still enough to furnish outlets for all the possible productions of her soil and industry. "Her agricultural products," says Loudon,[1] "include all those of the rest of Europe and most of those of the West Indies; besides all the grains; for the production of which some provinces are more celebrated than others, and most of them are known to produce the best wheat in Europe." Her soil and climate are as various, and the face of the country is as diversified, as so unlimited a range of products could require. Mountain and valley, plain and *vega*, vineyard, cornfield, pasture, and sheep-walk,—all contribute their shares to the bounty of her agriculture. Nor are the treasures beneath the soil less varied and abundant than those which spring from it. Copper and lead are found in large quantities, and in the most valuable combinations. The quicksilver mine of Almaden is inexhaustible, Zinc abounds in La Mancha and the Asturias. Black-lead of the first quality is to be had abundantly through Andalusia. Alum, saltpetre, and salt are the riches of various districts. Iron of the best quality, and in inexhaustible deposits, is to be found throughout the whole kingdom, especially in the northern and more industrious provinces, and at Marbella on the Mediterranean, not far from Malaga, where there is a mountain almost entirely composed of it. Of the coal mines of the Asturias, Widdrington says that "the quantity is inexhaustible, the quality excellent, the working of extraordinary facility, and the communication easy with the sea." Near Villanueva del Rio, by the Guadalquivir, there is also an extensive deposit of coal, which is used for steam-navigation on that river; but it is, like the most of the mines which have been referred to, only imperfectly worked.

---

[1] *Encyclopædia of Agriculture*, Sec. 721.

Baron Liebig,[1] speaking of the extensive formation of phosphate of lime, which was explored, in Estremadura, by Dr. Daubeny of Oxford, observes: "This is one of the treasures, of which Spain has so many, sufficient, perhaps, at no distant period, to pay a part of the national debt of that country." "It is deeply to be regretted," he adds, "that the railways projected seven years ago, which, crossing each other at Madrid as a centre, were to unite Portugal with France, and Madrid with both seas, have not been executed. These railways would render Spain the richest country in Europe."

With these and similar inducements to create all possible channels for internal intercourse, nature has undoubtedly mingled an infinitude of obstacles, which in some degree excuse the paucity and imperfection of the facilities which at present exist. It would be difficult to devise a more unfavorable topographical arrangement for the construction of improvements of all sorts. The immense central plateau of the Castiles is more than two thousand feet above the level of the sea, towards which the descent, in many places, is sudden and precipitous,—obstructed often, in the most important quarters, by mountains of painful declivity and ruggedness. The chief mountain ranges which cross the Peninsula do so transversely, and in such a manner as to present as many lines of impediment as possible, in the directions which the most valuable works must take. The rivers, in their upper portions, run mostly in narrow channels, between high and rocky banks, difficult of access, often, in an extreme degree, for the purposes of canal construction. The long droughts in many districts, and the paucity of streams where most desirable, present other

[1] *Letters on Chemistry*, p. 498, note.

difficulties in this regard, which are almost insuperable. In the presence of natural obstacles so numerous and real, it is not difficult to understand how a nation, sparsely peopled, vexed by invasions and civil discord,—with an exhausted treasury, an impoverished agriculture, and broken industry,— should have shrunk from encountering what, under the most favorable auspices, must be a gigantic labor, and involve an enormous expenditure.

Bad, however, as the means of communication and transportation undoubtedly are, in many parts of Spain, the common ideas of other countries in regard thereto are very much exaggerated. It is gravely stated, in many respectable books of reference, and believed, with a shudder, by travellers, who would otherwise enjoy the pleasure and profit of visiting the Peninsula, that a tourist can scarcely see any thing except from his saddle, and that mules and donkeys are almost exclusively the common carriers. There is no foundation whatever for such notions. Through the most important parts of the kingdom, and especially between the principal cities, there is every facility which good carriage-roads and excellent diligences, constantly running, can furnish to travellers; and the *galeras*, or wagon-lines, for the transportation of merchandise, are numerous,—often very well conducted and reasonably prompt, the mountainous nature of the principal routes being taken into consideration. Those persons who desire to explore the country,—to penetrate its romantic recesses and enjoy the wildness of its most secluded scenery,—will undoubtedly be compelled to do so on horseback, and trust their valuables to the next mule-driver. But in such cases the adventurousness of the journey would seem to be an attraction, rather than an inconvenience; and one can hardly expect the appliances of civilization, when expressly seeking the beauties of primitive, uncultivated nature.

It may be well to say in this place, that the dangers of Spanish travel have been quite as much the subject of hyperbole as its difficulties,—perhaps, indeed, more. Since the civil war ended, the improved security and profit of peaceful labor, and the consolidation, in a more permanent and effective form, of the elements of real government, have so removed the temptations to lawlessness and increased the probability of its punishment, that robberies and murders upon the highway have become of comparatively infrequent occurrence. The new road-police—the *guardias civiles*—are an excellent and effective corps, and by their numbers, activity, and energy have become a great terror to evil-doers. They are to be met in all directions, traversing the country on horseback and on foot, well armed and accoutred. The justice to which they bring the criminals whom they arrest is so decided and summary, as to have diffused already, when I was in Spain, that salutary dread of the vigorous and active administration of the laws, which is the most effectual preventive of crime, and especially of open violence.

So far as the construction of carriage-roads is concerned, but little could be added to the energy and industry with which the system of improvements has been prosecuted, since the final establishment of peace. There is a Board of Engineers of Roads,—originally organized towards the close of the last century, which, after having been suppressed, during the war of independence and the despotical reaction of 1823, was placed upon a secure and permanent footing in 1836, when a school for the education of its future members was established. The construction and improvement of the chief national and provincial highways is under the charge of this corps, while that of the minor (or, as we might call them, country or township) roads is intrusted to certain "Directors of By-roads and Canals for Irrigation," who were created a board, by royal decree, in 1848. The funds for the construction of the last-mentioned works are raised by the proper provincial and municipal authorities, in a manner provided by law. Those which are of a national character are dependent upon the Treasury. The amount designated for their support, in the budget of 1850, was $1,452,360, over and above $84,657, appropriated to the pay of the engineer board and the support of its school. Some members of the opposition contended that a very undue proportion of the amount applicable to the construction of highways was absorbed in the *personal* of the service,—that is to say, the perquisites, expenses, and it may be the pickings and stealings of the various officials concerned in it. Doubtless there was truth in the charge,—for it was made openly and responsibly; but it was equally true, that the roads in progress of construction were advancing with much rapidity, to the obvious and almost incalculable advantage of some of the most important districts. In many places also, they were reducing the grades of the old roads, with great benefit to their practicability for heavy transportation. If, however, on the whole, the new highways shall be constructed with the masterly skill in the engineering department, and the solidity of the bridges and masonry, which are conspicuous in the older works, a small extra appropriation to the *personal* may be regarded as a pardonable sin.

In the matter of railroads and canals, there is less to be said for the actual improvement of Spain, although projects without number, and especially of railroads, have been for some time occupying public attention.

"Six are the canals for navigation which we have," says Mellado, in 1849, "but none of them finished,—in accordance with that sort of fatality which has always persecuted Spain, and in virtue of which every thing useful is left to be done (*se queda por hacer*)." The only one of these works really worth noticing is the Canal of Castile, referred to in a preceding chapter. Eighty-one miles only were finished; but the work was done in the most substantial and permanent manner, so that its continuation, now so actively undertaken, will not be embarrassed by the necessity of extensive repairs. It runs through a productive country, abounding in the best breadstuffs, and can be readily and copiously supplied from the Pisuerga, which washes the walls of Valladolid. Its completion, which is now a matter of no doubt, will give, as I have said, a most important impulse to the agriculture of Castile and the commerce of Santander. The canalization (as they called it) of the Ebro was the subject of a good deal of interest and discussion when I was in Spain, and it seemed likely then to be realized; but I have not been able to learn whether any actual progress has been made in the enterprise.[1] It was commenced during the reign of Charles the Third, and finished, from the neighborhood of Tudela, nearly to Zaragoza. Tortosa was its contemplated terminus, and such are the manifest advantages which it would confer upon a most productive

---

[1] It is now announced that the work is in the hands of contractors for speedy completion.

region, that it is hard to understand how even the most adverse circumstances could have prevented its completion. A similar observation may with propriety be made, in reference to the lateral Canal of the Guadalquivir, a work of national and consummate importance, a portion of which was under contract, in 1850, and which seemed to have been taken up energetically by both the government and private capitalists. How far it was to be connected with a former noted, but unsuccessful, scheme for deepening portions of the channel as far as Córdova, I was unable to ascertain; but the consummation of either project would make an epoch in the national prosperity.

When I left Spain, the railway between Barcelona and Mataró, a distance of fifteen miles, was the only one in active operation. I did not pass over it, but was informed that, although an excellent road, its construction had involved no great difficulty or expense. I have since seen an announcement in the journals, of its continuation to Arenys, some nine miles farther. In the autumn of 1850, the railway between Madrid and Aranjuez, a distance of twenty-four or five miles, was opened with great magnificence, in the presence of the Queen and Court. This road, of itself, is not of very great usefulness to trade, because, although directly on the routes between Andalucia, La Mancha, Valencia, &c. and the capital, it still forms but a small portion of the immense lines which it terminates. Its completion, however, must be of extreme importance in another point of view, by bringing those who work the springs of government at the capital in direct and unavoidable contact with the wisdom, value, and practicability of such enterprises. It thus may be, not only the beginning of a great central work, which will unite the plains of Castile with the shores of the Mediterranean and the wealth of the West and South, but perhaps the means of giving a direction to the public mind and energy, which will produce general results now hardly to be anticipated. Already, its continuation to Almansa, on the route to Alicante, is under contract and rapidly advancing.

The line of Langreo in the Asturias, established for the purpose of developing the immense resources of the coal region mentioned in the last chapter, was considerably advanced at the time of my departure, and its completion was looked for towards the close of 1850. The want of coal in Barcelona was suggesting also, to the people of that enterprising capital, the necessity of a railway to San Juan de las Abadesas, and it was accordingly projected and commenced, with the usual energy of the Catalans. Its construction would occupy, it was supposed, but little over two years, so that by this time it must have nearly approached its termination. During the present summer (1852) the provincial deputation and the municipal corporation of Barcelona have petitioned the government for leave to construct a railway to Zaragoza, nearly one hundred and seventy miles,—a work of great difficulty, and which must of necessity be protracted and costly. If there be any province in which such an enterprise could be successful, it is Catalonia, and there is sufficient wealth and commercial and industrial activity among the inhabitants to render it altogether practicable. Recent accounts treat its consummation as certain. The very desire of so shrewd and calculating a people to take so heavy a responsibility on their own shoulders, is evidence at once of the probable productiveness of the work, and of the spirit which is awake in the nation.

I have referred, in another place, to the railway from Santander to Alar, with its projected continuation to Valladolid and Burgos. Important as this must be to the whole North, it will be rendered doubly so by the completion of the great line now contemplated between Madrid and the frontier of the Pyrenees, at Irun. The government seems to be really in earnest, in regard to this latter work,—having but lately decreed the sale of the communal property in the provinces through which it is to pass, for the purpose of devoting their proceeds to its construction. It is scarcely possible to overrate the benefits with which the successful prosecution of so gigantic an enterprise would be pregnant. The Pyrenees would then, indeed, exist no longer,—not levelled, as the ambition of Louis the Fourteenth would have had them, that Spain might be an appanage of France,—but removed for ever, as a barrier to European intercourse and the march of European civilization. Emboldened, perhaps, by the action of the government in regard to this great Northern highway, or awakened at last to a sense of their necessities and resources, the people of the South have also laid their hands to the work. The authorities of Seville, according to the last advices, have sought permission to devote the proceeds of their communal property also to the construction of a railroad, which is to extend at least to the Sierra Marena, at Córdova. The nature of the country is such as to present few formidable obstacles to this enterprise, and its success would develop the riches and command the trade of the very garden of Spain. From Cadiz to Jerez and to Seville a line is in process of active construction.

It is unnecessary to mention a host of minor enterprises, projected, or more or less advanced, and which, though many of them may fail, must nevertheless result in something, here and there, of great and permanent advantage. While I was yet in Madrid, a Committee on Railroads, appointed by the House of Deputies, was holding its sessions during the recess of the Cortes. It was headed by Don Salustiano de Olozaga, the distinguished *Progresista,* an able and enlightened public man. Its meetings were attended by several accomplished engineers, foreign and native, and by many prominent capitalists and enterprising and public-spirited citizens, who were summoned for the purpose of consultation. The committee was active in seeking, from them and from other trustworthy sources, such practical and scientific information as would enable its members to report the most judicious and promising scheme of general internal improvement. What was the result of its labors, in view of the dissolution of the Cortes and the change of ministry which followed, I have never ascertained. It was, as I learned, the first parliamentary inquisition ever held in Spain, and was regarded with great favor and interest, on that account and as a valuable precedent.

Pending the action of the Cortes, a royal decree was promulgated, prescribing the mode of applying for, and the conditions of obtaining, the privilege of railway construction. It involved—as the Spanish policy in such matters, by analogy to the French system, now always involves—a participation by the government in the control of the companies, which is foreign to all our notions of private enterprise and of a judicious and politic *laissez faire.* It provided, among other things, for a guaranty by the government to the companies of a minimum interest of six per cent. on their investments,—to commence from the completion of the works,—together with a sinking fund of one per cent., upon certain conditions. All the guaranties of the government were to be of no obligation, in case the works should cease, or the operation of the roads be suspended, by the default of the stockholders. The one per cent. sinking fund was to be continued, until the capital should be extinguished, or, in other words, until the government should become the purchaser of the works.

It is not to be denied, that the exercise of a little more control, in our own country, by government, over the immense corporations on which railway privileges are conferred, would be exceedingly salutary,—conducive at once to the interest and safety of the citizen, and not unjust or disadvantageous to the corporators. But the mania which possesses the governments of the Continent to mingle themselves with every public enterprise, and be part and parcel of every speculation in which two or three are gathered together, is one which a constitutional system must counteract, if it would avail any thing. It often, in the long run, works its own retribution. The powers which control every thing, for their own advantage, are often made to bear the brunt of every thing, to their sorrow. The government is seen in so many things, that it is believed to be in all. When the crops failed in France, the peasantry of Louis Philippe could with difficulty be persuaded that it was not all the fault of *" ce diable de roi"!* And the *diable de roi*, poor fellow! paid dearly for it at last.

Although there is a great deal of disposable capital in Spain, —much more than is commonly believed in other countries,— the success of the railroad enterprises in contemplation must depend in a great degree upon the readiness of foreign capitalists to embark in them. This, in its turn, must depend upon their confidence in the permanency of existing institutions, and in the preservation of peace. Capital cannot possibly be led into channels,—no matter how tempting,—which may, at any moment, be diverted or be drained by the outbreaking of revolutions, or the fluctuations of civil war and an irregular government. The same rule, indeed, applies to domestic as well as foreign capital, for the root of all evil is not often watered by patriotism, and Spanish capitalists heretofore have been wise enough to know the difference, in the matter of investment, between the British and the Spanish per cents. Of late years, however, things have changed greatly in this regard. Capital has begun to abandon its former absenteeism, and now stays, for the most part, at home, to produce where it is produced. The same confidence which has caused this, has given the same direction to much foreign wealth. British stockholders are largely interested in the works already completed, and many of those projected have too many probabilities of success and of large returns, not to command a similar support. The knowledge of this fact,—of the prosperity, the development, the power it will bring,—and a conviction that peace and permanent institutions, steadily administered, are necessary to secure these blessings,—will, of equal necessity, tend to preserve that peace and permanence. Nations, for the most part, are governed by the convictions of the mass of their citizens,—especially by their convictions as to matters of interest; and thus is true, for another reason, what was observed in the opening of this chapter,—that the internal improvement of Spain is as vital to her civilization and good government, as to her material prosperity.

XXVII.

Improvement in Agriculture and its Causes.—Improved Value of Land.—Territorial Wealth and Production.—Practical Farmers.—Espartero.—Agricultural Education.—Economical Societies.—Agricultural Bureau and its Action.—Irrigation.—Geological Chart.—Colonization of Waste Land.—Irish Colonists.—Dairy of Madrid.—Advancement in Manufactures and Commerce.—Prohibitory Duties.—Exports and Imports.—Steam Coasters and Coasting Trade.—Manufactures.—Catalan Monopolies.—Manufacturing Resources of Spain.—Modifications of the Tariff.—Silk and Woollen Fabrics.—Flax, Hemp, and Iron.—National Arsenals and Foundries.

THE subdivision of the Church property in Spain, and its passage into the hands of the laity, would alone be sufficient to account for the improvement in agriculture since the establishment of the constitutional system. The immense tracts of land accumulated in mortmain were always regarded, by the wisest agricultural economists of the kingdom, as the chief cause of the torpor formerly so prevalent in that important branch of public industry. Though always administered considerately, and with becoming forbearance towards the tenants, the estates of the Church—in addition to the other evils which their possession involved—were notoriously mismanaged as to productiveness. There were, of course, exceptions to the rule, but poverty and raggedness surrounded the wealthiest ecclesiastical endowments so generally, that to say a neighborhood was "clerical," (*de clérigos*,) was, emphatically, to apply to it the strongest proverbial phrase for wretchedness and desolation.

Other and most serious impediments to agricultural progress have been removed by the abolition of tithes and other ecclesiastical dues and perquisites, as well as by the suppression of the multiform prescriptive imposts formerly levied by the state upon real property, and the substitution of a uniform system of assessment and taxation. Notwithstanding the unequal manner in which the present tax-laws occasionally operate in their details, the evils which result from them are purely administrative, and susceptible of practical remedy; but the old system was so vicious in all its principles, and so manifestly partial and oppressive, that its existence was altogether inconsistent with the possible prosperity of the landed interest.

It will not have escaped the reader, that the internal improvements referred to in the last chapter, as actually completed, must be an item of controlling importance in all calculations of agricultural promise. Those in progress, also, or serious contemplation, cannot fail to give great encouragement to rural labor, and increased value to real estate. In some districts, it is a familiar fact, that the wine of one vintage has to be emptied, in waste, in order to furnish skins for the wine of the next,—the difficulty and cost of transportation to market being such, as utterly to preclude the producer from attempting a more profitable disposition of it. Staples of the most absolute and uniform necessity—wheat, for instance—are at prices absurdly different in different parts of the kingdom; the proximity to market being such as to give them their current value in one quarter, while in another they are perhaps rotting in their places of deposit, without the hope of a demand. Until such a state of things shall have been cured, it will be useless to improve the soil, or stimulate production in the secluded districts; and of course every circumstance which wears the promise of such cure must enter into the calculations of the future, and avail in them, according to its probabilities.

Other important pieces of legislation, which may not be enumerated here, such as the abolition of entails, &c., have, no doubt, combined with those just mentioned, to give an impulse to agricultural industry and the public good-will in its behalf; for it is a significant fact, that, notwithstanding the immense amount of land thrown into the market by the Church confiscations, the value of agricultural property, and of real estate generally, has been steadily increasing throughout the greater part of the kingdom, since the termination of the civil war. Indeed, the Church property itself has commanded an average of nearly double the price at which it was officially assessed, according to the standards of value at the time of its seizure. If any reliance is to be placed upon the statistical information which Mellado has collected in his *Guia del Forastero,* the territorial wealth of Spain was estimated in 1849 at $369,400,000, being nearly $116,000,000 more than it was supposed to amount to in 1803. It is stated in the same work, that the yearly product of the soil is now nearly $3,000,000 greater than at the last-mentioned date, while the quantity of land in cultivation, which then scarcely amounted to one-ninth of the whole soil, has now risen to more than two-sevenths. What scope there yet is for the wisdom of the government and the industry and enterprise of the people, the last-mentioned fact will sufficiently show.

There is no better sign of a healthy national feeling, in regard to agriculture, than that many persons of influence and position have begun to take a personal interest and participation in the superintendence and cultivation of their farms, and the adoption of the improvements suggested by modern science. Of this— a thing until lately altogether unknown in Spain—the Ex-Regent Espartero is a most respectable illustration. He derived from marriage an excellent estate near the venerable Castilian city of Logroño, in a fertile and delightful quarter, on the borders of Aragon. Having retired to it, since his return from England, he has devoted his time and attention almost exclusively to the development of its resources, and the application of new methods of cultivation. These it is his effort to make as general as possible among his neighbors, and I am informed that the influence of his example has been materially beneficial already. It is more than probable that he will thus establish another, and a just, though modest, claim, to the title of public benefactor. To that title,—where it involves the outlay of private fortune, without any chance of remuneration, with usury, from the public chest,—there are but few *pretendientes*, and the Duke may probably flatter himself that he has at last reached one position, which he may retain,—as long as he is content with it,—without fear of jealousy or exile.

The existing scheme of national education makes provision for the delivery of public lectures on agricultural science, and the instruction of students in matters connected with that branch of industry. There are other institutions, besides, under the care of the various Economical Societies, in the provinces, which are, perhaps, still more useful. These societies, originating in the enlightened views of Jovellanos and men like him, have been of incalculable service to the general industry of the nation, since the comparative freedom of later days has given scope to their investigations and reports. Many papers of great ability have proceeded and continue to proceed from them, and they are constantly diffusing information upon all matters connected with the material development of the nation. There is an excellent periodical conducted, in Madrid, by the society of "Friends of the Country" (*Amigos del Pais*), in which the most creditable essays are constantly appearing, and the experience and discoveries of more prosperous nations are applied, with great industry and assiduity, to the removal of prejudices and the extirpation of antiquated notions and methods. In some of the other cities, I am informed that similar journals are successfully dedicated to the same work. As an evidence that they are not without effect, I may mention, that in Catalonia, Valencia, and Murcia, where innovation was, not long ago, a sin, the use of guano as a manure has been adopted, to a considerable extent, within the last two years. I have occasion to know, that its application has been so successful, and the demand for it has begun so to increase, that Spain is now looked to as a growing and prospectively important market, by those who regulate its distribution.

The interests of agriculture, until October, 1851, were protected by the same Department which presided over commerce, education, and public works. They now depend upon the new Department of *Fomento*. About $100,000 were appropriated to the agricultural branch, by the budget of

1850,—over and above the expenses of the board for the superintendence of canals for irrigation,—an indispensable part of the system of cultivation in some of the most fertile portions of the kingdom. While I was in Spain, many measures for the improvement of agriculture, in its various branches, were adopted by the Department, of its own motion and upon the suggestion of the Economical Societies. I remember being amused by a royal order, with a long preamble, directing the Royal Academy of Sciences, at Madrid, "*sin levantar mano*" (without lifting hand from the work), to offer proposals for the best essay on the causes of the constant droughts in the provinces of Murcia and Almeria, together with the means of preventing them, or counteracting their effects. It was possible to understand that the consequences of the droughts might, to some extent, be remedied artificially, but as the preamble asserted, in round terms, that the want of rain was their cause, there seemed no recourse for the Academy, in the matter of prevention, except to Professor Espy or the astronomer in Rasselas. The minister, however, seemed quite willing to get what he could out of the weather-makers for the almanacs, and, in addition to the prize, offered to compensate liberally the author of any scheme which might turn out to be effectual. I never was able to ascertain what the result of the *concurso* was. Probably it never had any. Many of the other movements of the Department were of an eminently practical character. New plans of irrigation were attempted. Premiums were offered for successful essays on agricultural subjects, and successful efforts in cultivation. An appropriation of $7,500 was made, in 1850, towards the completion of a geological chart of the kingdom, already then in progress.

Horses and cattle were imported, and schemes devised for the improvement of the native breeds of domestic animals. Inquiries were instituted into the causes of the failure of particular branches of agricultural production, once valuable but now almost extinct, and plans were matured for their restoration.

It was but lately that the papers of Madrid gave the details of an arrangement, said to have been entered into by the government with an association in London, for the establishment of colonies of Irish Catholics on some of the waste lands belonging to the crown, many of which are admirably adapted to agricultural purposes. The capital of the company was said to be £500,000, actually paid in, and the scheme, as reported, was a very feasible one. There has always been a decided sympathy between the Irish and the Spaniards; indeed, in many points, the Andalusian and the Irish character, mental and moral, are strikingly alike. The movement, if successful, would be of infinite importance to Spain, and would furnish the colonists with a congenial asylum, and the opportunity of acquiring a comfortable competence. It is, I believe, a just observation, in regard to the Irish, that, although reckless and improvident in poverty, and of small resource in devising means to escape from it, they are industrious and energetic in prosecuting what they have practically discovered to be profitable, and careful, to a singular extent, in preserving and increasing the proceeds of successful labor. Of this their career in the United States furnishes constant illustration. If the Spanish government and the company having a colonial movement in charge would be careful to bear these traits in mind, and to leave no stone unturned for the establishment of the proposed colonies, from the first movement, on a substantial and permanent basis, there is every reason to believe that such a plan would now have a far different result, than that which attended the *nuevas poblaciones* of poor, persecuted Olavide, in Andalucia.

The traveller visiting Madrid will be quite edified by seeing on many signs, in some of the principal streets, the words "*Casa de Vacas*" (House of Cows), with an accompanying illustration, in oil colors, of a cow in the process of milking. Additional signs will inform him, that "the cows will be milked in the purchaser's presence, if desired," so that it will be his own fault if he labors under the slightest uncertainty as to the orthodoxy of the fluid which enters his household. He will find, too, that from these establishments, or from the agents of the royal dairy at Moncloa (hard by the city), he can obtain fresh butter at his will, without paying a more than moderately exorbitant price for it. If he desires to be economical, and is not particular, he can procure excellent salted butter, direct from the Asturias, at a very reasonable rate. As a matter of creature comfort, he will not find these facts altogether unimportant to him, but this would hardly justify referring to them in a book, did they not furnish an illustration of the progress making in a material department of rural industry. If he should chance to have been in Spain before, or to have recently sojourned in any of the districts where things continue to be as they were in the beginning, he will rejoice in his deliverance from goat's milk and the butter prepared from it, or that insufferable compound, *manteca de Flandes* (Flemish butter). One who has been exposed to these things will deserve to be pardoned, if, before looking on the promised land as Paradise, he distinguishes in regard to the milk with which it is to flow. Among many of the Spaniards, however, even in Madrid, Capricornus has still a bright place in the Milky Way. Towards sunset, every evening, flocks of goats may be seen descending the streets which lead from the gates into the heart of the city. They have been, all day, upon the arid hills about the neighborhood, refreshing themselves with what goats only could construe into pasture; but their distended udders illustrate the moral, of the fulness which a little may bring to an easily contented spirit. As they go by the houses of their customers, the maids run out with their milk-vessels in search of the evening supply. The goatherd seizes the nearest of his flock, and proceeds to business in the middle of the street, while the rest of his company, immediately conscious of a pause in the march, bivouac on the stones till the milking is over. A signal, which they only understand, then sets their bells in a moment to tinkling, and the procession advances, at its leisure, until the calling of another halt. It is a pleasant little *rus in urbe*, to look at, but, like many other picturesque objects, its appearance is the best of it.

As this work in no wise pretends to give detailed information of any sort, but merely to present, as generally as may be, the results of the author's observation, and of such knowledge as he could acquire from sources which he had reason to believe authentic,—it will not be expected that he should dwell, with any particularity, upon those specific details which would enable the reader to form a precise idea for himself of the present state of commerce and manufactures in Spain. As has before been observed, statistics do not exist which would furnish trustworthy data, to any extent, and accident avails quite as much as industry in the acquisition, by piecemeal, of such facts as bear importantly on these subjects. Enough, however, may be easily ascertained, to satisfy an inquirer, that both the great interests referred to have profited much by the impulse which the last fifteen years have given to the nation.

It is a very illustrative fact,—and one which ought to have made the suicidal policy of prohibitory duties as obvious as light,—that, while the exportation of Spain has considerably more than doubled itself since the beginning of the century, the increase in imports has been but little more than one fifth. Not only that, but the amount of exports, which in 1803, or thereabouts, was not more than half that of the imports, is now nearly equal to the latter, with the increase which has been mentioned.[1] It of course hardly requires to be remarked, in view of these statements and of other facts which have been mentioned in the chapters immediately preceding, that the advancement of Spain in the value of her importation must depend upon the freedom with which her ports are thrown open; and her exportation must be greatly governed by the success of the schemes devised for the improvement of her agriculture, and the perfecting of her facilities for internal communication. That the spirit of the government, in these regards, is what it should be, has been already stated; but the number and magnitude of the obstacles, both moral and physical, to be overcome, and the Spanish proclivity to the *poco á poco* (little by little) policy, in all things, will prevent

---

[1] In 1850, the imports were about thirty millions of dollars, an increase of five millions over 1849; the exports were about twenty-four millions, an increase of about half a million.

a more than small delay from being at all remarkable. Some alterations, too, will be required in the navigation laws, which are now far from being liberal; but these will necessarily follow. A robust natural growth is very sure to burst asunder almost any artificial bonds. It is only when that growth is hindered at its sources, that vigorous expansion is prevented. The weakness of the plant has effect in that case, not the strength of the restraint.

The reader, whose interest in the facilities of travelling may be blended with his curiosity as to the commercial progress of the Spaniards, will be gratified to know that the whole coast is now visited, almost daily, in its most important points, by excellent steamers, provided with all desirable accommodations for passengers. There is a line established between Malaga and Havre, which touches regularly at Cadiz, Lisbon, and Vigo, and there is constant intercourse, by other lines, between Marseilles, Barcelona, Valencia, Alicante, Cartagena, Almeria, Malaga, Gibraltar, and Cadiz. With Madeira and Cuba there is regular steam-communication also, though of course not quite so frequent. This state of things, in itself, goes to show a most material improvement in the coasting-trade, which cannot fail, in its turn, to develop the interests that serve it. As has been observed in another connection, it is both an effect and a cause,—as significant in the one point of view, as it must necessarily be important in the other.

In the "Glimpses of Spain" I had occasion to note the improvement in manufactures which was making itself conspicuous in 1847. It is in my power to add but few details to those which were there given. The public documents furnish but little precise information, and such matters have not been much inquired into by writers of authority. A good deal of exact and trustworthy statement might, it is true, be collected from the Geographical Dictionary of Madoz, to which reference has already been made; but, from the nature of that work, its details are spread over so wide a surface, as to make the task of grouping them almost endless.

The Catalan cotton-manufacturers were besieging the Cortes, in 1849-50, with memorials and remonstrances of a most doleful character, in which it was set forth that they had been compelled to close many of their factories, and had been brought, generally, to the brink of ruin, by the alteration of the tariff on imports. I had information from a source on which I could rely, that the closing of the few factories in question was a dramatic performance for the benefit of the monopolists engaged in it, and that the looms were straightway set in motion again, when the scheme was found ineffectual with the legislature. As the genuine manufactures of many of the Catalan establishments are really not worth protecting, under any system of political economy, and as a large quantity of the wares which they sell as their own are manufactured in England, and smuggled into Barcelona, with the names of the ostensible makers already on the bales, it would be little short of a blessing to the legitimate production of Spain, if such of them were closed never to be opened. The large capital which the Catalans have acquired, under the restrictive system of so many years, gives them, in a great degree, the command of the home market; enabling them to undersell—and to smuggle *ad libitum* for the purpose of underselling—their more honest and less wealthy competitors. Many of these last, however, have begun to thrive, notwithstanding, under the auspices of the modified tariff,—restrictive as it still is; and all that any of them can require to insure success, is sufficient capital to sustain them against the first onslaught of the monopolists.

There is, in fact, no reason whatever, in the nature of things, why domestic manufactures should not succeed in Spain. Water-power may be readily commanded, in advantageous locations. Coal is abundant, for all possible applications of steam. Iron is excellent and cheap, for every need of the workshop. Labor can be had upon the most moderate terms, and the cost of subsistence is so trifling, that the operative may thrive and be happy on the limited fruits of his toil. Ingenuity and industry are as accessible as elsewhere, and sobriety and frugality are pervading characteristics of the people. No effort, made with ordinary prudence and backed by sufficient means, has yet failed in turning these natural advantages to account. Should the tariff undergo a thorough modification,—as sooner or later it must,—protective duties, of a moderate character, will probably be necessary, for a while, to enable the new establishments to take root; but legislative aid will not be long desirable. The Catalans ought to be ready to encounter foreign competition at once; for if, with their capital, experience, and energy, they are not able to protect themselves, after so many years of restricted importation, manufacturing industry must be an artificial thing with them, and there is no reason why the rest of the country should be taxed to encourage or maintain it. At all events, the duties which will be proper to develop manufacturing production—in those parts of the kingdom where it does not exist, but in which nature and circumstances indicate the policy of its establishment—will be all that the Catalans can ask, to enable them to hold their own. It is more than likely that they will avail themselves of any protection, to crush their rivals at home; but Spanish taxation has internal facilities, which may meet even this difficulty, and though they should not, the new establishments must be content to pay the price, which one need not be a manufacturer to know that all experience in this world costs.

Of late years there has been a considerable effort to extend and improve the production and manufacture of silk, and the result has been very favorable. The silk-worm, formerly confined, in a great degree, to Valencia and Murcia, is now an article of material importance in the wealth of the two Castiles, Rioja, and Aragon. The silk fabrics of Talavera, Valencia, and Barcelona are, many of them, admirably wrought, and are sold at rates which appear very moderate. I had particular occasion to note the cheapness of the damasks which are sold in Madrid from the native looms. It is not easy to imagine any thing more magnificent, of their kind. The woollen cloths, too, of home manufacture, are, some of them, very admirable, and the coarser kinds supply, I believe, a considerable part of the national demand. In cheapness, I have never seen them surpassed. The finer qualities do not bear so favorable a comparison with the foreign article; but those who were familiar with the subject informed me, that their recent improvement had been very decided. Many laudable efforts have been made to render the supply of wool more abundant, and to improve its quality; and there has been a considerable importation of foreign sheep, with a view to crossing on the native breeds. The sheep-rearing interest is so very large in Spain, that any material improvement in the quality of the wool must add greatly to the national wealth, as well as to the importance of the woollen manufacture and its ability to encounter foreign competition.

In the general movement towards an increased and more valuable production of the raw material for manufacture, the flax of Leon and Galicia and the hemp of Granada have not been forgotten. But the article in which the most decided and important progress has been made, is the great staple, iron. In 1832, the iron-manufacture of Spain was at so low an ebb, that it was necessary to import from England the large lamp-posts of cast metal, which adorn the Plaza de Armas of the Palace. They bear the London mark, and tell their own story. A luxury for the in-doors enjoyment or personal ostentation of the monarch, would, of course, have been imported from any quarter, without regard to appearances. But a monument of national dependence upon foreign industry would hardly have been erected upon such a spot, had there been a possibility of avoiding it by any domestic recourse. In 1850 the state of things had so far changed, that there were in the kingdom twenty-five foundries, eight furnaces of the first class, with foundries attached, and twenty-five iron-factories, all prosperously and constantly occupied. The specimens of work from these establishments, which are to be seen in the capital and the chief cities of the provinces, are such as to render the independence and prospective success of the nation in this particular no longer matters of question. In the beginning of 1850 the Marquis of Molins, then Minister of Marine Affairs, upon the petition of the iron-manufacturers, directed inquiries to be made, by a competent board, into the quality of the native iron, and the extent to which the home manufacture might be relied on for the purposes of naval construction. The result was so satisfactory, that in March of the same year a royal order was issued from the Department, directing all future contracts to be made with the domestic establishments. This, indeed, had been the case, since 1845, at the arsenal of Ferrol, which had been supplied altogether from the iron-works of Biscay. The government, however, had determined, for the future, to be chiefly its own purveyor, and national foundries at Ferrol and Trubia, constructed without regard to expense, were about to go into operation when the royal order was published.

XXVIII.

Fine Arts.—Galleries.—The National Museum and its Treasures.
—Academy of San Fernando.—Marshal Soult.—Murillo.—
Architecture.—Public Edifices.—Domestic Architecture.—
The Escorial.—Fountains of Madrid.—Bronze Equestrian
Statues.—Spanish Academy.—Academy of History.—National
Library.—The Armory.—Bull-Fights of 1850.—Montes, his
Exploits, Death, and Story.

THE state of the fine arts in Spain, at this time, is not such as to deserve particular consideration. Sculpture has hardly any votaries,—none, certainly, of note,—and, with a few exceptions, painting seems to lie under the same ban. The Royal Academy of San Fernando, intended to be the nurse, has proved—as academies will sometimes prove—to be but the stepmother of art; and the pictures of the present day, which hang upon its walls, are, for the most part, as bad as if they had been made so to order. The younger Madrazo is unquestionably a man of talent, and he and a few of his contemporaries are doing what they can to elevate the national standard; but there is, nevertheless, no distinctive Spanish school now in existence, and no art in any degree worthy even the *décadence* of a people, whose earlier masters stood so near the summit.

There are several private collections in Madrid, which well deserve the traveller's attention; but the National Museum, on the Prado, is such a world of art,—so full of the most remarkable monuments of genius,—that, except for the gratification of a casual curiosity, or for the purpose of visiting the few great works at the Academy or the Trinidad, no man of taste will care to carry his researches beyond it. Some writers complain of the *Museo,* as imperfect in some of its departments, and deficient in the works of particular epochs and painters, Spanish as well as Italian. Yet the collection is so various, and its wealth is so prodigal,—the gems of the masters and the periods represented are so many and so precious,—that it is little short of wantonness to be dissatisfied because the measure of perfection, in all things, is not filled to overflowing. A collection which (according to Ford's enumeration) can boast of ten Raphaels, forty-three Titians, sixty-two by Rubens, sixty-two by Velazquez, forty-six by Murillo, fifty-two by Teniers, twenty-two by Vandyke, ten by Wouvermans, ten by Claude Lorraine, and more than two thousand pictures in all, —ranging through the most diversified and most exalted walks of excellence,—may well deserve the title, so often conferred on it, of "the finest gallery in the world."[1] It contains the choicest spoil of church and convent,—the treasures of the Escorial and the Palace. Its riches were gathered from Italy, when Spain ruled at Naples, and from the Low Countries, when she had her viceroys there. Titian and Rubens dwelt at Madrid to paint for it; Velazquez searches the repositories of Italian art, to fill it, and left to it the priceless endowment of his own most perfect works. All that royal munificence

[1] See Vol. II. of Ford's Hand-Book, p. 744, where a great deal of interesting critical and historical matter may be found, in the author's peculiar style.

could do, was done lavishly,—at times, too, when Spanish kings had taste, with wealth and power to serve it.

The Academy of San Fernando has fallen heir to a few very fine pictures, among which is the celebrated St. Isabel of Hungary, painted by Murillo for the Hospital of La Caridad, at Seville, and carried off by Marshal Soult, with the rest of his precious booty. On its return from Paris, after the visit of the Allies, the St. Isabel, with two other masterpieces of the great Andalusian, was arrested at Madrid, by the intrigues of the Academicians, whose influence with Ferdinand was sufficient to prevent the restoration of all three to the sanctuaries from which they had been stolen. It was by consent of his Majesty, I believe, that the free-booting Marshal was allowed to retain his individual share of the spoil, and thus occurred the singular spectacle, lately exhibited in Paris, of the Queen of Spain bidding, at an auction, for the rescue of works of art of which her country had been barbarously plundered.

The complete and excellent treatises of Head and Stirling have made the works of the Spanish painters so well known to the art-loving world, that it would be idle to comment at length upon the collections at Madrid, even if my familiarity with the subject, or the scope of this volume, would render such details appropriate. I may observe, however, that an admirer of Murillo will be more than ever satisfied—after seeing his pictures at the capital—of the entire truth of the remark, that this great master can only be fully understood, and appreciated fairly, at Seville, where he won his fame. It is there that by far the most exquisite of his productions still are,— the most interesting subjects, most ably treated; and it is there only that he can be seen, in his own colors, unspoiled and unpatched by Vandal or Academician. In this judgment, almost every one who has visited Seville will probably concur. The further conclusion of my own, with which I venture to accompany it, will probably find fewer supporters, though it has the countenance of some whose criticism does not lack authority. It is, that, after using the opportunity presented by the *Musco*, of contrasting Murillo's paintings directly with the masterpieces of the greatest artists,—with a vivid remembrance, too, of the *chefs-d'œuvre* of the Italian galleries—I cannot find it in me to place the Spaniard, in point of genius, below the loftiest of them all, Raphael not excepted. In the incarnation of beauty, ideal or merely human,—in a sublimity and dignity which borrow nothing from the Grecian chisel, yet have the purity and grace, without the coldness, of its marble,—in simplicity and tenderness of conception,—in a magic of coloring, where tints blend imperceptibly and warmly, as they melt into each other in the clouds and sky,—I confess that my uneducated taste gives him no equal. There are, no doubt, defects which I cannot see, and details which others may surpass; but in the perfect expression of a poet's highest thought, his canvas is, to me, unrivalled.

With the exception of the Royal Palace, which is certainly one of the most splendid structures in Europe, Madrid has little to boast in the higher walks of architecture. There is not a church in the whole city, with the exception of that of the Convent of Salesas Reales, which deserves to be mentioned as an effective work of art, in a European sense, although to Cisatlantic eyes many of them would seem very imposing, both in style and dimensions. The Custom-House, on the street of Alcalá, and the General Post-Office, in the Puerta del Sol, are large and stately buildings, but both of them, and particularly the latter, derive their principal effect from their size. Substantially, the same thing has already been said of the new Palace of the Deputies, and it may with equal propriety be repeated in regard to the massive edifice on the street of Atocha, which is dedicated to the *Facultad Medica*. On the roof of the portico of this latter building sits a statue of Æsculapius, reminding one exceedingly, by its position and ponderosity, of the effigy of Queen Victoria, mounted, in like case, upon the Royal Institution at Edinburgh. The crushing effect of both brought forcibly to my recollection the exclamation of John Kemble to the tyro in Hamlet, who did not stare sufficiently aghast at the awful words of the ghost:

"But look! amazement on thy mother sits!"

"Imagine me, Sir," cried the enraged tragedian, "imagine me, sitting on your mother!"

I fortunately had no familiarity with the Medical Faculty of Madrid which gives me any right to know, from experience, what Æsculapius has done for them to show his gratitude. The medical school ought to be a good one, and the number of physicians who have had all the advantages of Parisian education must certainly have infused into the Peninsular system the spirit of modern science. I had occasion, however, to obtain some information in regard to the death of a grandee of Spain, which took place but a little while before, and could not help being struck with the extraordinary circumstances under which he was reported to have departed this life. "*Falleció*," says the parish certificate, "*de resultas de un ataque cerebral, con asfixia del corazon, procedente de un espasmo general, segun certificacion de dos facultativos."*—"He died from the result of a cerebral attack, with asphyxia of the heart, proceeding from a general spasm, according to the certificate of two physicians." It is the duty of every man to make what humble contributions he may to the cause of science,—and I report the case for the benefit of the profession and the good of humanity and diagnosis.

Within a few years past (to return to our subject) the domestic architecture of Madrid has wonderfully improved, and some of the more modern palaces, as well as private buildings of less pretension, are in excellent taste and of imposing appearance. I have already alluded to the stately beauty of the street of Alcalá, with the splendid triumphal arch to which it leads; and there are other of the public ways which would do no discredit to any capital. The taste for buildings of immense dimensions has taken complete possession of the Madrileños, so that the number of houses is actually smaller than it was some years ago, although the population has increased considerably, and household facilities and comforts have multiplied, in a proportion still larger. The sites of many of the suppressed monasteries have been used for the erection of dwellings, and the peculiar taste referred to has been illustrated, remarkably, in the magnitude of some of these. The Casa de Cordero, or *del Maragato*, as it is sometimes called, is probably the most extensive of these new structures. It occupies the grounds of the ancient convent of San Felipe el Real, a large square on the Calle Mayor, near the Puerta del Sol, and is distributed into an almost incredible number of suites and establishments, public and private. Its fronts of dressed stone are in admirable taste, and all its appliances are of the most complete and highly finished character. Some idea may be formed of its value and extent, from the fact that its daily rent exceeds two hundred and fifty dollars. The owner, Sr. Cordero, belongs to the singular tribe of *Maragatos,* in Leon, and is one of the wealthiest and most enterprising capitalists of Madrid. He was a Deputy to the Cortes and an ardent *Progresista.* His hand is in every enterprise of public benefit, and no one, perhaps, has done more to awaken and sustain the public spirit, of which Madrid is reaping the advantages so signally.

While on the subject of architecture, I may express the disappointment, in many particulars, which was the result of my visit to the Escorial. That famous edifice is certainly of extraordinary dimensions, but the effect of its size is almost entirely lost, as you approach, in the dwarfing contrast of the mountains which lie behind it; and although, as you wander through the innumerable courts and corridors and quadrangles, a wearying sense of vastness creeps over you, it is not one which is at all coupled with an impression of architectural grandeur. Indeed, the building was never intended as a triumph of ornamental art, but merely for the purposes of a monastery, and with the necessary adaptations. It is, therefore, no discredit to the original architect, Juan de Toledo, that he made it what it is,—nor indeed to Philip the Second, that he did not cause it to be made otherwise. The gridiron, it is true, might have been left out of the plan, but it may be doubted whether—adopted as latitudinarily as it was—it did not furnish an excellent mode of arrangement, for a building which required long passages, small apartments, and many and small windows. It is the traveller's mistake, if he looks for a palace, where nothing was designed but a shelter for cenobites.

The disappointment caused by the general aspect of the monastery was lost in a feeling of the deepest admiration, when we entered the great chapel in its centre,—the most impressive adaptation I have ever seen of classic architecture to the purposes of Christian worship. It is, throughout, of dark gray granite, of the simplest and severest Doric. Its dimensions are colossal, as those of a cathedral; the piers beneath its lofty cupola as massive, in proportion, as those which uphold the dome of St. Peter's. Every detail is in solemn keeping with the austerity of the architect's conception,—the very light, even at midday, seeming to steal with shadowy awe, as into the presence of something holy. It was towards sunset of a stormy evening, that we were conducted, through long galleries and dreamy cloisters, into the front of the great choir. But for a distant, half-heard chanting, we should have thought ourselves alone with the twilight. There was no painted glass,—no fretwork,—no quaint device or cunning tracery,— to fill the waning light with shapes of beauty or of fantasy. The sublimity about us was that of darkness and silence, in a temple meet for them.

In singular contrast with the simplicity of the chapel is the *Panteon*,—the burial-place of the Spanish kings, far down beneath the high altar,—a work of later days, the florid elegance of which could never have been tolerated, in such a connection, by the chastened taste of Herrera or his master. Every thing that is gorgeous, in bronze and gilding and jasper, is lavished upon the charnel-house. The walls of the descent to it throw back, like mirrors, the glimmering of the tapers that you hold, and you are warned to be careful, lest the polish of the marble that you tread, should afford no security to your footsteps. Save the reverential aspect and bent body of the old monk who is your guide, there is nothing in the sepulchre or its appointments to wake one solemn thought of death, or lift the mind towards the uncertainty beyond it. Were it not for the grandeur of the temple which is above it, —the fame of some few of the monarchs who occupy its urns, —and the dignity and awe with which the genius of Quintana has associated it, in one of the noblest efforts of the Spanish Muse,—the *Panteon* would be but a tinselled chamber, without taste, appropriateness, or moral.

In speaking of the works of art which adorn Madrid, the attention of the reader may very well be called to the sculpture of the fountains in the Prado, which, though not of the highest order, have, nevertheless, a great deal of merit, both in composition and execution. The size of the groups and figures is so colossal, that they form conspicuous features in the evening view, when the great walk of the capital is crowded with its cheerful thousands; and there is beauty, as well as freshness, in the glancing of the waters which they scatter so copiously round them. The group of Cybele is perhaps the most admired, but I was particularly struck with the great fountain of Neptune, in the winter season, when the breezes blew chill from the Guadarrama Mountains. There was infinite spirit and effect in the gallant style in which the sea-god's horses seemed to be flinging the icicles from their manes and nostrils.

Of the bronzes in the public places it may, I think, with justice be said, that Madrid can furnish one of the best and one of the worst equestrian statues in the world. The latter is the effigy of Philip the Third, in the wide old Plaza Mayor which was the work of his reign. It seems scarcely possible that the sculptor could ever have seen a horse, at all events as the animal exists at present. The monarch's steed is absurdly swollen, and his action, in the sort of amble to which he is condemned, is ingeniously unnatural and clumsy. The whole work would suggest the idea of Bacchus astride a barrel, but that the attitude of the rosy god has generally a graceful *abandon*, of which the awkward and unknightly seat of the king bears not the slightest trace. Yet the statue was modelled, horse and man, by John of Bologna, who certainly knew better, and was finished by Pietro Tacca, the author of the admirable work with which I am about to contrast it.

The statue of Philip the Fourth, formerly in the Retiro gardens, and now in the Plaza de Oriente, is quite another affair; but Tacca was aided, in this task, by a drawing from the hand of Velazquez, still extant, and there breathe, throughout the whole production, the fire and spirit, which have made the equestrian portraits of that master perhaps the finest in the world. The attitude of the horse is rendered somewhat artificial, by its conformity with the rules of the *manège*; but the nostrils are distended, the fore feet beat the air, and even the hind feet, on which the whole weight rests, appear to spurn the earth. The seat of the rider is matchless,—light, graceful, and yet firm as a centaur's. The touch of the bridle-hand is as delicate as the best training for the lists could make it, and the lace-work of the sash seems floating from the armor like gossamer upon the wind. I am induced particularly to refer to this work, not only because it is, beyond dispute, a masterpiece, but because a statement has recently been going the rounds of the American press, in which a projected cast, by an ingenious native artist, is spoken of as the only attempt to make an equestrian statue depending altogether for support on the hind quarters of the horse.   Philip the Fourth, having perhaps the dread of his predecessor's effigy before him, insisted that his charger should be cast as in the gallop, and availed himself of the influence of Christina of Lorraine, then Grand Duchess of Tuscany, to secure the services of Tacca for that purpose.   It was not without some remonstrance on the part of the sculptor, that the will of the king had its way. A full account is given, by Ponz, of the mode in which the difficulties of the subject were overcome; and an artist of the present day would doubtless find matter in it made worthy his consideration by the triumphant success of the Florentine master.   The weight of the statue is eighteen thousand pounds, and the tradition is, that the sculptor was aided in his distribution of the mass by the suggestions of Galileo, his contemporary and friend.

If it were any part of my intention to give a narrative or descriptive character to this little volume, there are many interesting public institutions in Madrid to which I might profitably direct the reader's attention.   They will all be found mentioned in the guide-books, and a more particular reference to them would be foreign to my present purpose. Those, however, who are interested in the purity and preservation of the Spanish language, will be pleased to know that the *Academia Española* still continues its labors, and that they are about to take a more profitable shape than of late, in the production of a new and complete grammar and dictionary.

The latter is not to be merely the republication, which has periodically appeared for some years past, but a thorough and copious work, such as signalised the learning of the Academy in its earlier history. Both the grammar and dictionary are imperatively called for, by the variations in orthography, syntax, and the vocabulary itself, which the last few years have introduced into the works of even the most approved writers. The Academy has many members peculiarly qualified for such tasks, and the result of its labors may therefore be awaited with interest.

The Academy of History, to the sessions of which the unmerited honor of a corresponding membership gave me admission, was occupied, as diligently as its moderate means would allow, in the publication of historical manuscripts,—treasures of which yet lie, undeveloped, on its shelves. Some of the unpublished books of Oviedo's History of the Indies were in a state of preparation for the press, nothing being wanting but a portion of the manuscript, belonging to the Queen's private library,—to which access, strange to say, is difficult, even for Academicians. The Padre Baranda, a learned member of the Academy, was intrusted with a continuation of the *España Sagrada* of Flores, and the publication of several volumes of Villanueva's "Literary Voyage to the Churches of Spain," which are yet in manuscript. To the printing of these latter works a liberal contribution was made by the Commissary of the Bull of the Crusade,—their ecclesiastical merit and interest commending them a good deal more to such patronage, than to any general acceptation in the literary world. The Academy can hardly be said to be in a flourishing condition, so far as concerns its capacity for the dissemination of knowledge.

The library is a good, and in some measure a rare one, but the want of room renders its arrangement and classification extremely imperfect, so that—the catalogue being in manuscript and not clear to the uninitiated—it is necessary to depend, almost entirely, upon the personal familiarity of the worthy librarian with the sheep of his pasture. Under such circumstances, and in the absence of any but the most limited pecuniary resources, the institution is necessarily narrowed in the sphere of its usefulness, and principally serves to keep alive, in a small body of learned and indefatigable scholars, a quiet devotion to the literary antiquities of their country. Before I left Madrid, it was in contemplation to remove the collections of the Academy to a more favorable and commodious locality; and it may be that some impulse will thus be given to its labors, which will enable it to continue worthy of the days of Clemencin and Navarrete. So far as industry and learning may contribute to this result, there is enough of both, among the members, to insure it.

The National Library, with its collection of 130,000 volumes, is an excellent institution, so far as it goes,—a perfect model in its arrangement, and in the liberality with which provision is made for the convenient and satisfactory access of the public. The apartments are many and comfortable, and the attendants as numerous and courteous as could be desired. Those who are interested in coins and medals will find an extensive and admirable collection there,—probably unsurpassed by any of Europe in the Arabic department, which owes the beauty of its arrangement—so often praised— to the skill and learning of Don Pascual de Gayangos. The Library is obnoxious to the same complaint which has been made in regard to the more limited collection of the Academy of History,—the want of proper and complete indexes. Those which exist are very perfect, down to their date; but they have not been systematically added to for several years. Being in manuscript also,—of which there is but one copy,—they furnish the most limited facilities, even where they are complete; and it is necessary to resort to the officers in charge of them with a frequency which is a great obstacle to uninterrupted and elaborate investigation. The collection of books also needs modernising very much. It is unequivocally behind the times, and meagre in its stock of contemporary literature. But every thing cannot be done at once. Material necessities must be met, before intellectual cravings can be satisfied. Arms must have yielded long, before the toga can be worn as a familiar garment.

The lover of romantic antiquity will probably find nothing in Europe to delight him more, in that regard, than the superb *Armería* (Armory) near the Palace. It is not only rich in armor and weapons, the most complete, ingenious, and magnificent, in themselves; but suggestive, at every step, of all that is chivalrous and glorious in Spanish history. Suit after suit, bruised in the bloodiest frays,—swords which have names in song and chronicle,—shields and lances which have driven back, or onward, the tide of famous battle,—are all there, as they were worn, or borne, or wielded, by king and champion, Moor and Christian. Blades of the Paladins,—the mail of the Cid,—the halberd of Peter the Cruel,—the armor of Isabella, and Boabdil, and Gonzalo of Córdova,—the casque of the captive Francis,—the harness of the great Emperor, his victor,—of Columbus and "stout Cortes,"—of Guzman the Good,—of Ferdinand the Saint and Ferdinand the Catholic—and sinner! It is a place to read ballads and dream dreams, and ask no questions.

As an historical memorial, I was struck with an *adarga*, or Moorish shield of dressed leather, which belonged to Charles the Fifth. It is divided into four compartments, the upper one of which, upon the left, contains a representation of the surrender of the Alhambra. Ferdinand rides on the outside, on a white charger; the Queen, on a white palfrey, is between him and a gray-haired man, supposed to be the Cardinal Mendoza. They are entering at one gate, followed by their soldiery, while from another gate of the same tower sallies Boabdil, with but one attendant. The similarity of this picture to the bas-relief on the altar of the Catholic Sovereigns, in the Cathedral of Granada, entitles it to some consideration as illustrating a point on which the chronicles differ. I referred to the question in the *Glimpses of Spain*, and it is hardly of sufficient importance to deserve more than the present allusion.

It would be scarcely pardonable to take my leave of Madrid, without some reference to the bull-fights of the famous season of 1850. Not that there is any thing new to be said or sung upon the subject, in the general,—nor that I propose to say or sing what has been heard so often before; but that the veteran Montes, "the first sword of Spain," returned, during my visit, to the scene of his triumphs which he had for six years deserted, and his advent was an epoch in the annals of tauromachy. When it began to be rumored that he was coming, the newspapers were wild, and the people in ecstasy. He brought with him his nephew, the famous *Chiclanero*;

and the Duke of Veraguas, a grandee of Spain and the lineal descendant of Columbus, was one of the attorneys who contracted on their part with the directors of the Plaza. A procession of the fancy, noble and gentle, went out to meet him as he drew near Madrid, and, after feasting and congratulation, he entered the city in triumph. His first performance was on the afternoon of Easter Sunday,—a special honor to the day. The Plaza was crowded to overflowing, the *troupe* was choice and beautifully equipped, and the array of loveliness, fashion, and enthusiasm not to be surpassed. The great *matador* was received as a victor from a hard-fought field. He bore his laurels modestly, and addressed himself at once, like a man, to his work.

Though past the prime of life and of activity, Montes was conspicuous for his athletic form and perfect composure. He had

"The eye of the hawk, and the fire therein,"—

dexterity, which nothing but long practice, courage, and command of nerve can give, in the presence of such terrible and instant danger. When the bull came in, he would sit for a few moments on the barrier and watch his motions. Apparently satisfied as to the character of the animal by this brief observation, he would descend into the arena, and place himself where he pleased. He would call the bull,—attract and mock him with his cloak, backwards and forwards and again,—and yet not desert a circle of ten feet in diameter. Where the *banderilleros* would fly and leap the barrier, he would avoid the charge by the slightest inclination of his body, without a step to the right or left. Once I saw him call the bull, and as the furious animal rushed towards him, Montes confronted him with folded arms and steady gaze. The bull turned instantly aside, and attacked some other of the company. It seemed, indeed, as if his mastery over the wild brutes was absolute,—as if, to use the language of one of the journals, "they knew him and respected him." To me, I confess, it was incomprehensible,—to the reader it will, I fear, be incredible.

The killing of the bull by Montes was a very miracle,— no butchery, no side-blow, no loss of swords, no hurry, no help. In one and the same instant the sword flashed behind the crimson cloak, and the *matador* was wiping the blood from his blade, with the victim at his feet. I saw the whole Plaza rise, to a man, in admiration of one such blow. The newspapers were absolutely glorious in their accounts of the *maestro's* performances; but the details of their descriptions, though no doubt interesting to the fancy, were as unintelligible to me, as the history of a milling-match in Bell's Life in London. I endeavored to educate myself up to the proper level, by reading the treatise of Montes himself on *Tauromaquia*,—a work of considerable reputation; but I found it as scientific as a book of surgery, and as deep as one of Mr. Emerson's Essays. Having had occasion, at the time, to turn to Ford's Hand-Book,—which is full of knowledge and admirable description in regard to the sports of the arena,— I fell by chance on that singular passage, in which he gives vent to his nationality, by speaking of the "quick work" which "a real British bull, with his broad neck and short horns, would make with the men and horses of Spain"! I could not but feel curious to know what the patriotism of the writer might induce him to think of a boar-hunt, with prize pigs.

Since my return from Spain, Montes has fallen before a mightier *matador* than himself,—having died of a fever, or a doctor, at home, in his bed. The account which I have of his decease sets down his age at forty-six. In the ring, he appeared at least ten years older. "Six bull-fighters," says his chronicler, " bore his coffin in silent sadness. . . . . . He was of noble family, but was compelled, by the reduced circumstances of his father, to gain his subsistence with his own hands. The destiny of a day-laborer, however, did not furnish a field broad enough for the movements of his soul. In his straits, he sought a door to the temple of fame, —and he found it. He elevated his art to a height unknown before, and the whole world beheld with awe the triumphs of his skill and valor!"

What is glory, after all? And what lacks Montes, but his Homer, to live as long as Ajax? Is not the hero thrice blessed who slays only cattle?

XXIX.

Valladolid.—Simancas and its Archives.—Blasco de Garay and the Application of Steam to Navigation.—His Invention a Fable.—Burgos.—Vergara.—Visit to Azpeitia.—Valley of Loyola.—Jesuit College and Church.—The Basques.—Their Character, Agriculture, and Institutions.—Tolosa.—Ride to Bayonne.—The Gascon.

WHEN I left Madrid, the duty which called me homeward permitted but little deviation from the beaten track by which I had entered Spain. I took advantage, however, of a few days' leisure and the agreeable companionship of a fellow-countryman and friend, to visit the noble old city of Valladolid, and the works of art which are still so splendid in Burgos. A full account of our journey would be out of place here, and the objects of interest which we passed in review would be unfairly dealt with, if treated otherwise than in detail.

From Valladolid, an excursion to the Archives of Simancas was a matter of course. A drive of two leagues or thereabouts, along the banks of the Pisuerga,—which waters a beautiful and highly cultivated valley,—carried us to the base of a bold hill, whose summit is crowned by the village of Simancas. High over all rises the stern old castle, with its round towers, which once belonged to the valorous Henriquez,—the Admirals of Castille,—and in which are now deposited so many of the most important records of the Spanish realm. Making our way on foot up the precipitous and narrow streets of the town, we at last reached a stone bridge, which occupied the place of the old drawbridge and led us, across the moat, to the massive gateway of the castle. The occupation of the moat was as peaceful as that of the grim walls it girdled, for a harvest of luxuriant grain was growing along its deep and fertile round.

The kind letters of our friends at Madrid commended us so efficiently to the good offices of the courteous and learned *archivero*, Sr. Gonzalez Garcia, that we were soon introduced to the most interesting of his curiosities. The French destroyed many documents of value and removed others,—partly from wantonness and partly to obliterate the historical traces of some transactions and mischances of their own; but the *Archivo* is still a treasure-house of European history, and access is now obtained to it with so much greater facility than of old, that it is likely yet to revolutionize many received historical theories and dogmas. The History of Philip the Second, now in the hands of our eminent fellow-citizen, Mr. Prescott, will probably afford early evidence in this behalf.

The papers, throughout the whole *Archivo*, are capitally arranged and kept,—the most precious, in queer old *arcas* or chests, which are deposited in safes or small vaulted chambers, for which the solid walls afford excellent convenience. The state apartment contains perhaps the most valuable documents, in the shape of diplomatic correspondence. Some idea of the copiousness of the records here may be formed from the fact, that the letters of Gondomar, the Ambassador of Spain at the Court of James the First of England, fill eighteen folio volumes. Among the more curious papers may be seen the wills of Isabella the Catholic and her grandson, Charles the Fifth; the autograph letter of John of Austria, written in the flush of the victory of Lepanto, with a plan of the battle, drawn by himself; and the memoranda made by Philip the Second for the despatch to be written in reply. Philip was a pragmatical man of business, and made memoranda and notes of every thing, so that almost all the details of his reign may be traced here after his own hand. In some of the lower courts of the castle there were immense bales of papers lying, which had belonged to the archives of the Inquisition at Madrid. They had not been long remitted, and there was no room for them. An *auto de fé* would be a characteristic and appropriate disposition of them.

"Let the dead past bury its dead."

In the copying-room of the *Archivo*, we had the good fortune to find Don José Aparici, an exceedingly interesting person, to whom, also, we were recommended. He was a colonel of engineers, a man of science, and an antiquarian and scholar of no mean repute, to whom had been assigned the duty of preparing materials, from the records, for a history of the Engineer Department of Spain. To this task he had voluntarily added that of searching the archives for the annals of the artillery corps. He showed us some twenty or thirty volumes of copies, the fruits of six years' investigations, and yet covering only the history of the sixteenth and a part of the seventeenth century. He had searched, as far as he had gone, all the papers in the archives of the War Department, and contemplated going through all those of later date. The number of years which his labors were still likely to occupy was of course uncertain,—not less than six, however, at the least. Taking us to his house, he showed us a beautiful collection of fac-similes he had made of the signatures of all the distinguished persons—kings, queens, soldiers, statesmen, artists, and scholars—of the fifteenth, sixteenth, and seventeenth centuries. Among them we noticed the name of Blasco de Garay, the engineer, to whom has been attributed, by many, the first application of steam, with success, to the purposes of navigation. The reader who is familiar with either the history of Spain or that of the steam-engine, will remember that the experiment is said to have been triumphantly made by Garay, in the presence of Charles the Fifth, in the harbor of Barcelona, and that the prosecution of the discovery was arrested by a court intrigue. The details were given to the world by Don Martin Navarrete, in his *Coleccion de Viages*, &c., and were perhaps first republished in the United States in Mr. Slidell's "Year in Spain." To our surprise, Colonel Aparici informed us, that the whole story was a mere fiction. The facts which he related in regard to it bear so closely on a question of great interest, particularly in this country, as to induce me to depart from my original plan, by giving this account of my visit to Simancas.

There is no doubt that Garay—who calls himself, in his memorials, "*un pobre hidalgo de Toledo*" (a poor gentleman of Toledo)—was a man of a great deal of mechanical talent and proficiency in the physical sciences. The records of Simancas show many projects of his, which indicate an active and inventive mind. Among them is an ingenious plan for

converting salt water into fresh, at sea. The invention which
has given rise to his connection with the history of steam
navigation was nothing more nor less than the substitution of
wheels for oars in the royal galleys. He made four failures
in the harbor of Malaga. His fifth experiment, which was in
the port of Barcelona, was in a measure successful. With two
wheels, and relays of six men for each, he was able to move a
large galley, at the rate of something more than a league in
the hour. The crew of such a vessel, when moved by oars,
was required to number at least a hundred and fifty men.
The Emperor, who was to have been present at the experiment, was called off suddenly to the Low Countries, and
Garay lost the benefit of his personal inspection. When the
result, however, was communicated to Charles, he made the
same objection which has been urged, in our time, to the use
of war-steamers. He said that a cannon-ball might destroy
the machinery, and render the galley unmanageable at a single
blow. It was this opinion of the Emperor, and no intrigue
of the Treasurer Ravago, as stated by Navarrete, which put
an end to Garay's improvement. He died poor, and there is
extant, in the *Archivo*, a memorial of his son after his death,
asking the allowance of a hundred ducats, for the construction
of another machine according to the father's plan. It was not
granted.

These facts, which conclusively settle the question of
Garay's invention, were given to me by Colonel Aparici,
in detail, and with an offer to refer to the copies of the proper
documents. They are, of course, not made public here without
his permission. He told us that he had looked over every
paper in the *Archivo*, having any connection with the projects

of Garay, and that there is not, in any memorial, report, or *oficio* relating to the subject, a single allusion to steam, or to a *caldera* (boiler) or any thing which, directly or indirectly, suggests the idea of steam as a motive-power. He added, that the facts which he thus communicated to us were known to a great many persons in Spain, and particularly to the members of the Academy of History; but that there was a natural indisposition, on every one's part, to take the lead in giving them to the world. The invention was too glorious a one for the national pride to surrender without a struggle. The documents, however, he said, must one day appear. He himself had prepared some biographical memoranda for the press, which he showed us, in which the true state of the case was lightly alluded to, by way of preparing the public mind. To use his own emphatic and manly language, "he could not think that fame which was a lie, was worth preserving."

It is but justice to the learned and indefatigable Navarrete to say, that there is not the slightest imputation upon his candor or research involved in the fact of his having published a statement, which now turns out to be so far unfounded. The documents on which he relied were furnished to him from a responsible source, and he gave the results to the press in the best faith. Small portions of the latter part of Garay's correspondence were all that he received, and the allusions to steam were surreptitiously introduced, to impose on him. It is not known whether he was ever informed of the imposition; certainly he was not, if at all, until after his advanced age had placed literary labor of any sort beyond his powers. The memory of so able, pure, and accurate an historian deserves this statement. In the multiplicity and scope of his painful and protracted labors, he could not possibly see all things with his own eyes.

After two or three days spent among the wonders of the past and the discomforts of the present, in both of which Burgos is so abounding, my companion was called back to official duties in the capital, and I resumed my journey towards the frontier, pausing only for a slight deflection into Guipuzcoa (one of the Basque provinces), to visit the family of a valued friend whom I had left, an exile, in America. We diverged from the main road at Vergara,—the scene of Espartero's famous "Convention" with Maroto,—a sweet little town in a shady and romantic defile, by far too beautiful to be the witness of unnatural and cruel strife. For a league and a half our journey lay along the margin of the Deva, which is indeed a "wizard stream." The lofty hills between which it flows were cultivated almost to their summits, in every variety and shade of green, to which the iron-tinted soil, where freshly turned, gave charming contrast and relief. Here and there, whole hill-sides, covered with the yellow turnip-blossom, looked, in the sun, like fields of cloth of gold. White *caserias* (farm-houses) peeped out at every turn, from groups of trees; peasants were at work all round us; horned cattle, sheep, and goats, in large numbers, were cropping the luxuriant grass. Every inch of ground was converted to some useful purpose; every handful of soil was made to yield its double-handfuls of product. Defile came after defile, and gorge after gorge, all beautiful alike. Mountain streams rushed down, in foam, beside the road, and now and then leaped wildly across it. The Deva was full and turbid, from recent rains. The gray stone of the bridges over it was often covered with mosses and pendent vines. The walls, along its banks and on the upper side of the road, were green with ivies and lichens, and fringed with fern. Wild-flowers, blue and yellow, spangled the dark carpet on the lower grounds. Every thing told of moisture and sunshine.

After a while, as we advanced in our ascent, the scene developed itself into wider valleys, and the hills began to wear a savage look about their summits, well suited to suggest the presence of those "spirits and walking devils," with which old Burton, upon learned authority, has peopled the ruggedness of the Cantabrian mountains. We saw none of these, however; but as we were toiling upwards, near a hill-top, our path was suddenly and swiftly crossed by a party of *Pasiego* smugglers, after whom the custom-house guards were in full cry. They were stout, athletic fellows,—so well able to meet danger, that it was no wonder they despised it. Each of them carried a mountaineer's long pole, and they rushed over the rocks, and up through the forest, with an agility that was astonishing. My postilion wisely turned his back, so as not to see the direction which they took, and when the troops came up, he, of course, could give them no information. I dismounted and walked a half-mile with the officer in command, who was a pleasant fellow and asked me no questions. He told me that a party of his men were behind, with the main body of the *contrabandistas*, whom they had captured. I saw the poor *Pasiegos* pass along, afterwards, two by two, quite unconcerned. At the next *venta*, the soldiers bound their hands together, apparently with great reluctance; but the captives smoked their cigars very contentedly during the process. They were superb peasants, of the manliest mould, which was well set off by the tight, neat costume of their province. It was sad to reflect that a system of pernicious and unreasonable laws should tempt such stalwart fellows from honest labor, to waste their manhood in the squalid toil of the chain-gangs.

Ascent and descent, equally tedious but for the beauty of the scenery and the excellence of the road, carried us, at last, into the valley of Loyola, where, on the margin of a copious and rapid stream, bearing the musical name Urola, lay the delightful village of Azpeitia, the place of my destination. The town is famous as the birthplace of the great founder of the Society of Jesus, who, in the various colors of saint and sage, bigot and madman,—according to the predilection, or judgment, or prejudice of the painter,—has filled so many pages of the world's most serious history. The house in which he was born, with the arms of his family—two wolves, at a pot suspended by a chain—rudely sculptured over the entrance, is still in perfect preservation, at a short distance from the town. It is now incorporated into the buildings of the immense Jesuit College, whose founders once owned the wide and pleasant *huerta*, still green and plentiful about it. The church of the college is a superb *rotonde*, with a dome and lantern in fine taste,—the most remarkable building of its style in Spain. It is constructed of hard black jasper, which takes an exquisite polish. The front and the grand Corinthian portico look as if they were made of the costliest Egyptian marble. The good priest, who was our guide, showed me a magnificent block, in which the town, the smiling valley, and the hills about it, were reflected, as in a perfect mirror. The high altar and many parts of the interior of the edifice are remarkable for the variety and great beauty of the marbles,—all of which are Spanish; some of them from the Granadian mountains, but the most from those of Biscay. Some of the mosaics and inlaid work can with difficulty be surpassed. The church was deserted, being under the charge, for preservation only, of a solitary clergyman, once the prior of a convent in Azpeitia. The college was the property of the province, and then only used as the depository of the archives of Guipuzcoa. The whole establishment has since been restored to the Jesuit fathers.

But it was not to enjoy the beauties of architecture, art, or scenery, that the reader was invited to join me in this little pilgrimage. It was that he might observe the totally different characteristics of the Basque provinces, as compared with the rest of the kingdom, and attach the proper consideration to those accounts which deal with Spain as homogeneous in its physical, moral, industrial, and agricultural developments,—a nation to be sketched in a paragraph, with a flourish of the pen. The Basque territory is as unlike Castille, La Mancha, or Andalucía, as nature and man can make it. Instead of *dehesas* and *despoblados*,—wastes and depopulated places,—wide fields, without fences or hedges,—scattered and poor villages,—woodless plains or hill-sides,—it has small farms, well wooded and inclosed, with bright cottages, and cheerful little fields, not a foot of which, as I have said, but pays its contribution to the farmer. Where the plough cannot pass, the hoe or the hand does its work. Between the rocks, and along the precipices, every slip of soil is tilled. The very difficulties of the location seem to stimulate the energy of the laborer. Plantations of beech and chesnut reward his toil with timber and fruit. Crops of Indian corn spring up around him, with a luxuriance which might shame more fertile regions. On the whole, I do not remember to have seen a country more resembling those delightful tracts, among the Apennines, which M. de Sismondi describes with such elegance and just enthusiasm, in his Essays on Political Economy.

Indeed, as far as I was able to ascertain during my brief visit, the lands are held, in some sort, upon the principle of the *métairie* which Sismondi commends so much in Tuscany. The leases, for the most part, are very long, descending often from father to son among the tenantry, as the freehold passes in the family of the landlord. A small pecuniary rent is paid, nominally for the house, and for the land a reasonable portion of the crops is given. Attached to each *cascria* there is generally a tract of woodland, often at a considerable distance, upon the mountain; but sometimes only a right is reserved to cut wood for farming purposes and fuel. The relations of landlord and tenant are so well understood, and in general so satisfactory, that difficulties but seldom occur; the tenant, on the one hand, being beyond the risk of exorbitant exactions, and the landlord, on the other, quite as secure in the receipt of his moderate but sufficient income. What gives to the system its chief merit is the feature which renders it so attractive to M. de Sismondi,—the guaranty of the future which it affords the laborer. He has something before him. He does not toil for present support only, preparing the land for a stranger who may at any moment be put in his place. Every foot that he redeems from barrenness is so much added to his own stock and the heritage of his children. He labors, therefore, as if the land were his own, and the spirit with which he applies his hand to the work is as fruitful of independence and content to him, as of profit to the owner of the soil. He gathers his humble comforts about him with a sense of security and permanence. His condition is not that of a mere agricultural proletary. It is blended with the enjoyments and surrounded by the blessings of rural competency and a rural home.

As a consequence of this peculiar system, and of their provincial traits of frugality and industry, the Basques, though an extremely crowded population, are for the most part well fed, well clad, and physically comfortable. There is very little mendicancy or extreme poverty among them. By nature, they are manly, frank, and hardy, like mountaineers in general; and the freedom of their political charters has developed these qualities into a provincial character of the sturdiest independence. They are bold, active, and enterprising; remarkable throughout the kingdom for their trustworthiness and stern integrity. On the other hand, their good qualities often run into extremes, and they are sometimes obstinate, abrupt, close-fisted, and perverse. "*Larga y angosta, como alma de Vizcaino,*" ("Long and narrow, like the soul of a Biscayan,") is the proverb in which their compatriots have caricatured their peculiarities. As *pretendientes*, they are famous. Looking over the Madrid blue-book, it will be seen, by their unequivocable surnames, that they absorb a conspicuous portion of the public patronage; but all who are familiar with the conduct of Spanish affairs will do them the justice to admire the fidelity and ability with which they respond to the public confidence. Upon one point they have a provincial weakness; it is for the antiquity of their race and language. The latter, they gravely contend, was the one spoken in Paradise. If it was, Schlegel has omitted the strongest argument in favor of the improvement of the human species.

When I left Azpeitia, and the cordial hospitality which had welcomed me, and which gave me such regret at parting, I turned my face across the mountains towards the flourishing town of Tolosa, which was reached in a pleasant afternoon's journey. The next morning I mounted the diligence for the North. It was Sunday,—a soft and genial day,

"So calm, so pure, so bright,"

that George Herbert might well have called it "the bridal of the earth and sky,"—or even their courtship, which is a brighter thing. The roads and the village streets were lined with cheerful peasants, in holiday costume, and children played happily by the way-sides, in troops that would have saddened a Malthusian. At last, the blue Atlantic hove in sight, suggesting thoughts of the far land beyond it; then came the frontier,—the custom-houses,—France,—evening,— and Bayonne.

" *C'est bong, ça!* " said a fat Gascon *marchand de chevaux*, who rode with us, next day, towards Bordeaux. We were passing through one of those stiff and formal avenues, which make the landscapes so often, in the South of France, resemble the first plates in Euclid's Elements. " *C'est bong, ça! c'est très pingtoresque!* " repeated the Gascon, leaning heavily upon me and puffing his pipe in my face. Neither the sentiment itself, nor the mode of its delivery, was calculated to enforce conviction, in one who despised both tobacco and straight lines; but it awakened me to the first full consciousness that I was out of Spain, and I date my exodus accordingly.

XXX.

CONCLUSION.—POLITICAL PROSPECTS OF SPAIN.—EFFECTS OF PEACE.—ESPARTERO.—THE MODERADOS.—THE QUEEN MOTHER.—THE NOBILITY.—MONARCHY.—REPUBLICANISM.—INDEPENDENCE OF NATIONAL CHARACTER AND MANNERS.—LOYALTY.—TENDENCY TO FEDERALISM.—REASONS THEREFOR, AND PROBABILITY OF A CONFEDERATION.—ITS BENEFITS.—THE BASQUE FUEROS.—EFFECT OF INTERNAL IMPROVEMENTS AND DEVELOPMENT OF INDUSTRIAL RESOURCES.—EMPLEOMANIA.—REASONS FOR AMERICAN SYMPATHY WITH SPAIN.—JUSTICE DUE HER.

HAVING, to the best of my ability and information, placed it fairly within the power of the reader to draw conclusions for himself, in regard to the political future of Spain, I have little to add but deductions of my own. There are impressions, sometimes fixed upon the mind, when in the centre and bustle of affairs, which have the force of convictions, though one can scarce tell why. That such may have blended themselves, in the present case, with opinions which I can more readily trace and perhaps defend more satisfactorily to others, is altogether probable. The conclusions at which I have arrived would not seem to me less likely to be accurate, on that account; but it would be presumptuous to expect that the reader should be willing to take them equally upon trust.

The most obvious fact which the preceding chapters disclose, and a fact not to be gainsaid, is the revival of the prosperity of Spain within the last few years. The improvement may be less thorough, and less worthy of the epoch, than it should be. Its course may have been misdirected and interrupted. It may yet be diverted, nay, occasionally arrested altogether. Nevertheless it exists. It has been the result of causes, still operative, which were deliberately set in motion to produce it; of principles, which it was dangerous to broach, and which it has cost time and labor, agitation and blood, to establish. It has continued to go on, until its march, rapid or retarded, has grown into a custom,—a thing of course. It has wrought changes which it is now too late to undo, and has established reforms from which a relapse is now impossible, because the abuses reformed have been cut up at the roots. It has vitality, therefore, and strength, and foothold, and it must advance.

Nor are the causes of this revolution less obvious than its existence. Liberal institutions and peace have been the immediate and main agents of good. Without peace, liberal institutions would have availed but little; indeed, until the civil war was ended, their practical results were trifling, in comparison. With peace, a far less rational system than the worst phase of that which has prevailed would have yielded, by degrees, to popular development; indeed, the sternest despotism could hardly, at this epoch, have restrained it altogether. War has been, beyond all question, the bane of Spanish freedom and prosperity, as far back as history records. Foreign or domestic, it has been the perpetual background of the picture. To this eternal strife, more than to despotism in all its varieties and combinations, the decay of the nation is attributable; for it was this, in fact, which gave to despotism its opportunities, its pretexts, and its arms. Rest, therefore, more than all things else, had grown absolutely indispensable to moral and political regeneration,—even the most partial. Tardy as may have seemed to us the steps of the recent revolution we have traced, they would have been incomparably more tedious and unsteady, but for the peaceful though lethargic years preceding the death of Ferdinand the Seventh. It was then only that the scattered elements of change took form and energy, and were combined.

In view of this necessity, this paramount necessity, of repose to the nation, I have commended, in their turn, the "Convention" of Espartero with Maroto, and the subsequent policy of the *Moderado* party. The one produced peace,—the other has undoubtedly preserved it. In considering the wisdom and effect of public measures, the motives and the processes which led to them may well be left out of the account. It may be true that Espartero bribed Maroto,—as his enemies have said,—because he could not overcome the Carlists in fair battle. If so, the money was well laid out, notwithstanding. Narvaez and his compeers and successors may have strengthened the arm of government, not merely to save the nation from anarchy and its results, but because it was their own arm, and its strength was their strength. Yet if the salvation of the country was in fact the consequence,—if faction and discord were thereby kept down,—if leisure and opportunity were given and secured for industry and enterprise, and the prosperity and happiness that wait upon them,—what matters it that a constitutional provision, here and there, was, for the moment, ambitiously broken? Prosperous nations—confirmed in their prosperity—can afford to be technical, and may stickle even for abstractions; a prostrate land must have realities, not words. There are situations in which one material blessing may be worth a hundred of the holiest forms. Better, a thousand fold, to Spain, a brief, nay, a usurped dictatorship, with peace, than the nominal triumph of liberalism, with the certainty of reaction and desolation.

Those who see force in these suggestions will not distrust the reality of the good which has already been achieved in Spain, nor despair of the future, because of occasional arbitrary passages, and suspensions or infractions of the fundamental law. A moment's comparison of what is now with what but recently was, and a consideration of the obstacles which have been overcome, and the limited means by which the triumph has been won, will suffice to remove all doubts in regard to the present, and to justify the happiest augury. But the future has its own elements of promise, besides. When it is remembered that almost every man of eminence, in the ruling party and the opposition, has risen from the people, and owes his elevation, not to royal favor, but to the popular institutions which surround the throne, it is scarce possible to conceive an act of such wholesale suicide, as a serious attempt to re-establish an absolute government. The Queen, as has been said, is without ambition, or dangerous qualities of any sort. The Queen Mother, though, on the contrary, as scheming and ambitious as the blood of Naples can make her, yet, in spite of her large wealth, preëminent position, and talent for intrigue has never been able to secure a hold upon the popular regard. At this moment, though perhaps the most influential, she is probably the best abused and most thoroughly detested person in Spain. She can act only through her creatures, and they have interests of their own, which forbid their serving her beyond a certain point. As a class, the nobles have no political influence whatever; and as individuals, they are, almost universally, without the talents which could make them dreaded or useful.

But even if politicians and rulers were willing to break down the constitutional system, the first overt act would arouse the people to almost unanimous resistance. The lotos of freedom has been tasted, and it cannot readily be stricken from their lips. So long as the more important guaranties are not altogether violated,—so long as the government substantially dedicates itself to the public good, by originating and fostering schemes of public usefulness,—it may take almost any liberties with forms and non-essentials. Much further it will not be permitted to go, and every day diminishes the facility with which it may go even thus far. Every work of internal improvement which brings men closer together, enabling them to compare opinions with readiness, and concentrate strength for their maintenance; every new interest that is built up; every heavy and permanent investment of capital or industry; every movement that develops and diffuses the public intelligence and energy,—is a bulwark, more or less formidable, against reaction. Nay, every circumstance that makes the public wiser, richer, or better, must shorten the career of arbitrary rule. The compulsion, which was and still is a neccessary evil, for the preservation of peace, must be withdrawn, when peace becomes an instinct as well as a necessity. The existence of a stringent system will no longer be acquiesced in, when the people shall have grown less in need of government and better able to direct it for themselves. Thus, in their season, the very interests which shall be consolidated and made vigorous by forced tranquillity will rise, themselves, into the mastery. The stream of power, as it rolls peacefully along, is daily strengthening the banks, which every day, though imperceptibly, encroach on it. Sir James Mackintosh, in his comment on Burke's splendid apostrophe to Chivalry, has skilfully depicted a similar process and result, in the triumph of commerce and intelligence over the feudal and chivalrous institutions which fostered them into strength and independence. Hero points the same moral, in telling of the "pleached bower,"

> "Where honeysuckles, ripened by the sun,
> Forbid the sun to enter,—like favorites,
> Made proud by princes, that advance their pride
> Against that power that bred it!"

While, therefore, I should hardly be surprised at an attempt to assimilate the constitution of Spain, in some sort, to the simpler model of the "Prince-Presidency," I should regard its temporary success as an evil by no means without good. An enlightened despotism could not easily avoid laying, in the national prosperity, a solid foundation for the final establishment of a permanent free system.

Of the shape which the fundamental institutions of Spain will ultimately take, there is, in one particular, but little room for question. The traditions, and even the prejudices, of the people are monarchical altogether. In practice and from conviction, they regard loyalty as a virtue and a sacred duty.

There are really, in Spain, no republicans or democrats; or, at all events, no persons seriously contemplating the establishment of a republic or a democracy. The sense of personal independence is as high and scrupulous there, as it can be anywhere,—not excepting our own country. And there is a republican element, too, in the character and manners of the Spaniards, which I believe exists nowhere else, at the degree in which they possess it. Your American citizen will concede to you, if you ask him to do so, that other people are as good as he. But this is not the principle which he sets chiefly forth, in his life and conversation. It is the reverse of the medal,—it is the conviction, the practical demonstration, that he is as good as other people. He will not deny—he dares not deny—the equality of others with himself; but he goes about always asserting his equality with others. The Spaniard, on the contrary, has a sense of equality, which blesses him who gives as well as him who takes. If he requires the concession from others, he demands it, chiefly and emphatically, through the concessions which he makes to them. There is so much self-respect involved in his respect to others, and in his manifestation of it, that reciprocity is unavoidable. To this, and this mainly, is attributable the high, courteous bearing, which is conspicuous in all the people, and which renders the personal intercourse of the respective classes and conditions less marked by strong and invidious distinctions, than in any other nation with whose manners and customs I am familiar. It is this, perhaps, more than any other circumstance, which has tempered and made sufferable the oppression of unequal and despotic institutions,—illustrating "the advantage to which," in the words of a philosophic writer, "the manners of a people may turn the most unfavorable position and the worst laws."

But with this eminently republican temper, the continued loyalty of the Spaniards to their monarch is perfectly compatible. There is no servility in it. It is homage paid to the individual, as identified with an institution. The prince is the embodiment of their nationality,—the representative of past glory and present unity. They rally round the throne, in spite of the frailties or crimes of him who fills it. They are no worshippers of Ferdinand or Isabella,—no martyrs for Carlos,—but liegemen to the person whom they believe to be the rightful monarch of the Spains. It is a matter of great uncertainty, therefore,—and perhaps of great indifference, as affecting the question of freedom,—whether the most perfect system of liberal institutions which the Spaniards may adopt will be without some modification of the monarchical feature.

The political horoscope, in other respects, is not so easy to cast. The general, though perhaps the remote tendency, is, I think, towards a federative monarchy. The relations between Spain and Portugal, and the feasibility of uniting the whole Peninsula as one nation, were the subjects of frequent and practical discussion, public and private, when I was in Madrid, and have more than once furnished topics of serious diplomatical consideration. It seems difficult, indeed, to understand how such a measure as a Peninsular Union, so forcibly suggested by so many natural circumstances, has been so long deferred, or can continue to be postponed, now that the public good has become so controlling an element in national relations. The doctrine of public policy and morals, called " geographical necessity," has obviously not yet been expounded in Europe, with the same efficacy as among ourselves.

But, leaving Portugal out of the question, the Spanish kingdom has more of the federal elements than any nation that I know of in Europe. The provinces, mostly segregated from each other by natural barriers, are quite as much so by their peculiar and respective characters, customs, and laws. The sturdy Biscayan, the Switzer of the Peninsula, is as different, in his personal and provincial characteristics, from the stolid and uncouth Galician,—the industrious, but choleric and selfish Catalan,—the witty, flippant, gallant, bull-destroying Andalusian,—as is the burgher of Amsterdam from the sun-loving Neapolitan. And so of the other provinces. Their forms, prescriptions, ideas, are all different. Their interests are different,—frequently conflicting. Their costumes and dialects are totally distinct. The soil they till, the products they consume, are as the soil and products of remote nations. Some of them are mountaineers,—some dwellers upon boundless plains,—some fishermen, or sailors, or shepherds, or manufacturers, or cultivators of the deep green *vegas* that beautify the borders of the sea. Yet, over all, and binding them and all their diversities together, is the iron band of a beloved and time-honored nationality. Catalonians, Biscayans, Asturians, Castilians,—they are all Spaniards. It was this national sentiment which animated and sustained the heroism of their resistance to Napoleon, notwithstanding the local institutions, jealousies, and rivalries which deprived it of unity and concentration.

Nor is the present administrative system of Spain otherwise than favorable to the formation of federal habits and ideas.

The general government, as has been seen, presides directly over the foreign relations of the country, and has immediate control of all general and national affairs. Each province, however, has its own civil governor, appointed by the crown; representing, within his sphere, the Minister of *Gobernacion* (the Interior), and in effect the executive ruler of the province. For purposes of consultation, he has his Provincial Council, of three or five persons, likewise nominated by the Queen. The Provincial Deputation, an elective body, to which I have already referred, has duties and powers of a comprehensive and more active nature,—watching over the welfare, regulating the contributions, and developing the resources of the province. Each province, therefore,—thus taking care, in form at least, of its own interests, and in a measure controlling them,—concerned in the assessment and levy of its domestic taxes,—having its wants and wishes represented by its own officers, near the central authority,—is in many respects a separate, though a dependent state. Then, too, there is the municipal feature, the independent action of the *ayuntamiento* within its allotted sphere,—as distinct as that of the provincial authorities within their jurisdiction. In these particulars there is great similarity to the political condition of the American Colonies prior to the Revolution. The ingredients—the rudimental and elementary ideas—of a confederacy are all there, as developed in the beautiful analysis of the subject made by M. de Tocqueville, in his treatise on Democracy in America.

The very existence of these various elements—so suggestive of confederation, and so likely to produce prosperity under and through it—must render it nearly impossible to uphold the present centralised and centralising system, for any length of time, after the causes of improvement, which are now at work, shall have made it as easy to carry out, as it now is to discover, what the national prosperity demands. The very distinction in provincial characteristics—which would be the main stay of a federal union, constituted to adopt and perpetuate it, as far as useful—is productive only of discord and discontent, where provincial wants and interests are merged, as now, in an absorbing consolidation. Centralisation—which, modified by federal institutions, would be a blessing to every part, and communicate to each the vigor of the whole—now crushes, of necessity, what it attempts, unnaturally, to amalgamate. Two things, each, in its sphere, a good, are thus linked together for evil. Two healthful ingredients are combined, by bad chemistry, into a poison. This cannot last, when those who suffer from it grow able to reform it. There can be but one true policy for a people in such a condition, and that is, to give to the national and the provincial element, each, its appropriate sphere,—to surround the throne, which shall represent the nation, with the guaranties which shall be drawn from prosperous and independent states, confederated to form the one and to defend the other. I am aware that a writer [1]— whose opinions on such subjects are more justly entitled to be held oracular, than those of any other reasoner upon government—has pronounced a confederation, "of all systems, the most complicated, the most difficult: that which demands the greatest development in the intellect of men, the greatest empire of general interests over particular interests, of general ideas over local prejudices, of public reason over individual passions." Yet the requirements of a confederacy

[1] M. Guizot.

—growing up of itself, and not created by a constituent assembly,—suggested by geographical and natural causes, and arising spontaneously from national circumstances, in their ordinary germination and development—would hardly be so multiform and absolute. The causes which produced, would in such case preserve. It may require art and constant outlay to keep the walls of the Escorial as they came from the hands of the builder; but the mountain parapets, behind it, have become a changeless part of the nature which formed them.

Taking it for granted that a future confederacy is possible in Spain, there can be but little doubt that the wealth and power she would draw from it would make Portugal a suitor for its privileges. If not, the wealth might buy the freedom of the great rivers which pass through Portugal to the Atlantic,—or the power might give to Spain attractive views of "annexation," which its present uses will scarcely suggest to her. So seriously were plans of the sort which I have indicated broached in the political circles of Madrid, that there were many who believed the formation of a confederacy would be the basis of the next general movement of the people. The increasing tendency toward centralisation seemed to be regarded, in all quarters (except among the rulers and their immediate followers), as the leading evil of the times. During the administration of Espartero, the *fueros*, or provincial privileges of the Basque provinces, were to a great extent suppressed. As a piece of national legislation, this was altogether wise,—though the *fueros*, in themselves, were, many of them, relics of the best days of early freedom. With the existence of a federation they would have been eminently compatible; but the obstacles were infinite which they raised in the legitimate path of the existing system, and they were the source of great discontent and much ill blood among the other provinces, which could see no reason why the Basques should be thus preferred. The *Moderados* have carried out this portion of Espartero's policy, in the main, and the inhabitants of the "Free Provinces," when I went among them, were in no better predicament than the rest of their countrymen. As a sort of prelude to a federal movement,—a preparation of the public mind for it,—there was a project, when I was in Madrid, to restore to the Basques the most important of their *fueros,* and thus lead the people of the other provinces to insist on similar concessions. The idea was not a bad one; but I have seen no evidence of its having been carried out. It was but a means, however, and the end may be attained as readily in other ways.

Whatever may be the ultimate political destiny of Spain, it is certain that the development of her resources, and especially the completion of her great works of internal improvement, must in some measure precede its consummation. There are two obstacles to her entire political prosperity, which are not likely to be removed till these ends shall have been, to a great extent, accomplished. The one is the *empleomania,* or mania for place, which has already been the subject of remark; the other, the advantage which the government has over the people, in its greater facilities for prompt communication and action. The first is mainly the result of the few opportunities, hitherto offered, for the profitable exercise of industry and capacity. Until the cause shall have been removed, the evil must continue. But although the desire of advancement in the public service, which springs from lofty aspirations, is self-sustaining, as all things noble are,—hanging for subsistence on the favor of the little great, is a calling which few will consent to follow, who have access to any thing worthier. Custom, it is true, may demoralize men, till they feel no humiliation in that or any other sort of mendicancy. Want may sometimes break the proudest spirits to the degradation of dependence and servility. But the young and earnest—on whom the hopes of nations rest—must loathe such things, at first, though they have no other refuge from starvation. Let channels but be opened for industry and intelligence,—reasonable inducements held out to honest toil,—reputable and remunerative occupation given to the hands or to the mind,—and the throngs which bow in the antechambers, or scowl and plot in the Puerta del Sol, will soon be reduced to the few who are beyond demoralisation. It would of course be going too far to say that, even then, the evil will be eradicated altogether. Our own national experience has sadly failed to demonstrate that the utmost opportunity for the acquisition of pecuniary independence will, of necessity, withdraw men from the pursuit of politics as a trade. But if the good of a diversion be not absolute, it will, at all events, be a good, and Spain is in no case to despise the smallest of these. The evil is certainly that which retards, more than any other, the establishment of a free system, and its uncorrupted economical administration.

Upon the other point little need be said. The government is a vast, connected, organized system,—moved by a single will, and working with rapidity, certainty, and concentration. The people, broken into provinces,—without facility of access to each other,—have no opportunity for the speedy formation or expression of a public or national opinion,—no means whatever of prompt, united action. They can be anticipated and overawed,—kept apart, and crushed in detail. With all needful intelligence and spirit, they cannot bring either to bear, except under the greatest disadvantages. With abundant, but scattered strength, they are unable to concentrate or direct it. The difficulty is chiefly a physical one, and material agencies alone can remove it. When the telegraph shall flash its tidings through the whole land at the same moment, and the power of steam shall be at the bidding of the spirit which they may awaken, then the people and their rulers will be fairly in the lists, and with an equal sun the wrong must needs go down.

There may be persons to whom the views and anticipations expressed in the foregoing pages will seem too flattering, —the result, perhaps, of partiality for a favorite nation. This impression may not be altogether unfounded. The partiality is not denied, and it may have produced its natural effects. Insensibly too, from dwelling on a subject, the judgment may be moulded to its shapes. "In contemplating antiquities," says Forsyth, translating from Livy, "the mind itself becomes antique." The author has endeavored, as far as possible, to guard against this, and, even if unsuccessful, he is persuaded that his opinions have been affected far less by his predilections, than he has found those of many of his predecessors to have been by the prejudices of creed and education. Impartiality is no doubt the philosophic frame of mind, but not the impartiality of indifference; indeed it may be questioned, greatly, whether sympathy is not a necessary element in all capacity for national, as well as other appreciation. Antipathy, at all events, is not a promising one.

But if the author should not be fortunate enough to merit entire coincidence with his opinions, he trusts he has at least established, that Spain should not be coupled, as she usually is, with Austria and Russia, in our popular and daily denunciations of despotism. Surely she deserves, if any nation can, the encouragement and sympathy of the friends of rational liberty. For half a century—through blood and fire at first, and then through sad oppression and strife, and through the calmer but severer trials of peaceful revolution— she has been indomitably working out her gradual redemption. Her institutions may differ from ours. Her system may be imperfect; her power may, as yet, be far below its ancient scale and that of our present predominance; but the fortitude and perseverance which have gone thus far will go farther,

"ever reaping something new,—
That which they have done but earnest of the things that they shall do."

If we are devoted to human freedom for its own sake,— whatever be the shape it takes,—it becomes us to welcome a constitutional monarchy which has been reared upon the ruins of a despotism. That monarchy may be devoted, in appearance, rather to the cause of order than the cause of progress; but in Europe order is the road to progress, and there have been, of late, too many unhappy illustrations of the truth that the worst of despotisms is that which follows an abortive and too hasty effort to be free. All cannot be altogether like ourselves. All need not be, to flourish. To sympathize with none but those who adopt our forms, is to reverence but the reproduction of ourselves,—to forget that which is in us and in our forms, and alone makes them and us what we are.

But whether we give or refuse sympathy, let us at all events do justice. The one is our own, to dispose of as we please,—the other we may not honestly withhold. There is no law by which a man may be compelled to love his neighbor as himself, but there is legislation on the subject of highway robbery. Spain has the sorest need of her resources, in her toilsome struggle for happiness, development, and freedom. Let us not give it to history to say, that she was compelled to waste the means of her deliverance in defending herself from republican cupidity. Strange as it may appear to some of our political philosophers, there are such things as right and wrong, and they are not to be measured by the wants and desires of a people, any more than by the ambition and unscrupulousness of a prince. It is easy enough to write state papers, speak speeches, pass resolutions, and invent pretexts, in defence of profitable usurpation. Men of great intellect, and flexible temper or integrity, may be purchased or flattered by temporary popularity, or awed by general opinion and the public will, into the support of any heresy. Great names have never been wanting to sanction, or great abilities to justify, any national iniquity that promised heavy returns. Truth and justice exist, nevertheless, and magnanimity and fair-dealing with the weak are still valued among men. Injustice will survive the best gloss that we can put on it. Campbell could not preclude the verdict of history, by all the lyric splendor of the "Battle of the Baltic." If the annals of the world show any thing, it is that national power, in its utmost duration, is not so lasting as national shame.

POSTSCRIPT.

The changes which have taken place in Spain, since the period to which the body of this volume more particularly refers, do not affect, in the main, the correctness of the sketch which has been given. It may be well, however, to notice the general direction of those which have not been fully adverted to already.

Notwithstanding the very large majority of the *Moderados* in the Cortes chosen in 1850, it became apparent, soon after their session had begun, that the preponderance of the party furnished no guaranty for the permanence of the existing administration. The Count of San Luis had overshot his mark. He had controlled the elections, but could not manage the elect. In December, Bravo Murillo retired from the cabinet, and the dissensions which followed resulted in the resignation of Narvaez himself, and the dissolution of the ministry which he had formed and kept together. His downfall was believed to be the work of Queen Cristina. Recent events seem to indicate his return to power; and it is impossible that such a man can fail, for any length of time, to make his influence felt in one shape or another.

After the retirement of Narvaez, the reconstruction of the council was entrusted to Bravo Murillo, who continued until recently to occupy its presidency. Various cabinet changes and dissolutions of the Cortes have taken place in the mean time, but the *Moderados* have managed to retain the control of both departments of the government. Neither of the great parties has been without its troubles and schisms. Sr. Pacheco has developed the secret of these, in a single phrase. "Parties," he observes, "which were framed upon public principles, have split upon private interests." The laborers, on both sides, are out of proportion to the harvest, and some of them are fain to turn their reaping-hooks into swords. Among the *Moderados*, the advocates of extreme doctrines have had the ascendency, as the acts of the government show. The most unfortunate evidence of their predominance is to be found in the restraint imposed on the press. The spirit of the enactments on that subject, lately promulgated and enforced, is almost identical with that which has prevailed for some time past in France. Indeed, upon all subjects, the tone of the Spanish officials and their organs, until the recent change, had grown less and less deferential to the constitution, and more avowedly and openly absolute.

The *Progresistas*, forgetful altogether of the obvious truth, that no opposition can be effective without unity, have been wasting their strength and opportunities, for the most part, in the unprofitable discussion of abstract questions. While they debated as to the degree of rapidity with which progress should advance, they were imperceptibly throwing away the chance and their ability to secure any progress at all. Of late, they appear to have regained their wisdom, and with it their organization and their strength. In the Cortes recently assembled, they had a formidable array of numbers and parliamentary talent. The *Moderado* opposition, too, was full of vigor, ability, and influence, with some of the first names of the nation on its lists. A combination of the opposing elements resulted in the entire defeat of the ministry upon the organization of the Congress of Deputies. Martinez de la Rosa was elected President; but almost his first duty was to announce that the Queen had been pleased to dissolve the Cortes. Before taking this decided step, the government had submitted to the legislature several projects of constitutional reform,—all of them tending towards a reduction of the popular power, and the assimilation of the Spanish system to that of Napoleon the Third. The fate of measures so unnecessary and absurd was too obvious, in the Cortes as they then stood, and there was no alternative but a dissolution of the cabinet or of the legislature. The next Cortes will assemble in March, 1853. The people will have the views of the reactionists fully before them in the elections, and it can hardly be doubted that the result will strengthen, more than ever, the hands of the liberal constitutional party. Indeed, the news of the dissolution of the Murillo ministry, received as these sheets are going to the press, would seem to indicate that the question is already substantially settled.

But for the proximity of France, and the unavoidable influence of the imperial doctrines and policy, a Spanish cabinet would hardly have ventured, at this day, upon the suggestion of such changes as I have alluded to. So obvious is this, indeed, that the government organ in Paris has felt it necessary to disavow all connection of the Emperor with the matter. There is not a nation in the world which has furnished fewer pretexts than Spain for reactionary legislation. The Spaniards have used the degree of freedom which they have enjoyed, with prudence and extreme moderation. They have committed no excesses,—run wild with no theories,—organized no conspiracies,—invented no infernal machines. They have dedicated themselves, soberly and steadfastly, to the development of their material resources, asking nothing but to be protected, or at all events let alone. They have not required so much as a sham-fight on the Prado, or a single display of fireworks, to keep them in perfect good humor with their rulers and themselves. Even a government confessing itself arbitrary, would therefore be without excuse for interfering with the constitution. How the idea of such a thing could occur to a constitutional cabinet,—composed of men whom the constitutional system had created,—passes all understanding. The pernicious influence of the Queen Mother is probably the immediate source of the movement. The progressive tendencies of the people and the unequivocal revolution which old ideas and systems have already undergone, may be trusted to counteract it.

It must not be denied, however, that, under the policy of the Murillo cabinets, the prosperity of Spain substantially and steadily advanced. This is especially true in regard to her financial affairs. Nothing practicable was neglected, to secure an economical administration of the government and the faithful collection and disbursement of the public moneys. The measures which were adopted in regard to the debt were statesmanlike and earnest,—

indicating a due appreciation of the national responsibility and faith, and a determination to provide, to the extent of the national ability, for the payment of the interest and the gradual extinguishment of the principal.

It would be tedious to enter into a detail of the administrative reforms which the last two years have consummated. One of the principal of these was the suppression of the Department of Commerce, Instruction, and Public Works. The supervision of public education, which was one of the functions of this Department, has passed to that of Grace and Justice. Its remaining duties have been committed to a new department, called the *Ministerio de Fomento;* a title so peculiarly Spanish, that it can hardly be better rendered into English, than as the " Department of Public Encouragement." Agriculture, commerce, manufactures, internal improvements, and the general industry and national resources of the kingdom, are within its very comprehensive scope.

The administrative embarrassments which have been previously alluded to, as resulting from the suppression of the Council of Indies, seem to have suggested the necessity of a Colonial Department, to be called the *Ministerio de Ultramar.* At the last dates from Madrid, the details of its organization had not been promulged; but there appears to be no doubt of its establishment within a brief period. The magnitude of the colonial interests which are still controlled by Spain, would seem fully to justify the contemplated change. It is to be hoped that the colonial system will be so far modified under its auspices, as to remove all pretext for dissatisfaction with the government of the mother country. In view of the creation of the Department of *Ultramar,* that of *Fomento* seems likely to share the fate of its predecessor,—leaving its functions to be distributed among the other departments. The policy of assigning its important duties to officers whose labors are already sufficiently numerous and ill-performed, may well be doubted; but any permanent arrangement would be preferable to continued variation and experiment.

The *desestanco,* or removal of the government monopoly from salt and tobacco,—a measure of the deepest importance to the public interests,—lately occupied the attention of Sr. Murillo.

Whether it was suggested merely as a bid for popularity, or was really contemplated in good faith, must remain in doubt. Little could have been expected from the liberality of an administration which could promulgate such an edict as that recently published in regard to foreigners. "No foreigner," says its third article, "will be permitted to profess, in Spain, any religion but the Roman Catholic and Apostolic." Fortunately, there is no obligation imposed on strangers to profess any religion whatever, except in connection with certain legal acts. The article quoted is nothing new in the Spanish law, but it seems well-nigh time for something better. "Of old things," some "are over old."

January, 1853.

www.ingramcontent.com/pod-product-compliance
Lightning Source LLC
Chambersburg PA
CBHW032023220426
43664CB00006B/349